Tasteful Nudes

DAVE HILL

Tasteful

Nudes

...and Other Misguided Attempts at
Personal Growth and Validation

ST. MARTIN'S PRESS 🐾 NEW YORK

www.stmartins.com

ISBN 978-1-250-00203-7 (hardcover)
ISBN 978-1-250-01403-0 (e-book)

First Edition: May 2012

10 9 8 7 6 5 4 3 2 1

For my parents, Bob and Bunny Hill.
I apologize in advance for most of the pages that come after this one.

CONTENTS

Introduction   1

Desnudo en el Mar   7

Loving You Is Easy Because You Live
Pretty Close to My Parents' House   21

As of Now, I Am in Control Here   34

All the Right Moves   47

On Manliness   61

The Lord's Work   74

Tasteful Nudes   90

Rocking Me, Rocking You, and Probably Some
Other People, Too   99

A Funny Feeling   114

Northeastern Ohio Velvet   125

Pedicab Shmedicab   136

Witness the Fitness   148

I Kind of Remember You in the Chelsea Hotel   159

The Streets Are Hell   173

Big in Japan   186

The Time I Went to Prison   199

Bunny   212

Epilogue   223

Acknowledgments   228

• • • • • • • •

Introduction

(ABRIDGED)

Dear Reader,

Hi. How are you? I'm pretty good, mostly. Thanks so much for asking. I just wanted to thank you in advance for reading my book. I typed it all by myself and I really hope you like it.

You seem nice,
Dave Hill

Introduction

(UNABRIDGED)

Dear Reader,

When I was first approached by the editors at St. Martin's Press about writing this book, I told them to go fuck themselves. I am an artist. I pride myself on my integrity. And there was no way in hell I was going to cheapen my most important and beloved life stories by writing some fancy, overpriced hardcover for a stodgy old publishing house that would inevitably share shelf space in a bookstore or library with whatever drivel is being passed off as literature these days. Then they offered me four hundred bucks.

The results of my efforts, of course, you now hold in your hands. And to that I say, congratulations. I also humbly thank you for buying (or accepting as a gift—I'm cool with it either way) my incredible book. I typed it all by myself, mostly in the privacy of my own home, usually while wearing absolutely nothing at all. Needless to say, I'm pretty pleased with it, partly because it's my first ever book and partly because—wow—get a load of this font.

Still, it doesn't matter what I think of my book—it matters what you think, because you're the one who has to read it (yes, you have to). I just figured if I put the idea out there—the notion of my book's overall incredibleness—that it might somehow stick with you as you turn its pages. Then by the time you're done (yes, I am suggesting you finish it. Why are you fighting me on this? It's not that long, so just get over yourself already!), you'll be like, "Wow, this book was incredible! I can't decide whether to start reading it all over again from the very beginning or to strip my torso bare and press the book tightly against my flesh so that I might feel that sweet, sweet friction that is so easily generated by rubbing up against a cleverly designed hardcover edition with a tasteful matte finish[1] that was undoubtedly a bit pricey to manufacture, but entirely worth it for everyone involved when you consider the fact that the words swim inside of it like a mighty salmon boldly fighting its way upstream at the height of mating season in search of hardcore fish banging with any and all takers until it is grossly disfigured and soon-to-be dead."[2]

Naturally, I encourage the former. However, if my experiences with a first edition copy of Drew Barrymore's *Little Girl Lost* are any indication, I'm not exactly gonna call you names if you choose the latter. It's your book—do what you want with it. Write in the margins, lick its pages, give it the finger—I don't know your business and I don't want to. I mean, sure, if you see me in public with my pants fully secured and everything, by all means say hello and take a shot at some light chitchat. But let me say respectfully that I'm not interested in what you get up to behind closed doors.

I guess what I'm trying to say is I really hope you enjoy my book. A lot. It took me a seriously long time to write it. I mean, not, like, Bible-long, but definitely way longer than I thought it would when I ran out of the St. Martin's building with all the money. And it wasn't even the typing itself that ate up all the time. It was the sitting and

---

1 As I have written this introduction prior to the book actually going to print, I can only assume the St. Martin's Press people are going to follow through with their promise of making it a "cleverly designed hardcover edition with a tasteful matte finish" as discussed in that one meeting where they said I was talking too loud and that I couldn't bring lobster into the office anymore. Also, I requested that the book itself be really big and heavy, like an atlas or book of wallpaper samples or something, so that it might be readable by two or more people at the same time. If it turns out that the book you are holding is just normal size and you can easily stand there holding it all by yourself without any strain to the major muscle groups, I will only take it as further proof that the world is bullshit and you can't take anyone at their word.

2 "Stop it, you damn salmon," you want to tell him, "your insatiable sexual appetite will kill you in the end." But the salmon, he won't listen.

the thinking about what I was going to type. And also all the drinking that made it both harder to think and to type even though at the time it seemed like both were going really, really great. I think I checked my e-mail a couple of times, too.

But with my sitting and thinking and writing almost behind me, it just occurred to me there are all sorts of ways you may have come to be reading my book. You may not have bought it or gotten it as a gift—maybe you're just standing in the bookstore reading this right now, which seems creepy to me, mostly because of this thing I saw on the news once. Those bookstores—some of them are full of real perverts: "I have an idea. Why don't I grab a soon-to-be bestseller off the shelf, stroll on over to the New Age section, and expose my genitals to it. What the heck? I don't have to be at the clinic for another three hours." Promise me you're not one of those. You want to get some cheap thrills? Head on over to the photography section. Trust me.

The more I think about everything though, maybe I've been coming on too strong and maybe even been a bit judgmental and, well, kind of rambly. For that, and all of the above, I apologize. Why don't we just press restart on this whole thing?

Hi. My name is Dave and I wrote a book. This one. In it are stories from my life about things like stolen meat, prison, love, death, rock 'n' roll, and other stuff I experienced firsthand while I was just trying to live my life. I hope you enjoy them. If there are any life lessons in here, let me know. I probably missed them myself. But if you happen to stumble upon some on your own, well, there you go—the book has already paid for itself. Also, just as a heads-up, I sometimes use swear words in this book, not to be provocative or "cool" or anything, but just for emphasis, and also because the people at the book company said I could if I wanted to. (In fact, Dad—if you're reading this—the book company people said I had to use profanity. Seriously—they were kind of dicks about it. They say it "sells books.") So if there are small children around, do the right thing—shield their eyes from this book's pages, and for chrissakes, don't read it out loud unless you want them to end up joining a goddamn street gang or something.

Don't worry though—you invite me to dinner, a Bar Mitzvah, a wake, or whatever and I promise I won't be anything less than perfectly mannered, delightful even. Also, I smell really nice. Ask anyone.

Before I go, I'd like to address one last time those of you who might still be standing there reading this in a bookstore. Look, I'm not going to tell you how to live your life or anything, but, just as a suggestion, how about marching this bad boy up to the register? Not because I need the money, but just because I want the money. Yeah, I know, my book isn't exactly cheap (unless it's been discounted or put on clearance and, if so, what the hell?), but I promise you it's worth every penny, even if you don't read a word beyond this page. You take it home, you put it on your bookshelf with the cover clearly displayed, you invite someone special over to the house, and then you just stand there in your best outfit or maybe even nothing at all and lean in close to that spot where my book is impossible to miss. Take your time with this sexy, sexy pose—don't rush it, make it count. Once you're good and settled, whisper to that special someone (in a saucy kind of way, not in a "I'm calling you from a blocked number, I can see you right now, and I hate wearing pants" kind of way), "So— what would you like for dinner?" If my experience with Craigslist has taught me anything, eight times out of ten, his or her answer will be "You." And for that, my friend, you're welcome. In fact, I was going to call this book *The Date Impresser* but then St. Martin's got all *"Impresser* isn't a word" on me so I had to come up with something else.

Of course, if money is tight, you forgot your wallet, or you just don't feel like parting with [insert really-high-but-completely-worthwhile price here], I say you slowly shut this book, tuck it under your arm, have a quick look around, and run, run as fast as you can for the exit. I'll get my cut anyway, so don't worry about me.

Once you get outside, the temptation will be to keep running as fast as you can away from the bookstore until you feel you are no longer in danger of getting caught, put on trial, and then thrown in a jail cell with someone who will sell you for a pack of cigarettes or maybe have sex with your face. I understand the thinking here.

However, I encourage you to stop about fifty feet from the exit of the bookstore and wait for one of the employees (or maybe the security guard if it's one of those really big bookstores. Don't worry—he doesn't really have a gun, no matter what he might tell you. It's just his finger.) to come outside after you. At this point, you should hold my book high in the air, do a fun little dance, and yell, "You just got your ass handed to you, by [insert a good criminal nickname for yourself here]!" (A word to the wise: don't use the Unabomber or the BTK Killer or anything. They caught those guys already. And besides— it's just a book—keep it light. What the hell is wrong with you?) After that you should probably keep running.

Keep shining,
Dave Hill, famous writer person

· · · · · · · ·

Desnudo en el Mar

I've never been entirely comfortable with nudity, at least not my own, anyway. Even though I live alone, for some reason, I can never get myself to sleep in the nude, no matter how many great things I hear about it or how much I drink before bed. (And I've tried. A lot.) And just about the only thing I can do in the bathroom with the door wide open is that thing where you look in the mirror and say "Bloody Mary" three times.

When it comes to other people showcasing their goods, however, I say bring it on. In fact, you might say it's been a bit of a thing with me for some time now. I spent my childhood dreaming that some doctor or dentist would accidentally leave an old issue of *Playboy* in the waiting room magazine rack. Or that my family would somehow stumble upon a nudist colony on one of our camping trips. And I remember being changed forever at the age of twelve when, one balmy summer day at Jones Beach, I saw one girl lose her top in the waves and another accidentally display her butt while trying to clean sand out of her bathing suit. In the car home later that day, I felt like a man, and it was awesome.

The occasional brush with fate or some romantic date's poor judgment aside, I still wanted more in the nudity department. Then as luck would have it, I was asked to cover a "clothing-optional dinner" by a now-defunct radio program.

"We couldn't talk anyone on our staff or even someone not on our staff into doing it," they told me. "Then your name came up."

"I'll do it! I'll do it!" I said, remaining perfectly calm.

As an inquisitive and occasionally hard-hitting journalist, I felt obligated to accept. The fact that I'd be hanging out with a bunch of totally naked people and actually getting paid for it made me feel like I was creating my own destiny. It was as if I had been working toward this moment my whole life.

The group behind these clothing-optional dinners held events every few months, usually in some restaurant with a spare banquet room, an open-minded waitstaff, and—presumably—chairs that wipe down easily. But the stars magically aligned and the dinner I planned to drop in on would be taking place on a small cruise ship that would sexily wend its way around New York City's sexy surrounding waters as sexy naked people enjoyed what would undoubtedly be one sexy, sexy meal. My great-grandfather was a sea captain,[1] so it was almost as if my past and present had joined forces to give me what would undoubtedly be one of the greatest and most important nights of my life. I was born to be on that boat, dammit.

It was a rainy evening as I hopped in a cab headed for the water with John, a tech guy the radio show sent along with me to record everything the naked people and I said, and my friend Lucy, who was coming along both for emotional support and in hopes that this naked cruise was going to be every bit as awesome as I kept telling her it would be.

"Everyone on the boat is going to be fully nude and just kind of free, y'know?" I told her excitedly. "There's also supposed to be a very nice buffet."

"I'm sorry," Lucy said. "It just doesn't sound like my kind of thing."

"Please, I really need this."

"Fine, but you owe me one."

"You got it!"

I figured if things didn't go as planned, at least I'd be on a boat

---

1 It's true. He had the outfits and everything. It was really cool.

with a good friend, which is always nice. Also, to be honest, whether I took my clothes off or not, I didn't feel secure enough in my masculinity to go out there with just another dude.

The naked boat was setting sail from Sheepshead Bay, an area of Brooklyn that looks like it was once the stomping grounds of sailors, convicts, and whores but is now a port of call for sexy, sexy people with both a taste for adventure and a distaste for clothes, which is to say, people I totally could not wait to hang out with. I was certain the boat was going to be teeming with open-minded, uninhibited, and totally butt-naked superfoxes and maybe a handful of dudes with their junk out that I would just have to accept as part of the deal.

As our cab pulled up to the docks, it wasn't hard to spot the naked party boat. It was practically radiating good times. Even from far away I could see large swatches of flesh passing sexily by the boat's windows.

"Come to us, Dave, you succulent man," I swore I heard them call from the distance. "We're waaaaiting. . . ." My expectations, however, were dealt their first blow as soon as we got a little closer and myopia was no longer on my side. There, awaiting our arrival in the boat's entryway, was Ron, the event organizer and—to his credit—the brains behind the operation. Pale, freckled, and fiftyish, Ron wore only glasses and had a build not unlike a lopsided baked potato with four toothpicks shoved into it. One gut picked up just below where the first one left off and, well, I was determined not to investigate any further south after that.

"Whatever, I'm not here to look at dudes anyway," I thought.

"Welcome," Ron said with a firm yet slightly-too-long handshake. "I'm so happy you've decided to cover our little event here!"

"It's my pleasure," I said before immediately questioning that statement.

"Wonderful," Ron said. "Now climb aboard, we'll be setting sail just as soon as everyone gets situated."

As I quickly learned, in Ron's vocabulary "situated" meant "pantsless." At this point, I was starting to think maybe this would be like the movie *Eyes Wide Shut* where all the men were old and flabby, but all the women were still scorching hot for some reason. But that delusion was shattered only seconds later as Ron led me to the main dining area of the boat. There I was greeted by about thirty absolutely nude men and women in their forties and fifties, a shameless sea of pasty flab, cellulite, and slowly graying pubic hair.

"Usually we have a bigger group," Ron explained, "but the rain has kept a lot of folks away."

"Are you sure it's the rain?" I wanted to ask him.

To be fair, this wasn't necessarily an unattractive bunch. They more served to illustrate the fact that most people should probably keep covered up at all times than, for example, the idea that ugly people simply can't wait to drop their pants in a group setting. The exception, of course, were the half dozen gay men seated together in one corner, who were uniformly toned and tanned from head-to-toe. (As I understand it, most gay men receive a gym membership in the mail immediately after even grazing a male crotch other than their own for the first time, so this wasn't a surprise, really.)

As I slowly made my way around the boat, I decided to take my shirt off in a show of solidarity. Pale, flabby, somehow skinny and fat at the same time, and with enough random patches of body hair to singlehandedly prove the theory of evolution, I'm not exactly headed for the cover of *Men's Fitness* any time soon myself. Still, I was confident my looks (or lack thereof) would land me squarely between Ron and the table of gay guys, so I figured I might as well go for it.

"You're not going to take off your pants?" Ron teased me.

"Baby steps, Ron," I told him. "Baby steps."

"Oh, come on, Dave," he persisted. "Why not just see how you feel without them for a bit? For me."

"What happened to the 'optional' part in 'clothing optional'?" I wondered. He could have at least offered to buy me a drink or told me how nice my hair looked first. But, among other things, tonight was about acceptance, so Ron let the whole thing about me keeping my wedding tackle under wraps slide as he began to further explain what exactly I was in for once we pulled up anchor and headed out into the extra-friendly waters.

"There's only one rule at our dinners," Ron smiled. "No hot soup."

He said that last part like it was the group's official slogan. I wanted to suggest he get it printed up on T-shirts, but it seemed pointless. And as it turned out, there was another rule besides that one—everyone has to put a towel down on their chair before sitting, a courtesy that I'm guessing facilitates both sanitary table hopping and Ron getting his deposit back.

As Ron continued bringing me up to speed, I couldn't help but notice he was one of those people who stands just a little too close to you when he's talking, a detail greatly magnified by the fact that his senior vice president was flapping in the breeze as he spoke to me. Still, I had a job to do, so I held my ground and began asking the tough questions.

"What about erections?" I asked.

"What about them?" Ron replied.

"Well, are they frowned upon or . . . not at all?" I asked with a wink.

"It rarely happens," he explained as if he were reading aloud from some member literature, "but if it does, we ask that the owner simply be discreet about it and excuse himself."

"Good to know," I said.

"But I think you'll find this is a completely nonsexual environment," Ron continued.

I couldn't have agreed with him more, but I think my reasons were different than his.

A moment later, Ron's wife, Elaine, walked over to join in the fun. Again, I have no doubt she was a perfectly attractive woman with clothes on, but au naturel she was just further proof of what I've been saying since the '80s—no one should ever take their clothes off in front of another human unless there is either a medical emergency, the prospect of friction, or a significant amount of money changing hands. For starters, Elaine's personal lawncare choices made her look almost like she was wearing a snow-covered ghillie suit.[2] I'd go on but I'm kind of a gentleman.

"How are you enjoying yourself so far?" Elaine asked me.

"I'm just so . . . happy to be at sea," I said, struggling for an answer.

"Yeah, it's so nice and breezy," she agreed.

With Elaine at his unencumbered side, Ron quickly turned to her for backup on how their group dinners were more about enjoying a nice meal with like-minded folks than checking out other people's gender bits.

"The thing about our group is no one is going around looking at other people's privates or anything like that," Elaine said firmly. "It's just not what we're about."

"Of course not, Elaine," I agreed. "May I call you Elaine?"

"Sure. Anyway, one thing I always say to people about these dinners is that I've never had so many people look me directly in the eyes."

I didn't doubt it, but that just seemed to be about survival more than anything else. I had been on the boat for less than ten minutes and was already worried I'd need to be treated for post-traumatic stress disorder once I got back on dry land.

Once my conversation with Ron and Elaine ran, ahem, bare, I decided to make my way to the bar. Normally I try to avoid drinking on the job but I felt like I had plenty of excuses this time, so I ordered myself a beer. The bartender, an employee of the cruise line, evidently looking to join in the fun, was working shirtless tonight. Acknowledging each other's pants, we gave a "there but for the grace of God go I" look to each other before I turned around to do some sexy mingling.

---

2 A ghillie suit is a type of camouflage clothing designed to make its wearer appear to be covered in woodsy foliage. I saw a cop wear one on *To Catch a Predator* once and—while entirely unnecessary—it was still pretty awesome. The predator in question never saw it coming when the cop in the ghillie suite jumped up from the front lawn and tackled him to the ground. That's the fun thing about ghillie suits—that element of surprise. If you ever see one for sale, you should probably pick it up. That way if you are ever in a situation where it might be even slightly appropriate to don a ghillie suit—bam—you're all set.

By this time, Lucy, who had wandered off on her own shortly after we came aboard in order to let me wear my journalist hat, was already deep in conversation with a handful of naked people at a nearby table. The fact that she remained fully clothed must have rendered her exotic in their eyes as they were showering her with attention. As soon as I walked over to join them, however, they grew quiet. Thanks to Ron, word that I was a reporter had already made its way around the boat and no one was too eager to be outed as a practicing nudist by me, the guy with a notepad and completely fastened pants.

"People at my job wouldn't understand," a mustachioed man with a dangling earring explained to me.

"Really? That's strange," I said, trying to sound sympathetic. "So you're not exactly crazy about wearing pants—big deal."

"That's what I think," he agreed.

"Some men you just can't reach," I told him, shaking my head.

There was a reporter and photographer from *The New York Times* on the boat, too, but they seemed to be taking in the proceedings from afar, as if they were at the zoo, not getting right into the pen like I was. I suppose in that way, I was a bit more threatening. Plus, with the exception of the gay guys, I had the closest thing to a six-pack going on the entire starboard side, which wasn't saying a whole lot, but it must have been a little intimidating under the circumstances.

"Are you okay?" I whispered to Lucy as I tried to blend in with her and her new friends.

"Yeah, these people are really nice," she whispered back. "Really weird, but nice."

"Pretty strong words coming from the only person on this boat with all her clothes on," I said while pulling up a chair.

No sooner did I get settled in with Lucy and the naked people than Ron rang the dinner bell. Across from the bar was a banquet table covered in heaping trays of food. It turns out naked people eat pretty much the same stuff that clothed people do: salad, string beans, salmon, bowtie pasta, and a beef dish of some sort. The difference, however, was that in this scenario people's junk dangled just inches from the hot plates and Bunsen burners. I would have thought the situation called for a pud guard of sorts, but clearly this gang didn't have hang-ups like I did. I cringed as I watched a man's leaky faucet come dangerously close to plunging into a bowl of honey mustard vinaigrette.

"Sir, uh—" I said to him.

"Yes?"

"Never mind."

Suddenly, my hunger trumped any other issues I might have had at the moment, so I powered through, skipping the salad yet filling my plate to the edge like the hearty fourth generation seaman I am.

Settling in back at a table with the naked people, I attempted to get their stories. A fairly equal mix of men and women, some wore facial hair, some not, some wore pubic hair, some not. It was a good start, but I wanted to learn more.

"So, what brings you guys here tonight?" I asked. "Are you all nudists looking to mix things up with a little boating? Or is it maybe the other way around?"

Despite my sincere interest, most of them kept quiet and the ones that were willing to speak with me did so as if they had just taken a media training seminar for people who hate clothes.

"This isn't about sex, this is about being together in our natural state," a man with hair on his chest and nowhere else told me as the rest of the naked people nodded in agreement. I decided to take them at their word, mostly because I was whatever the opposite of horny is at that point, and it wasn't hard to agree that this night had absolutely, positively nothing to do with sex. Still, their answer didn't exactly explain why an attendee who introduced himself as "the Wolf" got dressed only from the waist up once a cool sea breeze rolled in.

"What's with the sweatshirt?" I asked.

"I'm cold," the Wolf said.

"Are you cold just from the waist up then or . . . ?" I persisted.

"No. I'm cold all over."

"Why no pants then?"

"I don't know."

"What do you mean you don't know?"

"I just don't know."

"So it really is all about having your beef thermometer out then, right?" I asked the Wolf as professionally as I knew how.

It felt like an "a-ha!" moment to me, but the Wolf just continued to dodge the question. That didn't stop me from getting at least a few answers out of him, though. Apparently the Wolf first got into nudism after seeing a sign for nude camping grounds while he was out for a drive one day. Wasting no time, he pulled over and joined in the fun. Even more impressive was the fact that this was the Wolf's first time at one of these "clothing optional" dinners and he had come alone.

I can't imagine circumstances that would cause me to show up somewhere all by myself for the very first time and just whip my master of ceremonies out like that. It was hard not to admire the guy at least a little bit.

Once the naked people and I had had our fill of the buffet, a gaggle of us headed to the upper deck to enjoy some of that sea air (though, admittedly, them more than me). Lucy stayed behind and continued to hold court with some other naked people. Her clothes still on, the naked people simply could not look away.

The upper deck was sort of an observation deck turned dance floor. There was another bar up there, so I decided to throw some more gasoline on the fire by buying another round for me and some of my new friends. Or so I thought they were. Separated from Lucy, I no longer had an ally and the naked people wasted no time in pressuring me to fully join their ranks.

"How about losing those pants?" a fiftyish, earth-mother type with a long, gray braid suggested coyly.

"You just want to see my package!" I protested.

Again, they all denied having any interest in that sort of thing and simply suggested I join them so that I might better understand what they were all about.

"You're a journalist," they pleaded. "How can you report on to-night without truly experiencing it?"

"I feel like I'm getting a pretty good sense of things," I said defensively while subtly making sure my belt was fastened and my fly was still up.

"Puh-lease," the earth mother said, rolling her eyes.

A few sips of beer later, I decided to throw the naked people a bone and took my jeans off. I had to admit the breeze was nice, even with my boxers still on. But with my assets still shrouded in breathable cotton, my gesture meant little to them.

"That doesn't count, Dave," the earth mother scolded. "Give us your underwear."

"Look, if you really want to see my dick so badly, why don't you just come out and say it?" I told them.

"No one wants to look at your dick, Dave," the guy with the dangling earring assured me.

"Okay, fine, so you just want to see my balls, then? Is that it?" I countered. Admittedly, the sometimes cruel rhythms of the sea had me a bit nauseous by this point, so I was starting to spout nonsense.

"We told you, we're not about any of that stuff," a woman with a full Brazilian chimed in.

"No, Dave," the earth mother seconded. "Now please join us."

"Yeah, Dave," the dangling earring guy chimed in with a New Agey grin. "Join us."

I don't know if it was the sea air, the alcohol, or Donna Summer blaring over the boat's sound system that did it, but I was starting to believe them. And as the fleshy mob slowly surrounded me, I was also beginning to think I had little choice but to lose my boxers or jump overboard.

"All right," I told them. "I'll do it!"

At that the naked people cheered in unison as if they had all won tickets to see a revival of *Oh! Calcutta!*

Kind of like submerging yourself in a freezing swimming pool, I figured dropping my boxers gradually would only make things worse, so I whipped them off in one swift, jerking, scream-filled motion.

And immediately following that motion my genitals practically caught fire from the amount of stares they received from the naked people.

"You're all looking at my package!" I screamed. "I totally just busted all of you!"

"Come on, Dave." The lady with the hairless infield blushed. "It's not like we're not gonna take a little peek."

" 'A little peek?' You were all just plain staring and you know it!"

Silence. These people disgusted me. Or did they? After all, I was now one of them. And I have to admit, after that initial tension subsided, I kind of liked it. No sooner had I dropped my boxers than the naked people suddenly dropped all that "It's not sexual" crap they had been trying to feed me all night.

"I'm also a member of a polyamory group," the earth mother cooed at me.

"I'm shocked," I deadpanned.

It turned out that, in addition to her office job, she ran an S&M-themed side business where her specialty involved strapping on a pair of high heels and kicking customers right in the clangers. And the guy with the dangling earring and lady with the bald vagina? Together, they were part of a swingers group and had been riding one another like a mechanical bull since the early '90s.

"You have a very nice package," the earth mother told me as if she were admiring my tie.

Admittedly, I had to ask her several times before she was willing to give me her opinion on the matter, but it was still nice to hear her talk so freely like that.

"Your stuff is, uh, nice, too," I responded, not sure what I meant but wanting to return the compliment somehow.

The more I opened up to the naked people, the more they opened up to me. With my dingle dangle twisting in the night air, I was no longer a journalist, but simply a fresh new face joining them for a night on the high and sexy seas.

"I can't help but notice you have no hair on your vagina," I said matter-of-factly to the woman with no hair on her vagina.

"Nope—I sure don't." She smiled. "You're a very observant young man."

"Thanks. I get that a lot."

It turned out she had been waxing her downtown real estate for years now and couldn't imagine turning back. The guy with the dangling earring seemed just as excited about it as she did.

"You should try it," she said eagerly.

"Yeah, you should try it," the guy with the dangling earring agreed, turning toward me.

The balls on this guy. Literally. Sorry, folks, you can take my dignity, but you can't take my shrubbery. I need that. For a lot of stuff.

With the playing field leveled and a full inventory taken of both my best and worst features by my fellow naked people, we decided to take a stroll together around the upper deck of the boat to take in a bit of the night breeze, which—with my boxers now draped over a nearby railing—really seemed to be picking up all of a sudden. To maintain some sense of decorum, I yelled down to Lucy to tell her that, in order to preserve our friendship, I really needed her to stay on the lower deck until the show was over. To her credit, she was fine with it. The naked people, not so much.

"Why won't you let her see you naked?" the earth mother asked.

"Because I don't want to scar her for life," I explained.

"But I already told you, you have a very nice package," she countered.

"Thanks. And it means a lot. But I'm really going to need everyone to respect my wishes here, okay?"

"Fine."

As we sexily made our way toward the ship's bow, we naked people happened upon the photographer from *The Times,* an attractive female twentysomething, who was busy snapping away like she had just spotted Jennifer Aniston on the town with a new boyfriend. I was surprised to find myself equally embarrassed and titillated as the fact that my chancellor had shown up to the party slowly registered across her face.

"Oh, no, the hot *New York Times* photographer can see my package!" half of me thought.

"Oh, cool, the hot *New York Times* photographer can see my package!" the other half thought.

As the *Times* photographer did her best to pull herself together at the sight of me, I continued to let the night air have its way with me. But no sooner had I grown accustomed to the all-new, all-nude me than the ship's fully clothed captain announced that the ship would soon be arriving back at shore, that dreaded netherworld where clothes were not only the norm, they were required by law. With that, my fellow skin aficionados and I headed for the stairs back down to the main level. Before I descended, I decided to put my boxers and pants back on. Not only did I not want Lucy to run screaming at the sight of me, but I didn't feel like sharing Naked Dave with those who had remained downstairs all night. Naked Dave was only for my fellow naked upper deckers, the ones who had really earned it.

Once back on the main level, I ran into big, butt-naked Ron again. Apparently the legend of Naked Dave had made its way down to the the main level well before my triumphant return.

"So, how did you like it?" Ron asked.

"It was nice," I told him. "But just so you know, the first thing everyone did was look at my package. You might wanna have a little talk with these people."

"Come on, Dave." Ron shrugged. "It's not like we're not gonna take a little peek."

Whatever.

As dry land slowly came into focus, my fellow birthday-suit boosters and I pulled the rest of our clothes back on like ancient slaves reluctantly refastening our own shackles. Not surprisingly, there was no shortage of tie-dye and batik ensembles, New Age jewelry, and other stuff I had already chosen to imagine them in during those moments when all that skin got to be a bit more than I could handle. And it was safe to say that—without exception—everyone was a whole lot more attractive covered up a little bit. I even wanted to tell some of them they looked so good with clothes on it was almost hard to believe how horrifying they looked naked, but suddenly it dawned on me how that might not sound like the compliment I meant it to be.

"That's a really fun top," I said to the earth mother instead.

"Yeah, it's okay," she said, clearly struggling with having to cover up.

Once we were safely docked, my new friends and I made our way back to shore where I noticed a handful of clothes-loving landlubbers loitering near the dock.

"Guess what. We were all just totally naked out there on that boat!" I wanted to yell out to them. "Butts, boobs, johnsons, hoo-has, everything!"

But in the end, I thought better of it. Sure, it would have been awesome, but it might not have been cool, especially with me being a serious journalist and all.

Before we went our separate ways, the earth mother, the guy with the dangling earring, the woman with the shaved infield, and I all exchanged business cards. They wanted me to get in touch with them as soon as my story came out and I wanted to see if their business cards said anything about how much they are totally into getting naked all the time (in case you're wondering, not even a mention. I know. I thought it was weird, too).

A couple days after my sexy night at sea, I received a coquettish e-mail from the earth mother.

"My polyamory group has regular outings to the beach. We have a bonfire and lots and lots of fun," she wrote. "You should really think about joining us sometime."

That was two years ago. I'm still thinking about it.

Loving You Is Easy Because You Live Pretty Close to My Parents' House

Love—it's a funny game, isn't it? One minute you're terrified you're going to die alone, the next minute you're pressing a stack of twenties into someone's hands just to finally get them out of your life once and for all. And yet we keep coming back for more, don't we?

My earliest memories of romance go all the way back to kindergarten. But as I sit here typing this, a for-the-most-part grown man, it occurs to me that chronicling my once burning desire for a five-year-old girl might come off as a little creepy. So—in the interest of preserving a modicum of decency in these pages—please allow me to skip ahead a bit and start things off by telling you about a twelve-year-old girl I once had the hots for.

It was a Friday night back in the seventh grade and I was spending it, as I did most weekend nights, sitting at the kitchen table, staring into the family room, trying and mostly failing to get the attention of my sisters' friends, who had come over for a bit of television watching and important girl talk. Suddenly, the phone rang. The odds of it being for me weren't great, but I went ahead and answered it anyway.

"Hello, Hill residence," I said. "This is the king speaking."[1]

"Dave?" asked the voice on the other end.

---

1 Okay, I might have made up that last bit, but it's just occurring to me now that that would have been pretty awesome.

"Hey, Marla," I said, recognizing the voice as belonging to one of the few girls in my grade willing to address me directly.

"I have a question for you," she said. "Who do you like?"

"Christina," I said without hesitation, naming the object of my burning desire since the third grade.

"Oh, uh . . ." Marla stammered. "Well, who else do you like?"

"Abbey."

"Who else?"

"Jessica."

"All right, what about Mary Jean?" Marla asked, cutting to the chase.

"Sure, she's cool," I told her.

"Would you ever go with her?"[2]

"Sure."

"Okay, hang on a second," Marla said. "I'll put her on."

"Hello? Who's on the phone?" yet another voice on the line said. "I need to use the phone this minute."

"Mom, hang up, I'm on the phone!" I yelled.

It turned out my mom had picked up the upstairs extension—as she often did—just as soon as things were getting good.

"Hurry it up," my mom said before slamming down the receiver.

A couple of seconds later, I heard another voice come on the line. It was Mary Jean. Finally.

"Hi," she said.

"Hi," I answered.

"What are you doing?"

"Just sitting here mostly. What are *you* doing?" I said, trying to sound about as sexy and coquettish as a twelve-year-old was legally allowed to at the time.

"Nothing," she answered.

"Cool."

---

2 When I was in elementary school, kids used the phrase "go with" to mean "go out with" or "date." These were simpler times, and we made the best of things with what we had.

"So, what do you think?" Mary Jean asked, subtly addressing our possible romantic future.

"Uh, um, yes, I would like to go with you," I said brashly.

"Cool."

"Cool."

"Okay, I'll see you in school on Monday."

"Okay. Bye, Mary Jean. See you Monday. Say bye to Marla for me."

By seventh-grade standards, shit was totally on. I showed up to school the following Monday with a bit of extra swagger in my step and some added attention given to my hair, which at the time I wore short, sometimes parting it on the right, other times parting it on the left without warning in order to let everyone around me know that I was a guy who had no time for rules.

As you can probably imagine, word spread pretty quickly around the seventh grade that Mary Jean and I were officially an item. Since she was pretty and a member of the "popular girls" clique, going with her gave me an instant bump in social status. And since I was neither good at sports nor school, Mary Jean gained herself a bit of street credibility by going with a fucking outlaw. Raising the stakes on things was the fact that Mary Jean and I weren't even in the same homeroom—risky circumstances that forced us to seize opportunities for romance wherever and whenever they came along. It was like something out of *West Side Story* only with less knives, dancing, and ethnic conflict. Most days, we had little choice but to express our love during class changeovers.

"Hey," I'd say to her as we passed each other in single-file lines between lessons, lingering for as long as possible without stopping the line in its tracks altogether.

"Hey," she'd say.

"How was history?"

"It sucked."

"That sucks. I'm . . . really sorry to hear that," I'd respond in an effort to let her know that I cared about her in a way that went way beyond just her good looks.

It wasn't much, but we made the most of it, like amorous dogs sniffing each other briefly before their owners jerk them apart and continue down the block. We rarely exchanged more than a few words in person, instead saving them up for our sometimes twice-weekly phone conversations, during which we'd talk about the important seventh-grade matters of the day until my mom insisted I let her use the phone. They were pretty good times. I was young and in love and I felt like anything was possible. One day, however, just a few weeks into our scorching-hot romance, everything changed.

"Mary Jean wants to talk to you," Marla said to me one day at recess.

I stood waiting anxiously on the small strip of cement in between the boys' area and the girls' area of the playground as Mary Jean cautiously approached. Right away I knew something was wrong. That familiar flicker of youthful romance I had come to know so well was suddenly gone from her eyes. Her skirt hung at a length that the nuns at our school would have had absolutely no problem with. And her hair, well, frankly it was like she wasn't even trying anymore.

"I . . . need to talk to you," she said.

Even at the age of twelve, I already knew it was never good to hear a woman say those words.

"I don't want to go with you anymore," she said.

"What? Why?" I whimpered.

"It's just not working for me anymore," Mary Jean said, staring into the distance.

"Is there . . . anything I can do t-to . . . ch-change your mind?" I sputtered.

"No . . . I-I'm sorry," she said before scampering away like a siren in some old French film.

And so it ended. Mary Jean and I were a thing of the past, a footnote in the long and sordid romantic history of my Catholic elementary school before we had even had a chance to share an awkward first kiss or hang out in front of the deli up the street from school or anything. It would be a long time before I could even think about loving a woman again.

The following year, I entered the eighth grade a changed man mentally, emotionally, and—perhaps most important—physically. I noticed similar changes in my classmates, particularly the girls, and, seemingly from out of nowhere, felt ready to love again. Unfortunately, I couldn't find any takers, which was especially hard on the thirteen-year-old me as many of the other kids in my class seemed to already be living out a lot of the stuff I saw happen in *Fast Times at Ridgemont High* on cable at my friend's house one weekend, at least according to cafeteria rumors anyway.

"Dude, Joey got to second base with Monica for, like, two hours straight this weekend in one of the upstairs bedrooms at Billy's house while his parents were out of town," a friend would say.

"No. Way," I'd respond.

"Way."

"Way?"

"Way!"

One Friday, I decided to join a bunch of my fellow eighth graders for something called "ski bus," a chartered coach that showed up in the parking lot after school and took seventh and eighth graders skiing at one of Northeastern Ohio's several nonthreatening ski resorts. We'd all hit the slopes for a few hours together, bundled in colorful '80s ski attire, and then be dumped back off in the school parking lot just in time to beat curfew. For reasons I still can't comprehend, there was no adult supervision on the bus aside from the driver, so naturally the ski bus quickly transformed into a caravan of raging, barely pubescent hormones, a veritable rolling Club Hedonism for twelve- and thirteen-year-old Catholic school children.

"Do you want to play Seven Minutes in Heaven, Dave?" Marla, pretty much my romance broker at that point, asked me as I sat shivering in long johns and jeans that were soaked from repeatedly falling into damp Midwestern snow for two hours straight.

"Huh?" I responded.

"Seven Minutes in Heaven," she huffed. "You pick out a girl and then you both go to the back of the bus for seven minutes and do, you know, *whatever.*"

I was still confused until I turned around to discover that the back of the ski bus was a sea of slobbering lips and clumsily roaming hands.

"Whoa," I thought. Suddenly I was standing at the outskirts of Makeout City and I wanted desperately to become mayor.

"Sure," I said to Marla, playing it cool. "Why not?"

Marla dragged me a couple of rows over to where four or five Catholic school girls were lined up like Thai prostitutes during Fleet Week.

"Which one do you want?" Marla asked.

At that point in my life, I would have settled for just about anyone recognized by the medical community as female, so to actually have a choice in the matter was almost too much for me to handle. And thanks to the social Darwinism of the ski bus, all the girls in question were at the very least pretty cute by elementary school standards, so I couldn't lose.

"I'll take Jenny," I said, pointing at the one girl who definitely wasn't taller than I was.

"Okay, head to the back," Marla said. "Your seven minutes start right now."

What happened next is still largely a blur, just as it had been immediately afterward. There I was, a thirteen-year-old boy still trying to piece his life back together after having his heart squashed all over the playground a year earlier, now totally about to make out with an actual girl for the first time in his entire life. Fortunately for me, Jenny had totally made out with someone before and guided me through the process, as I imagine most Thai prostitutes tend to do with their first-timers. As soon as we settled into one of the pleather-lined benches in the back of the sexy, sexy ski bus, Jenny wrapped her arms around my neck and shoved her tongue in my mouth, something I somehow never saw coming, not even after having seen *Fast Times at Ridgemont High* at my friend's house that one night. Taking my cues from Jenny, I shoved my tongue in her mouth and held on for dear life. My technique was crude, brash, and desperate— perhaps even more so than it is now. Fortunately for Jenny, exactly seven minutes later, I felt a tap on my shoulder.

"Time's up," Marla said, looking down at us like a tired and impatient madam who's seen it all.

I politely peeled myself off Jenny and dizzily stood up. Having passed what felt like a major milestone in my life, I was both exhilarated and relieved, at once thrilled to have the whole thing over with while severely disappointed that an entire seven minutes could fly by so quickly.

"Thanks, Jenny, that was really fun," I said before returning to my seat. "And thank you, Marla, for making it all possible. You're doing important work here."

After the bus dropped us back off in the school parking lot a short while later, I walked home through the icy suburban Cleveland snow as a man for the very first time in my life, dried slobber from both mine and Jenny's mouths glistening on my lips and cheeks like stardust in the pale moonlight. It totally ruled.

As much as I thought that anything-goes night of fun on the ski bus was just the beginning of my molten-hot love life, one that would involve making out with eighth-grade girls whenever I felt like it and maybe even a few seventh- and ninth-grade girls when I was feeling a little nuts, too, things cooled off pretty quickly afterward. In fact, it would be three long years before Lady Love would darken my doorstep once more.

Sheila was the older sister of Julian, one of my hockey teammates. We met after a school football game during my sophomore year. She had jet-black hair and olive skin and was the most beautiful girl I had ever seen in my whole entire life. And since she lived over a half hour away from me on the other side of town, she was also exotic, a temptress even. The only problem was that at the time she was dating some other guy in my class, so—to shield myself from heartache—I tried to forget she even existed. Then one day during my junior year, she sauntered back into my life, as temptresses so often do.

"Sheila was asking about you at the football game this weekend," my friend Todd told me at school one Monday morning.

"What?" I responded. "What do you mean?"

"I don't know," Todd said. "She was just acting all weird and asking everyone where you were."

"What did she say?"

"I don't know, dude. That chick's a weirdo anyway. Why don't you ask her brother Julian what the deal is?"

Todd was right—Sheila was a weirdo, if by weirdo you mean exotic superfox that I was now officially hell-bent on making my own. I ran into her brother Julian, a freshman, in the school library the next day.

"Sheila says hi," Julian said, beating me to the punch.

"What do you mean? What's going on?" I asked him while trying to keep myself from doing that thing where you grab someone by the collar and press them up against a wall in order to get them to start answering some tough questions.

"I dunno," Julian said. "I guess she likes you or something."

"Doesn't she have a boyfriend?"

"Not anymore. Why don't you call her?"

"Maybe I will," I said nonchalantly.

Since Julian was a whole two years younger than me, it would have been socially unacceptable of him to be protective of his older sister and not just go ahead and hand over his family's home telephone number (remember, this was all happening in pre–cell phone times), so he scribbled it down on a piece of notebook paper and sent me on my way.

I was officially freaking out. In case you couldn't tell, kissing Jenny that night on the ski bus was just physical. Sure, it was great and all, but feelings never really came into play. But knowing that Sheila actually liked me, Dave Hill, a not particularly cool kid from all the way on the other side of town, was practically making my heart explode.

That night, I snuck down into the basement of my family's house to call Sheila from the phone we kept in the laundry room, the most private place in the whole house since everyone in my family absolutely despised doing laundry.

The phone rang a few times. "Is Sheila there?" I asked the lady who answered.

"Just a second," the lady said.

It turned out the lady was Sheila's mom. And the twenty or thirty seconds I had to wait for Sheila to pick up the phone felt like an eternity.

"Hello?" she said, probably not trying to sound sexy at all but still sounding totally, totally sexy to me.

"Sheila?" I squeaked. "This is Dave Hill."

"Hi."

It was refreshing that Sheila didn't hang up as soon as she heard it was me, as that tended to be most people's reaction back then. In fact, it sounded like she was actually glad to hear from me. "Weird," I thought.

"How's it going?" I asked, trying and failing to sound like the coolest sixteen-year-old of all-time.

"Great," she answered.

Of course it was going great. She was the most beautiful girl in the whole world. Why wouldn't it be?

"How are you?" she continued.

"I'm really great. Thanks so much for asking."

I hadn't necessarily thought I would get that far into an actual conversation with her, what with Sheila being an actual girl and all, so I wasn't sure what to say next. Angel that she was, however, she took the reins of the conversation and I somehow managed to have a breezy, delightful discussion with her that—since my mom was at the grocery store at the time—lasted ten, maybe even twelve minutes as we chatted away about everything and nothing at all, finishing each other's sentences, and laughing hysterically at whatever hilarious thing one of us had just said. When my mom finally came home, I even managed to play it reasonably cool after she picked up the phone in the kitchen and demanded I hang up immediately.

"Sure thing, Mom," I said. "It was nice talking with you, Sheila. I'll give you a ring tomorrow."

I'm not sure where I got the moxie—nay, *balls*—to throw in that last line, but I actually did end up calling Sheila the next day and the day after that, too. And by the time the weekend finally came around, Sheila and I were hanging out. Together. We met up at my high school's football game like we had for the first time ever the year before, only this time instead of being there with some guy I wanted dead, she was there with me. It felt like the most important moment in my life thus far. When I walked into the football stadium, it could not be debated—I, Dave Hill, was there not only with a girl, but with the most beautiful girl of all-time. I felt like a champion, a champion of love, the best kind of champion. My hair looked good, too.

"So, do you like football?" I asked Sheila as we sat huddled together in the bleachers.

"No, I hate it."

God I loved this girl. I hated football, too. It was like we were made for each other. And, in an act of social defiance, Sheila and I left the football game early to go hang out at the Burger King near her house, where we made two Cokes and a large order of fries last as long as possible as we sat there figuring out what other stuff we both hated. Football, school, curfews, New Kids on the Block, at least half the people we knew in common—the list was endless.

I'm sure I had been happy plenty of times, maybe even most of the time before then, but being with Sheila somehow made me feel happy for the first time in my life. I couldn't get enough of her, either in person or on the phone. Since she used Finesse mousse on her hair, I even used to sneak down the hair-care aisle of the local drugstore and spray a little into my hand to tide me over until I saw her next. A little creepy maybe, but I was convinced she was my soul mate so I did what I had to do.

A few weeks into our courtship, I borrowed my parents' Chevy Impala station wagon and went for a wild night on the town with Sheila and a couple of other friends to Burger King, McDonald's, and maybe even Wendy's while we were at it. My friend Todd joined us and, since he lived on the same side of town as I did, over twenty long miles away from Sheila's house, he was the last one in the car besides Sheila and me when I went to drop her off at the end of the night.

"Dave, uh, why don't you walk Sheila to the door and I'll pull the car around so it's facing the right way for us to drive the rest of the way home?" Todd blurted as we pulled into Sheila's driveway.

A little awkward maybe, but I still thought he was the best guy ever for seeing to it that Sheila and I got a little alone time as, terrified sixteen-year-old that I was, I had yet to muster the courage to actually kiss her yet. It would not be a stretch to say that the line "Oh, God, my chance has come at last" from the Smiths' "There Is a Light That Never Goes Out" was running through my head over and over at that very moment. (In fact, I still hear it pretty much every time I find myself in that sort of situation.)

Sheila lived on a cul-de-sac, so Todd drove my parents' station wagon as slowly as possible, his foot barely on the gas pedal, all the way down to the other end before slowly turning around and heading back toward Sheila's house. It was freezing out, so because of that and the near-paralyzing fear I was feeling at the moment, I was shivering. I stood with Sheila in her driveway while knowing full well that I absolutely had to make my move before Todd returned if I didn't want to spend the following week anxiously waiting for another opportunity like this to come around.

"So, uh, that was fun tonight," I said.

"Yeah, thanks for driving," Sheila said.

"No problem."

Shit. There were literally seconds to spare as I saw Todd begin to lurch back toward us in the Impala, which by then looked like some slowly approaching phantom to me. Suddenly, a force I had never known before sent me hurdling toward Sheila's face, my eyes closed and my mouth open as wide as humanly possible. Sheila picked up on my brazen cue and did the same. It was pure magic as our lips finally met for the first time, the moon shining down on us through the trees as if we were the only two people on earth.

Until Todd pulled back into the driveway.

As the headlights of my parents' station wagon blinded us, Sheila and I slowly pulled apart to return to the awkward, stammering state we had been in only moments before.

"I'll, uh, talk to you tomorrow," I said as the biggest smile of all-time spread over my face.

"Okay."

"Good night, Sheila."

"Good night, Dave."

I climbed back into the Impala easily feeling like twice the man I was after that night on the ski bus back in the eighth grade. Even Todd, not normally the sentimental type, couldn't keep himself from giving me a high five.

"Awesome, dude," he said.

"Totally, dude."

Sheila and I continued our unbridled romance through the winter and it seemed like we were still going full-steam ahead by the following spring when she invited me out to her family's lake house one Saturday afternoon. It was our first official getaway, like we were a real couple or something.

As we wandered toward the water in front of the house in what I assumed was just some casual lovers' stroll, like the kind you see all the time in those karaoke videos, Sheila said to me, "I . . . need to talk to you."

Dammit. There were those words again.

"Um, okay," I said.

"My mom says I can't have a boyfriend until the school year is over because I need to get my grades up and boys are a distraction."

"Huh?" I gulped.

"I can't date you anymore. Because of school."

"Oh, you mean just for the rest of this school year and then when summer comes you can have a boyfriend again? Um, you know, meaning me, for example?"

"Yeah, something like that."

"But we can still talk on the phone and stuff, right?"

"No, my mom said I can't do that, either. Sorry."

I was devastated, but, blinded by love as I was, I figured that the school year would be over in less than two months and then Sheila and I could resume what I was pretty sure was the stuff of Harlequin romance novels, probably even better. As soon as we both finished finals, I went down into the laundry room and called her.

"Hello?" Sheila's mom answered.

"Hi, it's Dave, Dave Hill, from before," I said. "Is Sheila home?"

"Just a sec."

I waited breathlessly for Sheila to come on the line so we could pick up things right where we left off. Instead, however, Sheila's mom picked up the phone again.

"Sheila can't come to the phone right now," she told me. "So I guess she'll just have to call you back, maybe."

"Okay, great," I said obliviously before hanging up.

And then I waited. And waited.

A couple of hours later my sister Katy discovered me sitting on the dryer all alone. "What are you doing just sitting here?" she asked.

"Nothing. Get out of here!"

"Fine. Weirdo."

I spent the rest of the night in that laundry room and, while the phone rang repeatedly, it was never for me. Sheila did eventually call me again, but, looking back on it, it was most likely just to get me to stop phoning her house every five minutes. Do I still think about her, you ask? Of course I do. She was my first love and, unless you're made of stone or something, I guess you never quite get over that sort of thing.

I realize there might also be some people out there wondering if any other "stuff" happened after that night Sheila and I totally made out in her driveway. And to that I say yes, maybe it probably might have. But if you think for one second that I'm about to go into graphic detail about what two teenagers got up to in the back of a Chevy Impala station wagon just so some sicko can get a few cheap thrills from it, you've got another thing coming, thank you very much. Besides, it's not like any of that stuff really matters anyway. The important thing to remember is that I'm now a major, major celebrity and there are so many chicks out there who totally want to make out with me that it's actually a bit weird. Even so, there's just something about that first kiss in her driveway all those years ago that I'll never forget. In fact, not too long ago, in a fit of wistful and maybe just a little bit of drunken nostalgia, I decided to give old Sheila a ring.

"Hello," her husband answered.

He sounded like he might actually be a pretty nice guy. And if I didn't hang up right away, I bet I could have found out for sure.

· · · · · · · · ·

As of Now, I Am in Control Here[1]

It was the '90s and I had just graduated from Fordham University, shot like a cannonball from the warm, grassy bosom of a private liberal arts college and into what my guidance counselor kept trying to tell me was the real world, a place where my bullshit would not be tolerated. The original plan was to transition seamlessly from cafeteria-loitering undergraduate to globe-trotting rock star. I had the hair—curly, unwashed, and just long enough to make it clear to everyone around me that I was pretty much giving the finger to conventional society. I also had the guitar. I even had the rock band. The only things that were missing were the fame and money, those crucial pieces of the puzzle that would help all that rocking translate into no longer calling my parents collect to hit them up for cash all the time.

Since New York City rents had yet to reach fully ridiculous heights and my tastes at the time ran mostly toward wandering the streets drinking beer out of a brown paper bag and urinating between parked cars, my overhead was pretty low. Still, those forty-ounce bottles of

---

1 If you're a history buff, you may notice I borrowed the title of this essay from a press conference given by United States Secretary of State Alexander Haig on March 30, 1981, after John Hinckley, Jr., shot President Reagan in hopes of scoring a date with Hollywood's Jodie Foster, a plan that—against all odds—never really panned out. Alexander Haig, though—pure balls on that guy. How he said those words without giggling I'll never know.

whatever-was-on-sale weren't exactly going to pay for themselves, so—not wanting to move back home with my parents or make the most of my boyish good looks by trolling the West Side Highway in search of a quick buck followed by an awkward good-bye—I decided it was time to do the unthinkable and get a job.

I thought about working as a temp. My mother had run a temp agency back home in Cleveland, so showing up at some random office building to stuff envelopes for a couple of days only to disappear forever before I even had a chance to figure out exactly what sort of business was conducted there was practically in my blood. But the thought of someone seeing me on the subway dressed in a button-down shirt and a pair of Dockers[2] and thinking I had surrendered to the straight life was more than I could handle. Fortunately, my older and historically more responsible brother Bob already had a job as a case worker at a homeless shelter on the Upper West Side and suggested I might pick up some part-time work there until the whole rock star thing kicked in as planned.

Like the rest of the nine-to-five staff, my brother's job at the shelter involved actually helping people get their lives back on track, or at least as close to the track as possible. Then there was the skeleton crew that kept the residents fed, medicated, and out of trouble within reason the other sixteen hours of the day. This group consisted of a supervisor, who ran the show, a security guard, who mostly just answered the phone, and two program aides, who did whatever the supervisor or security guard told them to do. I had neither the experience to be a supervisor nor the air of menace to provide any sort of real security, so my brother figured working as a program aide was right up my alley. Being a legacy and all, I was hired after a brief phone call.

"Hi, this is Dave Hill," I said to Janet, the shelter's director, over the phone one day. "My brother Bob said you might need a new program aide and that I might be good at that sort of thing."

"Great," she said. "You can start next week."

---

2 The popular casual pant.

As best I could tell, all I really had to do at my new job was help serve meals, do bed checks at night, bake the occasional cake, and promise not to get drunk on the job. I took the fact that they actually had to include that last part in the job description as a sign that I would be working with a fun-loving bunch. For all this I would be pulling in a cool $7.77 an hour. Add to that the fact that I planned on helping myself to whatever food might be lying around the kitchen, I figured with even just a few snacks each shift I would be effectively making at least $8.88 an hour. Friends were impressed with my new job, as if working with the homeless were some noble deed.

"Wow," they'd say with a gentle smile. "You're a really good person for dedicating yourself to the underprivileged like that."

That thought never really occurred to me, though. I just saw it as easy work and easy money in what I chose to believe was an all-you-can-eat environment. It would almost be like getting paid to hang out at Sizzler.[3] I felt like the richest man alive.

My first day on the job was the following Saturday for the three-to-eleven shift. When I arrived, most of the shelter's two hundred or so residents were either out wandering the city or sitting in battered armchairs in the shelter's main room on the first floor. Depending on their age, mental stability, and the amount of prescriptions they might have been hopped up on, those in attendance either napped, played board games, or conversed with either themselves or whomever was sitting within shouting distance. Some of the residents had just lost or been kicked out of their homes, some had come from other shelters, and some had recently been living on the streets. Most, if they weren't native New Yorkers, were from Central America, the Caribbean, and South America. As a result, being a guy from the sleepy suburbs of Cleveland, I felt almost as displaced as most of them probably did. It felt like an even playing field, and I liked it. And having a different background from all the residents turned out

---

3 In case they don't have them where you live, Sizzler is a restaurant chain specializing in steak and seafood priced so low it's hard not to worry.

to be a good thing because it meant we had no choice but to relate to one another on a basic human level.

"What's for dinner tonight?" one of them might ask.

"Meat loaf," I'd answer.

"You fucking kidding me? Again? I fucking hate meat loaf."

"Me fucking too," I'd lie, solidifying our bond the best way I knew how—through mutual hatred. "As far as I'm concerned, that meat loaf can go suck a bag of dicks. I'm tired of its bullshit."

Other times we might discuss the possible merits of the temperature outside dropping or raising a few degrees, or exactly how many sugar and/or ketchup packets was a reasonable amount to carry on one's person at all times. Fifteen was deemed reasonable. Sixteen or more made you a nutjob. It didn't take long for me to realize that, hey, maybe we weren't so different after all.

By 5:00 P.M., however, the honeymoon was over. Freddie Russo, a Brooklyn-born seventysomething whose mood, I soon learned, often and quickly vacillated between playful bordering on delirious and irritable bordering on completely out of his fucking mind, came in after a long day of riding the bus nowhere in particular and needed a diaper change. Fast.

"Dave, can you assist Mr. Russo with putting on a new undergarment?" my supervisor asked. It was the kind of question you never really want directed at you.

"Sure." I gulped. "Th-thank you for the opportunity."

Unlike me, Freddie didn't seem to have too many hang-ups about the fact that—despite our having just met—we would soon be changing his Depends together. And I quickly learned, as we faced the task at hand in the fourth-floor corner room he shared with two other residents who had a cavalier approach to relieving themselves, the greater challenge in this situation was finding something, anything else to talk about while the diaper changing was taking place. Since it was Sunday, I figured I'd go with sports.

"So, uh, you gonna watch the game?" I asked him, not at all sure what game I might be referring to.

"I don't care much for sports," Freddie answered, the smell of fresh urine slowly mingling with the smell of stale urine already perfuming the air.

"Me neither. Uh, how about werewolves? Those things are pretty cool, right?"

He didn't take the bait, but that's okay—I wasn't sure what I meant by that, either.

I soon learned tasks like changing diapers were pretty much business as usual at the shelter. Disposing of lice-ridden mattresses (especially daunting given my aspiring rock star locks), administering breathalyzer tests to residents, and even collecting urine and stool samples is just a sampling of the fun I might get up to on an average day at the office.

Toward the end of each shift I'd poke my head into each of the shelter's sixty or so rooms to make sure every resident was in and accounted for by ten o'clock curfew. To rule out the possibility of someone's roommate simply yelling out "Here!" in the dark to cover for a buddy who might have snuck out for a drink or worse, I was required to actually see each resident in his or her room with my own eyes. As a result, I regularly barged in on one guy who, like clockwork, would be perched on the edge of his bed masturbating like he was in some sort of contest, no matter how many times I knocked first. I could never tell whether I was hurting or helping his mission by walking in on him like that, but regardless it was hard not to admire his joie de vivre. You can take away a man's home, and maybe even a little bit of his pride and dignity while you're at it. But, dammit, you can't stop him from living.

Another bed check all-star was a guy named Barry who had a hobby of collecting feces—animal, human, whatever he could get his hands on—in small plastic bags that the staff would have to delicately coax away from him each night.

"Good evening, Barry," I'd say. "You don't happen to have any bags of shit in here with you tonight, do you?"

"No. Why do you ask?"

"Come on, Barry, it's me, Dave. Now hand over the goods."

"Give me one good reason."

"Dammit, Barry, we've covered this before," I'd say. "And while I don't claim to have all the answers, I can tell you that having your own personal shit museum is just not cool no matter how good of an idea it might seem."

It was like trying to take a chicken bone from a dog—nothing could convince him he was better off without it. Still, all of the above was a delight compared to my time spent with a new resident named Ricky, who checked into the shelter with a mean case of scabies, the popular skin infection in which tiny bugs burrow under your skin, causing nasty sores, nonstop itching, and everyone around you to freak the fuck out. The guy was covered from head-to-toe and, somehow, whenever I showed up for work, needed to have lotion applied to each and every sore. Upping the ante on things was the fact that Ricky had a penchant for completely and repeatedly soiling himself over the course of the week and somehow never quite got around to changing his clothes. It was my job to not only apply a dab of lotion to each of Ricky's several hundred scabies sores but also dispose of his soiled clothing, supervise his shower, and make sure he put on a clean outfit when we were all done.

"The nuts—don't forget to wash behind the nuts," I'd suggest delicately as he lathered up.

"I already washed down there."

"Look, this is just one man's opinion, but you might want to take another pass," I'd tell him, noting the sort of buildup that's just part of the deal when you're the kind of guy for whom "going to the bathroom" does not necessarily involve dropping your pants or making use of an actual toilet.

Once Ricky's shower was complete, it was time for the lotion party. Young, paranoid, and totally not wanting any scabies of my own, I developed a rather elaborate ritual for the chore. First, I'd put on a pair of rubber gloves to handle the box containing the lotion. Then, I'd put another pair over the first pair to actually apply the lotion—I wasn't taking any chances. Duly protected, I'd apply a dab of lotion in a circular motion to each of his scabies sores, one at a time, like I was feeding little baby birds.

"So you're good mostly?" I'd ask Ricky as I gingerly applied a dime-size dollop of lotion to his left buttock.

"Yeah, things have been really great with me lately."

"Good to hear, good to hear."

"How about you?"

"Oh, me? Never better," I'd say. "Hang on a sec, I just need to get a little more . . . lotion . . . out of . . . this tube."

It was like some sort of extremely disturbing, alternate-universe *Karate Kid* exercise. Fortunately for both of us, his crotch was somehow spared from the outbreak. I'd like to think we both had our limits.

Spackled and dressed, Ricky would joke about whatever outfit I'd put together for him from the shelter's donation closet that day, usually nothing more glamorous than a clean pair of jeans and a button-down shirt.

"Everyone is going to think I'm from Paris," he'd say.

I couldn't help but love the guy.

The more I got to know the people at the shelter, the less I minded the more character-building tasks. And even those had the positive side effect of taking my mind off whatever existential crisis I might be having that particular day, hour, or minute. If I had to, I just pretended I had accepted some sort of dare to block out the reality of my situation. And no matter how gross things got on the job, I figured it still beat the hell out of temping at some boring office where almost nobody ever shit their pants or anything.

Sometimes I even managed to turn the otherwise cringe-worthy into fun. Swapping out a urine sample for apple juice and then pretending to accidentally drink it in front of my supervisor was a trademark move I remain especially proud of. Once the rumor that I was a pee drinker spread throughout the shelter, it gave me a mystique I really enjoyed. Another time I had to deliver a stool sample to a nearby hospital for testing and giggled uncontrollably to myself the whole way back to the shelter thinking about what I'd tell my supervisor when I saw him.

"How did it go at the hospital?" he asked as I entered the front door.

"Not too good," I snickered. "They told me to tell you they're not gonna take any more shit from you!"

My supervisor didn't think it was too funny, but all these years later it still feels like a home run to me.

The occasional prank aside, I was actually turning into a pretty good program aide. I began picking up extra shifts when others called in sick, and, eventually, when a supervisor was unable to make his Friday overnight shift, I was asked to jump into the breach and be supervisor in his place. I had never held a job long enough to be promoted before, and growing up I was never what one might describe as especially reliable, so I was surprised yet thrilled that someone might think I could actually handle more responsibility. Best of all, as supervisor of an overnight shift, with none of the regular staffers scheduled to return until the morning, I was effectively in charge of the entire shelter. I even got to be in charge of the shelter's hefty key ring, which hung from a short chain and held roughly nine thousand keys. Its weight felt good in my hands, like wielding a medieval weapon.

"This is it," I thought. "The big dance."

I was going to supervise the fuck out of that place. And I was pretty sure the rest of the staff was as excited about it as I was. Having me supervise would be like putting Michael Jordan in during the fourth quarter of a men's recreational league basketball game—total domination that no one would ever see coming in a million years.

I was so excited that I decided to show up a little early for my inaugural shift as supervisor, another employment first for me. As I walked through the front door, I imagined the theme from *The Good, the Bad, and the Ugly* playing in the background. There was a new goddamn sheriff in town and he wasn't about to put up with anyone's bullshit.

"So, anything I should *know about* before I put this shit on lockdown?" I asked the security guard on duty.

"Huh?" he responded.

Whatever. I didn't expect a mere security guard to understand anyway. I wanted to get the lay of the land, find out what sort of trouble may or may not have been brewing in the hours leading up to my shift—you know, supervisor stuff. And by the time 11:00 P.M. rolled around, I was in full-on supervisor mode, ready to bring the hammer down on any and all misconduct at a moment's notice. I couldn't help but have a little swagger in my step as I walked the halls of the shelter, looking for signs of mischief, disorder, or any other wrongs I would instantly right without even really trying. My supervisor key ring jingled with authority every step of the way. It was a lot for people to handle, even me.

As it turned out, most of the shelter's residents had already turned in for the night, so unfortunately it was up to me to keep the excitement coming. I decided to put my keys to work, locking and then unlocking doors that had been unlocked and also unlocking and relocking doors that had already been locked. I had the situation under control like a motherfucker.

I ended up running out of things to do about ten minutes into my supervisor shift, so I gave the security guard on duty a nod to let him know that I would be retiring to my de facto supervisor office, an old leather armchair just outside the employee restroom, until things started to heat up again. There I sat vigilant for a good fifteen minutes, partly listening for any signs of trouble and partly taking a nap, when Russell, the weekend cook, showed up unannounced.

"Hey, Dave," Russell said.

"Hey, Russell," I replied, my voice deepening in the way a man's tends to when he's suddenly making almost ten dollars an hour as supervisor.

"Who's supervising tonight?"

"I am, Russell," I answered, slapping the key ring for emphasis. "I am."

Apparently, no one told Russell that thing about how there was a new sheriff in town. And while he looked a little surprised to hear the news, I tried not to let that rattle me.

"You think I could borrow the keys?" Russell asked once it all sank in. "I need to get some meat."

Russell had to cook breakfast, lunch, and dinner for everyone at the shelter the next day, so I figured he just needed to defrost something.

"Sure thing, pal," I said, tossing him the key ring.

They landed in his beefy palm with a jangly thud.

"Just one guy tossing a huge key ring to another guy," I thought. I felt like a man, dammit.

After Russell disappeared with the keys, I tried to get back to being vigilant, but ended up mostly napping instead. About twenty minutes later, he returned with the keys and tossed them back in my direction. I snatched them out of midair while doing my best to hide any signs of the pain one tends to experience after having a giant knot of rusty old keys thrown directly at you by a guy who doesn't seem all that happy to see you in the first place.

The rest of my shift as supervisor held little to no action to speak of, so little in fact that I wrote "little to no action to speak of" in the supervisor logbook. At 7:00 A.M., it was time for the changing of the guard. I lobbed the key ring to the next supervisor and marched out of the shelter and into the city streets, confident in a job well done as the sun struggled up over Manhattan.

My next shift was at 3:00 P.M. that same day, so when I got back home to my apartment in the East Village, I lay down on the living-room futon that doubled as my bed when my roommates weren't watching television and caught a few hours of rest before heading back to the shelter. It wasn't a long sleep but it was a deep sleep, the kind authority figures tend to enjoy.

Though I returned to the shelter a lowly program aide for the three-to-eleven shift, I hung on to the boss-man swagger I had adopted the night before because I knew more supervisor shifts would be just around the corner for me. I could taste it.

"Hey, Dave," William, the security guard on duty, mumbled as I strode boldly through the front door.

"Hey, William. How's it going?" I said, collapsing into a chair across from him in the way that a guy who's used to being in charge tends to do.

"You hear what happened with Russell last night?"

"No. What?" I asked, concerned that something awful must have happened to him after he left the safe haven that I had made of the shelter just hours before.

"He stole three hundred pounds of meat."

"From where?" I asked, already feeling sorry for whatever chump managed to let that happen.

"From here."

"What do you mean 'from here'?" I pried, still convinced the crime couldn't possibly have happened on my watch.

"Someone gave him the keys to the freezer last night."

"Huh . . . that's weird," I said, slowly shifting in my chair. "And then what happened?"

"Then he tossed all the meat over the fence to his buddy."

Apparently William hadn't been brought up to speed on the fact that I had been in charge when the alleged beef heist went down. And while I certainly wasn't going to be the one to tell him, I wasn't ready to quietly slink away, either. There was still the matter of why one might steal what sounded like at least half a cow's worth of meat to get to the bottom of.

"Why did he do that?" I asked innocently.

"To sell it," William answered, growing impatient.

"Sell it where?"

"On the street!"

"But what kind of person buys meat on the street like that?" I asked, not even realizing meat had street value in the first place.

"I don't know. People who want meat. Anyone." William groaned, now convinced I was a moron. "They sell it for whatever they can get for that shit."

"I still don't understand why anyone would go to the hassle of try- ing to sell discount meat on the street like that," I continued, "espe- cially late at night when most people are done buying meat for the day."

It seemed like a reasonable question to me.

"So he could get money to buy crack!" William said.

"Huh?" I asked, that dusty-needle-dragging-across-a-vinyl-record sound effect playing in my head.

"Russell's a crackhead." William squinted at me. "Don't you know that?"

I had worked in the kitchen with Russell dozens of times over the last few months, chatting and laughing away the whole time while I helped him serve what he kept telling me was the best meat loaf ever. Somehow the whole crack thing just never came up. It's funny what you learn about someone after they steal three hundred pounds of meat out from under your nose.

Needless to say, the shelter bosses ended up firing Russell as soon as they found out about the meat caper since it was in violation of, well, all sorts of things really. Shortly afterward, William explained to me some of the shelter's other recent personnel changes.

"They fired Danny after they found him in the basement sucking on the glass dick,"[4] he said. "And they fired Michelle because they found her turning tricks right down the street for crack."

All of a sudden, I got really quiet in that way one does when you find out that two of your coworkers are full-time crackheads and another is a part-time prostitute. William then began rattling off a list of names as if he were simply reading off the shelter's time sheet, ending with his own. As it turned out, just about all the employees at the shelter who weren't a part of the nine-to-five staff were recovering crack addicts, William included. And, when an employee either quit or was fired, or simply stopped showing up for work one day, more often than not it was because their old friend had caught up with them. The exception, of course, was me, that guy from Cleveland with the cool hair and dreams of stardom. As it all hit me, I felt like Mia Farrow in *Rosemary's Baby* when she discovers that everyone in her apartment building is so into Satan it's not even fucking funny. It was seriously messing with my head.

---

4 Glass dick is a nickname for a crack pipe, so when someone's "sucking on the glass dick," they're, ah, you get it. It's a fun phrase to throw into conversation whenever appropriate (which is to say always). Friends will appreciate your colorful language.

"You mean to tell me you never smoked crack?" William asked me.

"No. I guess I just never got around to it for some reason."

"Then how'd you end up working here?"

"I dunno. Just lucky I guess," I said. I figured my brother might appreciate me not dragging him into things at this point.

As William's words continued to sink in, I was filled with feelings of sadness for my troubled coworkers. But being as thoroughly self-absorbed as any other twenty-two-year-old, it didn't take long before my thoughts turned back to myself. I had chosen to believe that my recent promotion was due to my overall sense of responsibility, my razor-sharp attention to detail, and that fact that I had yet to show up to work drunk. I now realized that what had really given me the edge over my fellow employees was that I simply wasn't on crack.

As word of the disappearance of three hundred pounds of meat on my watch spread among employees and residents of the shelter, however, not being a crackhead wasn't enough to keep me on top. Not too surprisingly, my inaugural supervisor shift turned out to be my last. My bosses never brought up the whole meat incident with me directly. But out of curiosity, I asked my brother if there had been any internal reports on the beef debacle, specifically with regard to my status as the guy who unwittingly helped make Russell's dream a reality.

"Oh, yeah, uh, that," he began before just sort of trailing off and shuffling into the next room.

I guess it was kind of like how one wouldn't bother scolding a newborn (or certain shelter residents) for shitting himself without warning. I would remain a program aide for life. And while I kept working at the shelter for another few months, I couldn't help but wonder whether everyone now viewed me differently. Or perhaps even worse, maybe they viewed me exactly as they always had.

· · · · · · · · ·

All the Right Moves

My grandfather was born and raised on a farm somewhere in Ontario, Canada. I guess technically what that means is that I'm a quarter Canadian. But what it really meant for me and my siblings was that we were all tossed onto an ice rink at around the age of three and forced to learn how to skate whether we liked it or not. From what I remember, I really seemed to like it.

My siblings' enthusiasm for life on the ice, however, varied. My oldest sister, Miriam, in particular, wasn't into it at all.

"I *hate* ice-skating," she said to my grandfather one night at dinner. "I'm not good at it and it's stupid and boring and dumb and stupid anyway!"

"What good are you if you can't skate?" my grandfather growled at her.

As a full-fledged Canadian, he took my sister's offhanded comment to be the equivalent of telling him to go screw himself. He shook his head in disgust and, as a quarter-Canadian grandson looking to stay in good graces with his fully Canadian grandfather, I shook my head in disgust right along with him. Was Miriam even a person anymore? It was hard to say.

Despite my sister's disdain for it, my family continued to go skating regularly throughout my childhood and I quickly grew to love everything about it—the sweaters, the organ music, the hot chocolate, even the actual skating part. Before long I was flying around the rink with what I presumed was not just Canadian proficiency but perhaps even a bit of Scandinavian proficiency, too. Soon after, I discovered ice hockey—the one thing that combined my love of ice-skating with my other boyhood passion: violence. And, like just about everything else I got into as a kid, I instantly became obsessed with hockey to the point of annoying everybody around me.

"The Canucks are playing the Jets tonight," I'd say to anyone who would listen. "Nothing like a bunch of British Columbians going head to head with a bunch Manitobans, right? Should be pretty nuts."

"Huh?" they'd usually respond.

My grandfather would silently nod in approval, though, which felt good. Still, there was no getting around the fact that Cleveland just wasn't a hockey town. We didn't have our own pro team and there were rarely hockey games on television, so I'd get my fix by reading every book I could find on the subject and plastering my bedroom walls with photos of hockey players I'd clipped from *Sports Illustrated* and *The Cleveland Plain Dealer*. My dad bought me a few hockey annuals, the kind with stats on every NHL team and player, and I memorized every page. To this day, I probably have a stronger working knowledge of obscure Canadian towns that happen to be the birthplace of a professional hockey player than any other United States citizen: Wayne Gretzky is from Brantford, Ontario; Bobby Clarke is from Flin Flon, Manitoba; and Clark Gillies is from Moose Jaw, Saskatchewan. I didn't even have to look any of that stuff up. I still know it better than any of my family members' birthdays.

To satisfy my growing hockey appetite, my dad drove me and my friend Kevin two and a half hours to Pittsburgh one weekend to see the Penguins play the Edmonton Oilers, whose star center, Wayne Gretzky, was just becoming a household name in America. We even got there a couple of hours early so I could wait outside the players' entrance and get his autograph. A few hundred other people had the same idea, so when Wayne finally showed up he was mobbed. To this day, I've never been so starstruck. Somehow I held it together long enough to get him to sign a recent issue of *Sports Illustrated* he had been on the cover of. I was so excited I practically required medical attention. I was convinced the magazine held magical hockey powers simply because he had touched it, so I kept it in a dresser drawer all by itself like some sort of minishrine for the next couple of years until one of my sisters threw it out for reasons I am still trying to get to the bottom of. And as awesome as it was for me to meet Wayne Gretzky—a hockey legend like I hoped to become myself one day—I was certain it was a pivotal moment in his life, too. I was completely out of my fucking mind.

Of course, with all my tireless hockey research, it didn't take me long to figure out that—at the ripe old age of eleven—I was getting an extremely late start in the game. Most of the pros I'd read about had a hockey stick shoved into their hands as soon as the placenta was hosed off them. I resented my parents for not doing the same with me. Gretzky was drafted by the pros at the age of sixteen. *Sixteen.*

"I've got a lot of catching up to do in the next five years," I thought. "From now on, it will be all hockey all the time, dammit."

To that end, I decided to take things to the next logical and manly step by signing up to play ice hockey in the local youth league. I wasn't particularly athletic, or even all that interested in sports for that matter, but as unpopular as hockey was in Cleveland at the time, I figured it made me a trailblazer of sorts. And perhaps best of all, playing hockey seemed like the most Canadian thing I could possibly do, so I was certain it would further ingratiate me with my grandfather. It would basically be the opposite of telling him to go screw himself.

I made my auspicious hockey debut by joining the pee-wee league in Cleveland Heights, the next town over. The league was comprised mostly of eleven- and twelve-year-old boys. There were a handful of girls in the league, too, but I tried to ignore that fact since most of them were better than me. My team was called the "white team," after the color of our jerseys. I didn't think it was possible to have a lamer name than our rivals, the "red team" and the "blue team," but somehow we nailed it.

To prepare me for the beating I was about to receive on the ice, my dad took me to the sporting goods store near our house and got me outfitted in hockey equipment from head-to-toe, including a combination cup and jockstrap. It was the first time in my life my testicles required formal protection and it made me feel like a man, a man with near-microscopic, prepubescent external genitalia, but a man just the same.

As I hit the ice for the first time, covered to the point of being unrecognizable in my sparkling new pads like some pathetic gladiator who would only be called to combat once everyone else had been killed, I was certain every parent in the stands would quickly take notice of the new kid and his uncanny natural ability to work magic with a hockey stick. Sure, my skating hadn't really improved all that much since the age of three and, yeah, I fell down just about every other time I tried to shoot the puck, but I was still convinced my raw talent was impossible to miss. It would be like the first time Streisand stepped in front of a microphone to sing, only slightly more butch. As I skated down the ice, I pictured someone in the stands secretly videotaping the whole thing for later use in a documentary about my unstoppable hockey career.

"There he is—Dave Hill," I imagined a baritone-voiced sports announcer saying over grainy footage of me doing my damnedest not to fall down. "Just eleven years old here, but clearly a hockey god in the making."

Despite my fearless efforts, however, my inaugural hockey season came and went without much fanfare. My team almost always lost and the most attention I ever got at the rink came after my family's golden retriever bit me in the face the night before a game.[1] Still, I had my eye on the prize, so I spent the following summer working on my ice-skating and playing street hockey all by myself in my family's driveway while all the other kids went swimming. Fortunately, my parents were extremely patient and barely complained

---

1 You can read about this incident in all its gory detail in the chapter "On Manliness." Don't read it at the dinner table, though. You've been warned.

when I figured out how to shoot the puck high enough to break all the windows on the garage doors. The first time it was an accident. But once I realized I wasn't going to get in trouble for it, I didn't exactly try to avoid having it happen. That summer, the sound of breaking glass was like hearing thousands of fans cheering for me on the ice. I was devastated when there were no windows left to break and my dad simply boarded them up rather than replace the glass and risk having me break them all over again.

Given the fact that hockey was the only sport I was ever any good at, my skill at it seemed more like a form of autism than actual athleticism. Much to even my own surprise, I managed to improve enough before my triumphant return to the ice the following season that it seemed like a reasonable enough idea to try out for the travel team, the one all the really good kids played on. Not only did they play teams in other cities, but they had cooler jerseys than all the other teams at the rink, were more handsome, and even had cooler names than everybody else, too—like Kip, Trip, and Torch, names that I'd never even heard of before but still sounded awesome to my impressionable young ears. The kids on the travel teams were usually dicks to all the players on the non-travel teams (or "house teams" as they were not-so-glamorously called), but I felt like they had somehow earned the right. I wanted to be one of them so badly my pancreas hurt. Despite making it past the first round of cuts for the team, I was still back on the house team in the end.

"You really impressed me out there, Hill," said the travel team coach, a guy with a thick mane of red hair and a much cooler outfit than any of the house team coaches ever wore, told me after I'd been cut. "You keep working hard and I think you'll have a real good shot at making the team next year."

"Really, coach?" I asked, beaming up at him. "Really?"

"I mean, sure. Uh, why not?"

I have no idea if he actually meant it or if he just felt obligated to say something nice to me so he could pass me in the hallway outside the locker room without things being too awkward, but either way I was pumped. Even with that mini-motivational speech, the house team is where I would stay for the next two years until it was time for high school. It was a long, cold two years, too—no cool jerseys, no trips to faraway cities to play other more handsome kids who probably had really cool names, too, no nothing.

My all-boy Catholic high school, Saint Ignatius, had its own hockey team, which felt like worlds colliding—my secret hockey world and the one my friends at school actually knew about. I figured I would finally be recognized among my peers as the best (if only) hockey player in our immediate social group and that felt great. I

This is the sixteen-year-old me trying to look as athletic as possible in my high school hockey uniform. I feel like I really nailed it.

still wasn't quite one of the greatest hockey players of all-time or even in my town for that matter, but I had at least gotten good enough by then that I ended up being one of only three freshmen to make the varsity team. The fact that the team was absolutely abysmal definitely helped matters, but it remains my greatest and perhaps only real athletic achievement to this day.

The Saint Ignatius team practiced before school, requiring me to get up at 4:30 A.M. and usually making me late for first period.

"And why are you late again today, Mr. Hill?" my Latin teacher would ask me.

"Because I'm a fucking champion," I wanted to tell him instead of just shrugging and collapsing into my desk as I did most days.

I was thrilled to finally be able to play hockey with guys I went to school with, and maybe even people besides the players' parents would show up to games, like girls, for example. But I quickly learned that being a freshman on a team full of juniors and seniors almost twice my size was like being in a really bad after-school special. Not only was I a hairless, hundred-pound doormat, but I had little in common with the other guys on the team aside from being a suburban white teenager. They were mostly jocks who also played football, baseball, and whatever else didn't conflict with the hockey season. And I was a shy, anxious semiloner who was obsessed with the electric guitar but still happened to play one sport and one sport only when he wasn't practicing scales in his bedroom or hanging out in a friend's basement listening to Led Zeppelin records. I might as well have gone ahead and taped a KICK ME sign directly to my crotch.

One day, I walked proudly into the locker room wearing a really tight, colorful sweater that I was certain made me look like Cheap Trick guitar player Rick Nielsen, one of my idols. It seemed like a really great idea at the time. My teammates, however, thought otherwise.

"Hill, you fucking pussy," one of them said. "How fucking gay is that sweater?"

It sounded like a rhetorical question, so I didn't answer.

"Does your mom know you wear her clothes?" another player asked.

I couldn't figure out why these guys weren't into what I was pretty sure was a totally awesome rock look. I also made a mental note to maybe not wear that sweater to the rink anymore.

Giving me shit about my fashion decisions was just the beginning of my hazing. As situations involving a bunch of young men coming to terms with an influx of testosterone tend to go, all three of us freshmen on the team were on the receiving end of a healthy share of abuse. And given my oddball status, I usually got it the worst. On more than one occasion, I'd close my eyes to rinse the shampoo out of my hair in the shower after practice only to notice a stream of warm water hitting me from somewhere other than the showerhead I was standing under. I'd open my eyes to discover one of my upperclassmen teammates urinating on me with a big smile on his face. I'd usually jump out of the way and punch him in the arm, sending myself bouncing off him and skidding across the shower room floor in the process. Since I was barely a hundred pounds, my punches were mostly symbolic gestures causing no actual pain to the recipient. But I felt it was important to send a message loud and clear that while I might very well tolerate being urinated on by just about anyone who tried, I didn't have to like it. It felt like the least I could do.

"Ha ha, Hill!" one of the other guys in the shower at the time would howl. "You got pissed on!"

Since he was merely stating facts, I rarely had a comeback.

In addition to the urinating, there was also a fair amount of towel snapping and other standard locker-room shenanigans. Occasionally, an upperclassman would use a freshman's towel to wipe his ass and then leave it on the towel rack in hopes that the freshman would dry himself off before discovering it (and now he) was covered in shit. Somehow I escaped ever having that bit of nastiness pulled on me, but I saw it happen to other guys. At the time it all seemed just really mean and gross, but looking back on it, it was also more than a little bit homoerotic. I guess I'm just lucky no one tried to make out with me or anything.

While it was practically raining men most days in the locker room, things were balanced out a bit by the drives home from practice on days we didn't have school afterward. I carpooled with a few of the upperclassmen and they would regularly threaten to drag me into strip joints or try to get me to proposition a hooker as we drove through Cleveland's seedier neighborhoods on our way back to the relatively whore-free suburbs. I was still a few years away from recognizing the entertainment value in that sort of thing, so I was terrified.

"What about her?" one of the guys would say, waving at a hooker as we rolled up to a red light. "Would you do it with her?"

"Please don't come over to the car, please don't come over to the car," I'd think to myself over and over as I prayed for the light to turn green before some woman wearing just a trench coat and underwear walked over to the passenger seat window.

"How much pussy do you get, Hill?" was another question I often fielded in the locker room.

"Um, what?" I'd reply. I knew there were probably other guys my age somewhere on the planet with active sex lives, but I was fourteen and still spent most of my weekends hanging out with my parents or watching a PG-13 movie in my friend Andrew's basement. Besides my sisters, I didn't really even know any girls. Eventually I realized the guys on my team were just messing with me, mostly just out of plain old teenage obligation, but at the time I was convinced I was a total weirdo for being a virgin who didn't occasionally hit the local strip joint or chat up a hooker whenever the opportunity arose.

I was never really bullied in elementary school, so I didn't understand why I had suddenly become the target of nonstop abuse. "Have I been a total punching bag my whole life and these guys are just the first ones willing to point it out to me?" I wondered.

But in spite of all the hazing and my teammates' frequent suggestions that I spend my allowance on sex, I still loved playing hockey, so I just did my best to ignore all of it. And, as cliché as it sounds, I knew that quitting would probably give my teammates too much satisfaction, so I refused.

"How was practice today?" my dad would ask.

"It was really fun," I'd lie, trying to save face. "My teammates are really nice guys. You'd like them."

Between the stress of his law practice and raising five kids, I decided hearing his son had gotten pissed on that day was something my dad probably didn't need. And, to their credit (I guess), my older teammates rarely gave me shit outside of the locker room or carpool. At school I was one of them, so while they weren't overtly friendly to me, they never tried to wipe their feces on me or anything, so I was still really proud to be a part of the team. Besides, those guys all graduated after a couple of years and before I knew it, it was my turn to be an unfathomable asshole to the younger players. But by then, I was too into the guitar to have more than a passing interest in urinating on anybody. And I knew at least one or two girls by then, too, which seemed like the greatest thing that had ever happened ever.

"Dave, look at Chris's retarded haircut," one of my fellow upperclassmen on the team might say in reference to one of the younger players.

"I've seen better, but it's not bad," I'd reply, unable to muster the necessary strength to ruin the kid's day.

My high school hockey career concluded with just slightly more fanfare than that first season I played back when I was eleven. I saw a lot of "ice time" (hockey lingo for getting to play in the game a lot), got a cool varsity letterman jacket, and even briefly had an actual girlfriend who would sit in the stands during games and occasionally agree to make out with me later that night. It was incredible.

I continued my unstoppable hockey career in college, albeit briefly. A couple games into my sophomore season, I realized it was interfering with my drinking too much, so I decided to pack it in. The coach was a little bummed to lose me but my roommates were thrilled because it meant I would no longer be stinking up our dorm room with my sweaty, moldy equipment. I didn't play hockey for several years after that. And during that time, it was hard to even watch hockey games on television. Sure, the integrity of the game probably remained intact after my retirement, but I still felt a little guilty about it since less than a decade earlier I was convinced the ice was my natural habitat.

Some years later though, with my grandfather in that great big Maple Leaf Gardens[2] in the sky, my half-Canadian mother managed to coax me back onto the ice again.

"I know a man named Paul who runs the men's hockey league down at the rink," she said to me sometime after my twenty-seventh birthday. "He said you could play on his team."

It sounded suspicious to me that my mom might "know a man" like that, but the prospect of coming out of retirement was too intriguing to let that distract me from the matter at hand. I had been away from the game awhile and was hungry for action.

"Oh yeah?" I said coyly. "What would I have to do?"

"Just call him. He said they could use an extra player."

I called Paul the next day and joined his team, the "yellow team," the following week. We played our games on the same ice I had started playing hockey on back when I was a promising yet delusional eleven-year-old, often at midnight or so, the time usually reserved for old men whose hockey dreams had been dashed by age, life changes, or just plain sucking long ago. The players ranged in age from their mid-twenties to at least one seventy-year-old. About half of the men had grown up playing the game and the rest picked it up as adults (you could usually spot them by how they had really new equipment and also fell down a lot).

After being away for so long, it was good to be back on the ice. Still, all that time away had left me beyond rusty. My brain would send a message to my body to do all sorts of really cool hockey moves like skating circles around my opponent, rifling the puck past the goalie, and other stuff I'd put on my imaginary highlights reel, but my body, nearly paralyzed from a decade's worth of beer and chicken wing intake, would rarely come close to getting it right. It was still a

---

2 As hinted at in the name, Maple Leaf Gardens was the home arena for the Toronto Maple Leafs 1931–1999. It was long considered to be hockey's most hallowed ground. There's probably more Canadian things you could do besides hang out at Maple Leaf Gardens, but I'm not aware of any myself.

lot of fun though, so between that and the after-game binge drinking my new teammates and I would get up to, it was enough to keep me coming back each week.

Somewhere toward the second season after my triumphant return, the yellow team was playing our archrivals, the blue team, whose scrappy, middle-age brand of ice hockey was legendary among the three other teams in the league. Early in the game, one of the blue team players began repeatedly hitting me in the legs with his stick, an illegal move known as slashing, every time we came near each other. I ignored it the first couple times it happened, but after he did it a third time I decided to let him know who was boss, so I punched him in the face, sending him crashing to the ice with a flabby, forty-something thud. Since everyone in our league wore helmets, face masks, and heavily padded gloves, punches were more a nuisance than actually painful. Still, he was pissed and came back for more. By then, the referee had blown his whistle to break up the fight, so we just wrestled each other for a few seconds before everyone else pulled us apart. Somehow during all the mayhem, however, the mask on my helmet unfastened, leaving my face wide open for pummelling. To his credit, my scrappy opponent managed to pull an arm free from whoever was restraining him and punch me directly in the face. Of course, I normally would have destroyed him after that, but my arms were being gently held back by the seventy-year-old I mentioned earlier, so there was nothing I could do. The fight was over and I was the only guy left with anything more than emotional wounds.

"You're a jerk!" I yelled at my assailant.

"No, you are!" he responded.

Tensions remained thick as both teams skated back toward their respective benches after the melee. Except for me, that is. I was determined to settle the score, so as soon as no one was looking, I skated back over to the guy who'd hit me and wound up on him as best I could, landing a solid blow that sent him crashing to the ice all over again. It was what some might call a "dick move," but I was still pretty pleased with myself. The referee, however, wasn't and decided to suspend me for what ended up being the rest of the season as there weren't many games left to play that year anyway.

Disgraced, I spent the next few weeks thinking about what had happened on the ice that night while hoping I wouldn't run into any of the guys from the league at the grocery store or elsewhere. Even if I were buying really manly stuff at the time, it would still be kind of embarrassing. In the end, though, it was my mother who ended up confronting me about what had gone down at the rink that night.

"I ran into Paul the other day," my mom told me one morning at breakfast.

"That's nice," I said, trying not to arouse suspicion. "How is he doing?"

"He's good," my mom said. "He said you got into a little trouble down at the rink."

"Really?" I said, trying to sound like I had no idea what she was talking about. "That's weird. What did he say happened?"

"He said you beat some guy up."

"Oh."

I was totally busted, so, being a fully grown man, I decided to just stand there staring at my feet and saying nothing.

"Well, did you?" my mom pressed.

"Yeah, I guess I kind of did," I told her.

I ended up giving my mom the play-by-play on what may have technically been the only real fight I had ever been in in my whole life.

"Are you mad at me?" I asked her when I finished.

"No," she said. "It sounds like he deserved it."

It was in that moment I remembered that while I may have been a quarter Canadian, my mother was twice the Canadian I was, so her tolerance for bullshit on the ice was even lower than mine. I both feared and admired her for that.

I've played hockey a few times since my controversial (to me and my mother anyway) expulsion all those years ago. But for the most part, I consider myself retired from the game. I still have all my equipment, though—it's hard to miss sitting in the middle of the kitchen like that. Sometimes I think about coming out of retirement and making yet another triumphant return to the ice. Maybe it'll happen, maybe it won't. If it ever does, though, one thing I know for sure is that as soon as I hit the ice, I'll hear that baritone-voiced sports announcer all over again.

"There he is—Dave Hill," he'll say as I drag my old bones to center ice. "He left the game completely years ago, leaving a trail of violence and destruction in his wake. . . . And while he very well might be a bit of a loose cannon, by golly if it doesn't translate to pure magic out on that ice. He's still got it, folks. He's still got it."

· · · · · · · · · ·

On Manliness

Masculinity is not something given to you, but something you gain.
—Norman Mailer (a very manly man)

I'm not the manliest of men. I condition, I moisturize, and I have worn a mud mask at least once more than most men who claim to prefer the company of women.[1] Similarly, I struggle to name a professional athlete unless he has either dated Madonna, been publicly accused of rape, or—ideally—both. And, frankly, the amount of time I spend gossiping about Prince William, Kate Middleton, and the rest of the Royal Family just makes me sound like a fucking bitch.

Making matters worse, I've never been in a knife fight. Not even once. Think about it: if you get in at least one knife fight in your lifetime, no one will ever question your manhood again. Just ask one of the Sharks or the Jets from *West Side Story*. Those guys sang and danced around like a pack of raging queens 90 percent of the time, but when they broke out those knives there was no question about it—these were real men. Men with a keen interest in choreography, but men just the same.

Despite all this, when it comes to exuding sheer, unbridled machismo, the kind that cannot be tamed by bullets, prison bars, or even some of the most insensitive name-calling you've ever heard, I do have one considerable edge over most other men: a jagged scar

---

1 You know, for intercourse.

This is me somewhere around the age of five, being really manly without even trying. That's my grandfather behind me. He used to make very large, sharp knives for fun. Manliness runs in our family.

running down my left cheek subtle enough so as not to send small children and house pets screaming into the night, yet rugged enough to let anyone who comes in for a closer look know that something really, really bad must have happened to me at some point. It's something I use to my advantage whenever possible. As any decent crime, gangster, and/or action film will tell you, the guy with the scar is probably not to be messed with. And I don't care if you are only in the sixth grade, you see a goddamn scar and you back the fuck off unless you're hell-bent on waking up dead.

Unlike most other traditional cultural signifiers of masculinity—alcohol, tobacco, and firearms, for example—a scar isn't something you can just go trying on for size one day when you're at the mall like a damn woman. Generally speaking, it has to happen to you. And once it does, a scar lets those around you know that you have come face-to-face with adversity—a pair of wayward scissors, an aggressive patch of shrubbery, or a box cutter–wielding member of a secret underground society of mole people easily given to handing out their own swift brand of justice—and managed to rise above it. Regardless, you'll definitely have a story to tell. Though, to be fair, you should probably never tell that story because, just as with sausage, drastically reduced consumer electronics, or motel carpet stains, you are almost always better off leaving others to speculate on its origin.

Scar or not, I realize at this point in my book there's probably no question in your mind as to whether or not I'm one of the biggest badasses that ever walked the face of the planet.[2] But as long as I'm on the topic, here's what happened to me.

I was eleven years old and was staying up late to watch a Beatles movie on television after the rest of my family had gone to bed. I had seen it a year or two before, so I already knew that Stu Sutcliffe— the fifth, sixth, or seventh Beatle depending on whom you ask— would be dead by the next commercial break. Then they'd all get better haircuts and the rest would be history, so I figured I might as well pack it in for the night. I had a hockey game in the morning and wanted to be well rested so I'd be better equipped to handle the inevitable loss. I got up from my dad's Barcalounger, clicked off the television, and headed for the family room door. In the doorway was Blazer, our ninety-five-pound golden retriever, sleeping peacefully, presumably dreaming about chasing some smaller living thing or licking his privates without interruption.

As I did most nights before bed, I got down on my knees to plant a great big, yet entirely masculine, kiss on Blazer's snout. I can't remember if my lips ever actually made contact with his fur, but I do remember Blazer quickly jerking his head and growling like one of those giant black and really pissed off bears I had seen on public television. His fangs tore through my left cheek like it was squirrel meat as my lips remained puckered and about as adorable as an eleven-year-old boy's can—pretty adorable I imagine, even under the circumstances— sending me reeling backward onto the carpet as I howled in a mixture of pain, confusion, and general holyfuckingshitness. Blazer, for his part, now entirely awake and also in a state of general holyfuckingshitness,

---

2 Author's note: I am.

scurried off to the kitchen, maybe to build an alibi for himself but probably just to get the hell away from a screaming child.

Up until that fateful night, I had always thought the expression, "Let sleeping dogs lie" was just something people said when they wanted someone else to stop whining. But as I lay there on the floor, my tears mixing with my blood to form a warm puddle on the carpet that would take a team of professionals to properly clean up, I got it. I totally, totally got it.

As is often the case when a human is attacked by an animal nearly twice his size, Blazer's strategic hit earned me a trip to the hospital, where I expected to be quickly stitched up by the nearest doctor and sent home. Instead, my mother—perhaps knowing I'd one day wind up on basic cable—held out for the man suggested to be the best plastic surgeon in the hospital's Rolodex,[3] a French doctor with a mustache and, presumably, a taste for serious carnage.

By morning I was all sewn up and sleeping off the anesthesia in a hospital room I was forced to share with some kid who got his head stuck in an escalator at the local mall.

"I got my scalp ripped off on my way up to menswear," he explained. "What happened to you?"

"My dog tried to rip my face off."

"Oh."

By that point in my life, I just assumed that escalators and most other machines existed to mangle, disfigure, or at least fall on top of children whenever possible, so—since I was the one who had suffered actual heartache by being maimed by my best friend—I figured I'd gotten it much worse.

The French doctor ended up going to work on my cheek once a year for the next three years like I was some sort of modern art project.

"Today, we're just going to apply an electric sander to your face to help smooth things out a bit more," he'd say before jabbing me in the cheek with a giant needle.

---

3 A Rolodex is an ancient phone-number-collecting machine.

"What?" I'd reply.

After the second round of surgery, I was no longer marked by the Beast, but instead looked more like an exceptionally young villain from a James Bond movie. After the third, I looked like I might be that villain's sidekick or something. And after the fourth, I looked like I might just answer the phone at the villain's office. Still, despite the French doctor's best efforts, it was hard not to notice the rather large, pitchfork-shaped scar on my face, something most kids at my school simply didn't have. Not wanting to put the blame on Blazer (whom, for the record, I never saw again), I usually made things up whenever anyone would ask about it, thus adding to my mystique and overall street credibility in the process.

"Oh, that." I'd laugh. "You ever do that thing where you fall down a flight of stairs and end up catching your face on a rusty nail on the way down? It sucks, right?"

"What?"

The look of horror on people's faces never got old. Other times I'd say I'd gone skiing and accidentally stuck a pole in my cheek while doing a sweet jump. Or tell them I'd simply been attacked by a pack of wild animals (which, given Blazer's lack of formal training, was kind of true, I guess). I tried to make the explanations as gruesome as possible so my classmates wouldn't have the stomach to investigate further and find out my own sweet Blazer was the culprit. But eventually the questions died down and I simply became known as "that one kid with the crazy scar on his face that no one wants to sit with at lunch."

All these years later, my scar still earns me plenty of tough guy points, especially under the right light, but rather than rest on my laurels, I've tried to declare my manliness through other, non-maiming-related means. The problem is, I'm generally pretty bad at it. I don't play in any recreational basketball leagues, I'm often accused of being too knowledgeable or (even worse) enthusiastic about women's handbags, and I'm the last guy any of my friends or family would call for advice on cars, lawnmowers, or anything else one might store in a garage.

More recently, I'm ashamed to admit that my manliness is rather frequently and directly called into question, specifically in the form of people actually mistaking me for a woman. I don't know if it's because of my delicate features, my penchant for wearing really fun, floral patterns, or because I have what some might categorize as "mom hair" (longish without being truly long, wispy, and generally well-suited for the on-the-go lifestyle). Whatever the reason, it happens every couple of months or so, often when I'm out to dinner with one of my sisters, a female friend, or even a romantic date (who is also a woman).

"Can I get you ladies anything to drink?" the waiter will ask.

Or I might be at a grocery store and, as I approach checkout counter, the cashier will ask, "Did you find everything you were looking for ma'am?"

In either case, the person making the mistake quickly catches themselves once they get a better look at me.

"Um . . . sir?" he or she will say.

There's no apology, though. They just call me "sir" as if I somehow hadn't noticed that up until a second ago, they were under the impression that I live my life as a woman. And to be honest, it's fine—I'm not mad. It doesn't hurt my feelings or anything. But I do feel sorry for the woman they imagine me to be—this lonely, dateless woman. Check out my photo on the jacket of this book and imagine I'm a woman who lives on your street or in your apartment building. Maybe my name is Peg or Jan or something equally unglamorous.[4]

"Hi, Peg," you say to me as I shuffle toward my door, juggling my keys and take-out as some old sugar and ketchup packets I carry with me at all times for some reason spill out of my bag onto the floor.

"Oh, hi," I mumble back to you as I slowly push open my creaky apartment door, a fog of cat piss practically tackling you to the ground.

Any way you slice it the female me is destined to die alone.

---

4 No offense if your name is either Peg or Jan. I think they are actually rather beautiful names. They just don't work for me.

The case of my mistaken sexual identity came to a head recently when I found myself in Washington, D.C., and craving a bit of Chinese food. So I headed to D.C.'s Chinatown, which seemed like a perfectly reasonable plan.

Located near a bus depot and the Verizon Center, Chinatown is often populated by drifters, vagrants, and other people who really seem to like hanging out and drinking in the streets for weeks and weeks at a time. And this time around, I had the Kung Pao chicken but for whatever reason couldn't finish it. So I asked the waiter to wrap my leftovers so I could give them to someone in need of a meal.

"This will be my good deed for the day," I thought. "Gosh, I'm a decent person."

Once I got outside of the restaurant, the first person I saw was a fortyish woman with a tallboy of Budweiser in one hand and an orange traffic cone in the other. She was dancing in place, cackling hysterically to herself, and seemingly having a really nice time.

"We have a winner," I thought.

"Excuse me, ma'am. Would you like some Chinese food?" I asked.

"Yes, I would like some Chinese food," she answered, momentarily taking a break from the action.

"Wow, this is working out great," I thought.

I began walking toward the woman while holding the bag of Chinese food out for the handoff. She, in turn, began walking toward me with her hand out, seemingly about to grab it. Then just as we were about to complete the transaction, the lady lunged at me with her other hand and tried to stab me in the chest with the traffic cone. Exceptionally lithe and catlike in nature, I quickly jumped out of the way.

"Hey!" I yelled at her. "Do you want the Chinese food or not?"

"Yeah, I want the Chinese food," she said as if she thought I had some serious hang-ups.

I decided to try giving her the Chinese food again, and again she approached me with her hand outstretched. And then, just as I totally swore I was about to make a successful handover, she lunged at me again, trying a second time to stab me with the traffic cone.

Needless to say, it was all starting to seem a bit weird. I guess the thing to do then would have been to just give my leftover Kung Pao chicken to someone else, someone more grateful, someone who might not try to stab me. But this woman was really pissing me off so I decided I was going to make her take my Chinese food, just to teach her a lesson. So, for what felt like the remainder of the afternoon, we continued our bizarre tango. I held out the food, she reached for it with one hand while trying to stab me with the other. On one side of our bodies, we were working as a team. On the other, I was under attack. Then finally, on my eighth or ninth attempt, the woman graciously and surprisingly accepted the Chinese food.

"Thank you, nice man," she said.

"You're welcome, nice lady," I replied, happy to finally be able to get on with my day.

I started to walk away as if nothing had happened, but I only got about ten feet before I looked over my shoulder to discover the woman was suddenly chasing after me.

"I'm a grown man," I thought. "I don't need to run from this woman."

Even so, she was coming at me pretty quickly, so I figured I should probably start running just to be safe. And before long, I found myself running as fast as I could. Even though the lady was carrying a tall-boy of Bud, an orange traffic cone, and my Chinese food, she still caught up to me pretty easily. I made one last gasp at an escape, but it was too late; she drew back the orange traffic cone like it was a medieval sword and lunged at me once more, this time fully connecting with what I guess would technically be known as my anus.

"Ow!" I screamed (because it really, really hurt). "Why'd you do that?"

At that she stopped dancing and cackling and looked me right in the eye.

"Your pussy stinks," she told me, three words a man almost never expects to hear about himself.

"Excuse me?" I replied while cleaning the wax from my ears and trying to think what else she could have possibly just said to me.

"Your pussy stinks," the woman repeated before resuming her dancing and cackling.

As I tried to make sense of it all, that's when it hit me. It's fine if a lot of people think I'm a woman. But apparently all of a sudden I was a woman with some sort of condition I needed to address. And as much as I'd like to think that lady with the orange traffic cone had no idea what she was saying, and as much as the fact that I am recognized by the American Medical Association as male should be reason enough to dismiss her words entirely, the more I roll them around in my head, it's hard not to start to thinking that maybe she had a point. Maybe my lady parts do stink a little bit. And to be honest, I'm not sure how to even begin dealing with that. The mind boggles. And presumably my lady parts continue to stink.

As a result of my bizzare Chinatown encounter, things have even started to seem kind of messed up at home lately, which is especially strange since I live alone. And sometimes I can't help but wonder how that whole scenario might have worked out differently. But I guess the real question here is does any of it really matter when it comes to the true measure of a man? This may be convenient thinking on my part, but I tend to think what makes a man a man more than anything else—far more than an interest in sports, an affinity for stuff that runs on gasoline, or even a complete lack of female genitalia, regardless of how good or bad it smells—is his ability to have someone else's back in a tough situation, what in simpler times was known as "manning up." And, truth be told, this doesn't even have to involve a knife fight necessarily (though, once again, knifeplay is preferable).

Manning up can be as simple as walking on the outside of the sidewalk to protect your companion from being trampled by wayward horses or splattered with the contents of chamber pots being emptied from overhead.[5] Manning up can also mean doing your damnedest to return a lost wallet to its rightful owner even though the easier thing would be to just stuff it in your pocket like it was

---

5 It should be noted that a time machine is usually required to properly pull off this move.

your own. And, of course, manning up can also mean letting your friends know that the ornery-looking guy who just walked into the bar in search of cheap booze, loose women, and trouble has a knife fastened to the tip of his right cowboy boot just before you totally kick his and all his friends' asses, not unlike Patrick Swayze in *Roadhouse*, a film that continues to both shape and define us as a people to this day.

It turns out that manning up is also something you can do as you ride on a crowded subway headed for Brooklyn during evening rush hour, minding your own business and totally not expecting to have to man up at all at any point during the journey. Let me break it down for you:

It was a rainy night, which only added to the foul mood of commuters forced to press up against one another in the name of getting from one place to another. I did my best to block it all out by reading a book held eye-strainingly close to my face, something by one of the more butch Brontës I think.

As the train swelled with more people at one of the stops, a couple of feisty male cross-dressers pushed and shoved their way onto the train, sending several passengers flying across the car, one of whom was an attractive young lady who just so happened to slam right into my chest. Naturally, my sturdy frame stopped her in her tracks. The poor gal must have felt like she'd just hit an especially sexy brick wall or something.

"Sorry," the winsome superfox offered while casting a disapproving yet sexy glance at the Feisty Cross-dressers.

"It's okay," I said to her in the way that a man who has absolutely no problem with having a pretty young thing slam right into his chest might.

As the attractive woman composed herself, a damp, middle-aged man began to chastise the Feisty Cross-dressers for so rudely shoving their way onto the train. He was swearing and everything and, as is often the case with Feisty Cross-dressers, they were not having it.

"That's just plain rude," the man said. "You should be ashamed of yourselves."

"No you di-in't," one of the Feisty Cross-dressers snapped predictably in return.

"Actually, yes, I did."

"No, you di-in't!"

Things were heating up pretty quickly as the Feisty Cross-dressers continued to insist that everything the man had just said or done had not actually happened at all despite the fact that—by all accounts—it clearly had. Were it not for the four or five passengers pressed between them, it seemed as if the middle-aged man and the Feisty Cross-dressers might have come to blows. The war of words continued for a couple more stops as everyone near them looked around uncomfortably, as if they thought a bomb might go off at any minute unless Hollywood's Wesley Snipes[6] were able to come to the rescue and quickly diffuse it.

Eventually, the train pulled into the station closest to wherever the Feisty Cross-dressers were headed and they pushed and shoved their way off the train, sending all in their path stumbling around the subway car and struggling for both balance and decency once again. Once the Feisty Cross-dressers were off the train, everyone on board heaved a sigh of relief. Everyone except for me, that is. As the train sat in the station with its doors still wide open, I intuitively sensed that the trouble had only just begun.

"This ain't over," I thought. "This ain't[7] anywhere *near* over!"

Now I was getting worked up. But, like any seasoned crime-fighter would, I pretended to be oblivious to my surroundings and continued reading my book. Meanwhile, the man who had been arguing with the Feisty Cross-dressers stood in the doorway with his back to the platform while the pretty lady remained next to me, still marveling at my rock-hard yet welcoming frame while I subtly stood guard on the opposite side of the doorway.

Of course my intuition was spot-on. And as the train idled in the station just long enough to incite groans of frustration from its

---

6 As best I can tell, he's great at that stuff.
7 Sometimes, in the pursuit of justice, proper grammar goes right out the window.

passengers, the Feisty Cross-dressers appeared once again, this time wielding a large closed umbrella. Then, as one hung back a few feet, the other swung the umbrella in the direction of the middle-aged man's head. It is at this point that the attractive woman stopped contemplating my chest and, presumably, our potential future together and gasped along with everyone else near the doorway at the sight of what would undoubtedly lead to bloodshed (and ultimately the cover of the *New York Post*) in a matter of milliseconds. As for me, well, I continued pretending to read my book while taking in the entire scene in my peripheral vision.

As you might expect, this whole scenario was all happening in slow motion for me. So, for dramatic effect, I waited until the umbrella was just about to connect with the oblivious middle-aged man's head before I slowly lowered my book and deftly reached out with a single hand to catch the umbrella just before it ripped the man's skull wide open. The sound of the umbrella hitting my hand was like a thunderclap, echoing throughout the station and probably some other stations like an alarm of justice.

Since the middle-aged man had his back to his would-be assailants, he was totally oblivious to what had just taken place. For all he knew, I had just mysteriously thrust my hand directly behind his head like some sort of crazy person. And, perhaps exhausted from arguing with the Feisty Cross-dressers earlier, he didn't even bother to question it. I imagine I could have explained to him how I had just saved his life, but, of course, that sort of thing goes against the hero code.

As for the Feisty Cross-dressers, one might expect them to have become enraged at me for foiling their attack, and reasonably so. But as I caught their umbrella in my hand, the look on both their faces instead seemed to say, "Wow, we were really hoping to split that damp, middle-aged guy's skull wide fucking open, but we gotta admit, what you did just now, well, that was pretty awesome! And while, sure, your delicate features and wavy locks do suggest the kind of femininity we strive to attain on a daily basis, we can honestly say, on behalf of all men who go to great lengths to give the outward appearance that they are, in fact, fully functioning women with lady parts and everything, that you, sir, are one of the manliest men we've seen in our entire gender-bending lives." And with that, they slowly backed away, presumably to reconsider the true meaning of the word *fierce*.

"But, Dave, what about the hot young superfox who couldn't stop thinking about your chest and probably other parts of your scorching-hot bod?"

And to that I say, calm down. I was just about to get to that.

As the subway doors finally closed and the train lurched out of the station with order restored, the hot young superfox slowly looked up at me with her big doe eyes and half-whispered, "Wow, you're good."

"Yeah, I know." I smiled back at her thoughtfully yet sexily.

Then I went back to reading my book, only this time for real. Then, as fate would have it, the seriously attractive young woman and I both got off at the next station.

"I wonder if she'll ask me to come directly back to her apartment to ravage me or if she'll want to stop off for dinner and sexy drinks first," I thought as she headed for the station exit just a few feet ahead of me, the clicking of her high heels echoing throughout the station like a goddamn mating call.

I waited what felt like an eternity for the seriously attractive young woman to finally turn around and say something, anything to me, but instead she just kept on walking out of that station and into the rainy yet sultry night.

I know, I can't believe it, either. I also never saw her again.

Sometimes I wonder if maybe I was the one who was supposed to say something before she disappeared into the night like that. Or maybe she took one look at my scar and decided being friends was just about all she could handle. It's hard to say, really. One thing I know for sure, though, is that it's not always easy being a real man. But guys like me—we don't have much of a choice now, do we?

· · · · · · · · ·

The Lord's Work

There's a phrase my friends in the the UK often use that I just can't get enough of—"could do," a seemingly innocuous pair of words that British people say to let someone down gently after they've suggested doing something that's pretty much guaranteed to suck. For example, if your friend Marty asks if you want take a bus across town with him to visit his incontinent great-uncle and help him finish up some expired cold cuts before taking turns wrestling him shirtless in his basement, you just say "could do" and you're usually off the hook. Sure, it sounds like the suggestion of possibility is there, almost like you're seriously considering it, but what you're really saying is something more along the lines of "Look, Marty, I recognize that what you've just asked me is indeed physically possible, but there's no way in hell I'll have any part of it—not today, not tomorrow, not ever. Seriously. No. F-ing. Way. Mention it again and I'll stab you. . . . Hey, we're still friends, right, Marty?"

"Could do"—it really packs a wallop.

One reason I like the phrase so much is because I've never quite gotten the hang of saying "no." As a result, I've found myself in countless situations I wouldn't wish on a Nazi or any other jerk, either, everything from having to sit through a community theater production of *Nunsense* in the middle of Long Island to catching last call with a friend of a friend of a friend at a bar called the Fat Cock in the

East Village that, as it turned out, wasn't nearly as chicken-themed as I was originally led to believe. Couple my inability to say the word "no" with my mother's inability to hear that same word and the results could be tragic.

This is the story of one of those many, many tragedies.

Shortly after my thirtieth birthday, at a time when most adults are out having lives and stuff, I had a date with my mother—one of our regular mother-son outings—another night of ice-skating at the local rink, all-you-can-drink instant hot chocolate, an organ player, and no one under sixty on the ice except for me. After a couple of hours of this, my mother was driving me back to my sister Miriam's house, where I had been living for the past few months while "plotting my next move." As we pulled into Miriam's driveway, I gathered my skates up from the floor of the car. Then my mother cut off the engine and slowly started to smile.

"There's going to be a benefit for retired nuns and priests at the new hotel downtown in a couple of weeks," she said. "I thought you might like to go."

"That doesn't sound like my kind of thing," I told her.

"Really?" she said. "There's going to be a nice buffet and there will be actual retired nuns and priests at the event."

She said that last part as if we had just won the lottery or a crime-solving monkey or something.

"I don't think so," I said.

"But, Davey, you haven't heard the best part yet," my mom said with a glimmer in her eye.

"It gets better?"

"A lot better. There's going to be a concert after lunch featuring none other than Maureen . . . McGovern," my mom said wide-eyed, the "F" word[1] in between "Maureen" and "McGovern" implied.

"Who's that?"

---

[1] As this is an essay largely concerning my mother, I cannot bring myself to use the actual F-word in it. I really need to keep things classy for this one. I hope all of you profanity lovers out there will understand.

"'Who's that?' You're kidding, right? I thought you were into music."

It turned out Maureen McGovern is the fiery chanteuse perhaps best known for singing the theme from *The Poseidon Adventure* and whatever other show tunes she could get her jazzy hands on. My mom was convinced Maureen McGovern was right up there with the Stones.

"I think I'm busy then," I lied.

"Okay. I guess you'll just let me know."

"I really don't think so, Mom."

"Well, you need to let me know soon because I need to make sure there'll be tickets left."

I'm not sure which was more disturbing, the fact that my mom was totally ignoring me or the notion that benefit luncheons for retired clergy followed by an afternoon of wall-to-wall show tunes actually had sellout potential. I kissed her on the cheek and jumped out of the car, something I should have done as soon as she slowed down to about ten miles per hour.

Not being an older Catholic lady, I didn't give much thought to the benefit after that. But a couple of days later, my mother called.

"Hi, Davey. Guess who I ran into up at church today—Father Aberdeen!"

Father Aberdeen was the priest in charge of music at the school masses back in high school. Since I played guitar, I'd play at mass because I could get out of class to practice acoustic renditions of songs like "On Eagle's Wings" and other church hits. It was awesome, almost like having an ejector seat I could use to get out of anything I didn't feel like doing during school hours.

"That's nice. Tell him I said hello next time you see him."

"You should tell him yourself. He'd love to catch up. In fact, I mentioned the benefit for the nuns and priests and he seemed really into it. Turns out he's a huge McGovern fan, too, maybe the biggest."

Then she paused and said, "Hey, Davey, I have an idea. What if you and Father Aberdeen went to the benefit together?"

I know she wanted it to sound like it was an idea she had just come up with on the spot, but it sounded more like she was reading it off cue cards she had written up the night before and been practicing with all morning. I saw through her little plan right away. As far as I was concerned, she was just trying to get me to spend some quality one-on-one time with a priest in hopes that I might become more "holy" or something. Older Catholic ladies live for that kind of crap.

"Uh-oh, that's the doorbell," I lied. "Gotta go."

"So I guess I'll just plan on it unless I hear otherwise," I heard my mom say as I pulled the receiver away from my ear. "Your father and I need to run a couple of errands before the benefit anyway, so it'll work out great if you and Father Aberdeen just head down there together. Thanks, Davey. This'll be fun!"

I suddenly felt like a shop owner in a mob movie who tells some henchman how he really doesn't need any protection and then the guy shows up to collect with a baseball bat the next week anyway. I tried to just put the whole thing behind me, but sure enough my mom called again the next day, asking if I'd had a chance to call Father Aberdeen.

"No," I told her through clenched teeth.

"He's expecting your call."

"Why would he be expecting my call?"

"Because I told him you'd be calling," my mom said as if we had just had this conversation moments earlier and I had a head injury and sometimes needed to hear things twice. "What am I supposed to do when I see Father Aberdeen at church and he asks me why you haven't called him yet? It'll be embarrassing. He'll think I'm some sort of crazy person!"

"And he wouldn't be alone on that one," I thought. Still, there was no denying this woman was good. Real good.

Reluctantly, I called Father Aberdeen the next day. I'd always liked the guy back in high school so it was actually nice to hear his voice and catch up. It turned out he'd recently been assigned to the church near my parents' house, the one I went to every Sunday as a kid. He was recovering from back-to-back heart attacks. And, as we spoke, he definitely sounded weary in that way one tends to get after having your ass handed to you like that.

"I ran into your mother after mass on Sunday," Father Aberdeen said. "She said you might be taking me to a benefit next week for retired nuns and priests followed by a concert by Maureen McGovern?"

"Um, uh, yeah, sure," I stammered, masking my rage.

"It sounds like it'll be very nice. Who knows? Maybe they'll even ask you to break out your guitar and play your famous rendition of 'On Eagle's Wings' from back in high school! Ha ha!"

"Ha ha! That would be both humorous and unexpected, Father. I can't even imagine! Ha ha!"

Panic began to set in as Father Aberdeen and I spoke for a few more minutes. Then I immediately called my mother to suss out how, despite my earlier unambiguous protests, it now seemed I, a thirty-year-old man with his whole life ahead of him, was attending a benefit for clergy followed by a Maureen F-ing McGovern concert with an actual priest who, from the sound of things, might very well have a third heart attack right in front of me.

"Father Aberdeen really wants to go," my mom said. "You can't not take him!"

"Yeah, I can."

"Great. So you'll do it!" my mom bulldozed. "Thanks, Davey!"

I was trapped.

My mother then started calling me every day about the benefit as if she were masterminding an elaborate air strike. There were a lot of details to hash out: what car would I be driving to pick up Father Aberdeen and would I be getting that car cleaned beforehand, what was I going to wear to the benefit and would I be getting that cleaned beforehand, did I need a haircut and, if so, would I be getting that beforehand, etc. And since he was trying to recover from those two heart attacks, Father Aberdeen had more dietary restrictions than a diabetic supermodel.

"I can't have anything with sugar, wheat, starch, saturated fat, unsaturated fat, trans fat, gluten, spices, preservatives, cholesterol, salt, chocolate, bleached flour, unbleached flour, dairy, caffeine, or flavor of any sort," he said, apparently not joking.

As best I could tell, if he had anything crazier than a glass of water and a Tic Tac, I'd be performing CPR. I figured this might be my ticket out, but I was mistaken.

"No problem," my mom assured me. "I'll bring a bag of sandwich meats. That way, if Father can't have anything they're serving, I can make him a sandwich right there at the table."

I was too beaten down to imagine how that scenario might make matters even worse, but more on that later. As the big day got closer, other frightening details came to light. For example, we wouldn't be sitting just anywhere for the Maureen McGovern concert. Our seats would be front and center so that we might better bask in that unmistakable McGovern glow. It would be like an audience with the Pope. Of show tunes. And since my mom was in tight with the organizers of the benefit, we'd all ride to the concert in a stretch limousine—a detail my mom seemed particularly pumped about.

"There's going to be a limousine, a stretch limousine—you know, the really long kind," she kept telling me. "And not just anybody gets to ride in it, either—just your father, Father Aberdeen, and me. Oh, and then you and some of the other ladies. It's a special stretch limousine just for us. The really long kind that's only for special people."

My mom wasn't normally flashy, so I was starting to think the benefit was totally corrupting her.

On the day of the benefit, a promising combination of snow and rain covered all of Greater Cleveland—nothing the locals weren't used to, but I still prayed it meant everything would be cancelled. No such luck though. Starting at 7:00 A.M., my mom called a half dozen times, going over every last detail yet again as if we were about to rob a bank.

"Be sure to leave yourself plenty of time to pick up Father Aberdeen," my mom stressed. "There could be traffic or construction or a funeral procession or a truck flipped over in the middle of the road or honestly there's just no telling. Don't chance it, David."

"Fine, Mom." I groaned.

"I mean it; we can't afford to have you picking him up last minute."

Perhaps in a subconscious act of rebellion, I'd stayed out late the night before drinking as much as possible with friends, which only added to my misery. Around ten, I got in my car and headed to church to pick up Father Aberdeen. When I pulled up, he was already waiting outside under an awning. He made his way carefully through the slush and got in my car. A few gray hairs aside, he looked unchanged since my high school days.

"So, still playing guitar I assume?" he asked as we began making our way downtown. I'm a sucker for guitar talk and was relieved that Father Aberdeen chose this as the opening topic instead of something tougher, like what I was doing with my life, for example.

"Yup," I answered. "You?"

"No," he said. "Not since these heart attacks. They almost killed me, so I really just have to rest up and get my health back."

As is usually the case when someone brings up almost being killed by something, you pretty much have to stop talking about everything else and focus on how they almost died instead—there's just no getting around it. So, as we made our way down to the hotel, I pretended to listen closely as Father Aberdeen told me about each of the heart attacks and all the hospitals, tests, and tubes that went with them. Mostly, though, I was trying to remember where the nearest hospital was and how quickly I might be able to get him there if things suddenly went south.

"You feel good though, now, mostly or . . . ?" I asked.

"Mostly I guess."

"Great. Anything changes, you let me know. And pronto."

About twenty minutes later, Father Aberdeen and I found ourselves exiting an elevator onto the second floor of the hotel, where about seventy people, most between the ages of sixty-five and nine hundred, mingled about, the men in various shades of gray and the women draped in either floral patterns or colors not found in nature. That unmistakable electricity that occurs when geriatric clergy members get together to make small talk with geriatric nonclergy members filled the air as the de facto Maureen McGovern tailgate party got underway.

"Hi, Father Winslow!" a woman with a short, blue perm said. "How's my favorite pastor?"

"I'm Father Henry."

"Hi, Father Henry! How's my favorite pastor?"

My mom quickly spotted us in the crowd and headed over with my dad and my aunt Helen in tow.

"Hi, Davey! Hi, Father Aberdeen!" my mom said. "Davey, why don't you get yourself and Father Aberdeen a drink?"

Now she was talking. For the first time I thought I might be able to get through this thing. All I had to do was keep a steady stream of alcohol coursing through my veins and everything would be okay. To that end, I made a beeline for the portable bar they had set up in the corner.

"Hello." The bartender smiled as I bellied up. "Can I interest you in a virgin mimosa?"

"That sounds nice, but I think I'll have something a little stronger." I smiled back.

"I'm sorry," he said, wrinkling his brow in faux sympathy. "No alcohol today."

"Die, you heartless prick," I tried to say in response with just my eyes. He looked to be about my age, so I figured he must have had some sense of the situation I had gotten myself into and how it might be greatly improved with ten or eleven drinks. I also knew that whatever supply closet he got all that orange juice and Sprite from was probably also home to at least a few bottles of vodka. In fact, the bastard had a mini liquor store sitting right there at waist level where no one could see it. I felt like grabbing him by the nose with his ice tongs and whipping him in concentric circles across the room until he begged for mercy.

"Fine. I'll take a virgin mimosa and a water." I sighed in defeat.

I returned with the drinks as my mother held court, pointing out the retired nuns and priests in the room as if they were former baseball greats trotting out to the field on Old Timer's Day.

"That's Father Murphy—he taught at Cathedral Latin for years," my mother said. "And that's Sister Patricia—she was at Saint Claire's throughout the seventies before disappearing entirely, never to be heard from again . . . until today."

She knew all the stats. It was creepy.

I knocked back my virgin mimosa, hoping the orange juice in it had somehow fermented. Then we all shuffled into a nearby dining room, where our group sat down at a large round table with a half dozen seventy-somethings. I plopped down between Father Aberdeen and my dad, with whom I briefly attempted to commiserate. My dad was never one for complaining, but even so I figured he might be willing to agree with me on the overall suck factor of the current situation.

"This blows," I whispered.

"I'm having a very nice time," my dad countered.

"Are you kidding? I'd rather be waterboarded."

"I don't know what you're talking about," my dad said, straightening up in his chair.

I wanted to ask my dad what he had done with the money he'd clearly been paid to lie through his teeth. But I was too flabbergasted to say another word to him for the rest of the day. Capitalizing on the lull, one of the grandmas at our table decided to chat up the fresh meat.

"So, David, I understand you play in a musical group," she said.

"Uh, yeah." I cringed.

"We should have you perform at next year's benefit!"

"Oh, I really don't think that would—"

"It'll be great!" She beamed while struggling up from her chair. "You stay right there while I go get one of the organizers so we can set it all up right now!"

By outward appearances, I probably just seemed like a guy spending a relaxing afternoon with an amiable group of senior citizens, but inside I felt like the victim of some bizarre psychological warfare. A minute later, my mom, who had gotten up from the table to work the crowd, ran over to me dragging a guy named Rick I knew from elementary school.

"Look who I found!" she screeched. "It's Rick! It's Rick!"

Rick and I played soccer together in the fourth grade. He was working at the event in some capacity and we chatted for a couple of minutes before he had to get back to things. As soon as he left, my mom came scrambling back over to me.

"What a nice young man." She smiled. "We should introduce him to one of your sisters."

None of my sisters were married at the time and my mom was determined to change all that, and fast. And although somewhere between fourth grade and the benefit, Rick had clearly embraced his gayness with open arms, my mom was somehow oblivious. I did my best to explain to her that the hunt would have to continue elsewhere.

"I dunno, Mom, I feel like he's not ready to settle down with a good woman just yet."

"A nice man like that? Please."

"Don't get me wrong, Mom. He's really, really nice," I agreed, "but also really, really gay."

"David, stop it!" she scolded.

My mom was born without gaydar, so she usually misinterpreted outward signs of homosexuality as heightened exuberance and tended to think calling someone gay was an insult, the sort of taunt fifth graders use on the playground.

"I'm not trying to insult him," I explained. "I'm just saying that while I think he and one of your daughters might become good friends, maybe even best friends, that's as far as it's gonna go."

"Well, if you won't ask for his number, I will!" she said before storming off.

Convinced I was just being an asshole, my mom returned to her seat. With her pissed off and my father suddenly a Stepford husband, I decided to check in with Father Aberdeen.

"Enjoying yourself?" I asked, assuming he was having as much fun as the rest of the pack.

"I have to be honest," he said hesitantly, "I'm not entirely sure why I'm here."

"Huh?" I grunted, thinking maybe that third heart attack was about to kick in.

"Well, I'm often invited places by parishioners and usually I understand why," he explained. "But I just don't feel much of a connection to any of these people."

I could totally relate, but I was also totally confused. My mom made it sound like Father Aberdeen lit up like a damn Christmas tree when he heard about the benefit, especially the Maureen McGovern part.

"I'm sorry, Father," I said. "My mom told me you were dying to come here today—sorry, no pun intended—so that's why I brought you."

"That's funny. She told me that you really wanted to come and that you really wanted to bring me," Father Aberdeen replied, his brow slowly furrowing.

We had been duped, set up by my mom, who was more than your run-of-the-mill manipulative Catholic lady. She was a full-on con artist.

As our reality sunk in, Father Aberdeen and I turned our attention to my mother, who was laughing it up on the other side of the table as if she were at her own bachelorette party. I hoped she would see us trying to burn a hole right through her with our eyes, but before she had a chance, a waiter announced that it was time to hit the buffet. Distracted by the prospect of food, Father Aberdeen and I set our mounting anger aside in hopes of stuffing our faces. Unfortunately, however, virtually everything on display appeared to have been breaded, double-battered, wrapped in bacon, sautéed in butter, covered in sour cream, marinated in Crisco, and then deep-fried a couple of dozen times before being hosed down with a mixture of gravy, hot sauce, and melted cheese. It was as if someone were on a mission to give Father Aberdeen that third heart attack. Still, I needed my strength, so I piled my plate high as Father Aberdeen grabbed a couple of carrot sticks and trudged glumly back to the table.

My mother, on the other hand, seemed almost delighted with the menu as it gave her the chance to break out that bag of heart-friendly sandwich supplies she had hidden under the table this whole time.

"Can I make you a turkey sandwich, Father?" she said while spreading assorted meats across the table like a guy selling fake Rolexes on the sidewalk. "I also have roast beef, corned beef, ham—basically if it comes in cold cut form, I've got it!"

"I don't think so," he said. "I can't really eat that stuff because of that thing about my two heart attacks and how I almost died."

"What?" another woman at our table asked, apparently alarmed.

"Nothing," my mother assured her. "Now, Father, what'll it be? Turkey sound good?"

"No, thank you," he said.

"All right, ham it is!" my mom said. "Davey, here, pass this slice of ham over to Father and if he likes it I'll make him as many sand- wiches as he wants. And don't worry, Father, my hands are perfectly clean."

While Father Aberdeen was beyond uninterested, I was just plain mortified, my eyes slowly glazing over in a way I recognized as hav- ing preceded the few fainting spells I'd ever had in my life. I was pulled out of it, however, when my mother announced it was con- cert time and we were all going to get McGoverned whether we liked it or not. Since she didn't want to make any of the other attendees jealous, my mom asked our group to play it cool as we made our way to the black stretch limousine waiting downstairs.

"If anyone asks, we're just taking a cargo van down to the concert—nothing fancy, nothing special, nothing anyone needs to get worked up about," she said. "Got it? Now everybody just keep moving."

There's something anticlimactic about piling into a limousine with a bunch of old ladies, a priest, and parents you stopped talking to an hour earlier. I had always thought these things were supposed to be filled with strippers, pulsing track lights, champagne, and maybe even Sinbad. My mom, however, seemed unfazed, her sheer delight increasing with each block as she went on and on about how nice it was to ride in a limousine to somewhere other than a ceme- tery for a change. "Tomato, tomahto," I thought.

At the concert, we sat in the dark enduring Maureen McGovern belt out show tune after show tune as she took just about every number from the American songbook that I never wanted to hear again and not only extended it, but made it "her own" in a way that had me feeling under my seat to see if someone had by some off chance left a gun. There were vocal acrobatics, spoken word intervals during which the band "brought it down," and a whole lot of cringe-worthy "selling it" in general.

"I'd like to dedicate this next one to my two little boys, Dante and Pepper," she announced before the string section kicked off yet another number. "They're Welsh corgis!"

I love dogs, but in that moment I wished nothing more than for Dante and Pepper to be lying dead somewhere that very moment. Even so, between that line and the rest of her stage banter, there was barely a dry seat in the house. Maureen McGovern had come to delight us all. Almost. As far as I was concerned, she represented everything that was wrong with the world. My mother, on the other hand, lapped it up, a "How does she do it?" expression plastered to her face. I thought to sneak out and call someone, anyone, who might be able to talk me through it all, but one look at Father Aberdeen and I saw he was at least as troubled as I was, and I felt too guilty to leave him behind. He must have thought celibacy was a breeze compared to this.

"How are you holding up?" I whispered to him as Maureen McGovern threatened to bring the house down once more.

"I-I'm f-fine," he answered, a desperate "I wanna go home! I wanna go home!" look in his eye.

About nine or ten hours later, Maureen McGovern finished her sixth and final encore and we slowly filed out of the theater and into the familiar Cleveland mix of snow and rain, like inmates fresh out of the penitentiary.

"Do you two want to join us in the limousine back to the hotel so you can pick up your car?" my mom asked us out front, still riding that unmistakable McGovern high.

"No, thank you!" Father Aberdeen and I shot back in unison before scurrying off in the opposite direction.

As we walked the few blocks to my car we both became giddy at the prospect of freedom.

On the drive home, I tried to engage him in a little trash talking, but he refused to return any of the shots I took at those old bastards we met back at the hotel.

"What about that crazy old bat with the soiled neck brace who kept double dipping and chewing with her mouth wide open?" I asked, hoping to get him going. "Ugh, I thought I was gonna puke!"

Nothing.

I couldn't even get him to revisit the fact that my mom had completely tricked us both. I was impressed by his self-control, but I resented him for not indulging my need for blood sport.

"Thanks for joining me," I said as we pulled back into the church driveway a short while later. By that point, I figured I might as well just pretend we'd had a lovely day together after all.

"Thanks for taking me. I . . . had a nice time," Father Aberdeen lied before stepping out of the car and into the slush.

As I headed back to my sister's house, I tried to figure out exactly why my mother would trick her own son and a Catholic priest, the closest thing to God on earth, into the nightmare we had just endured. I came up empty. Later that night, she called to check in.

"That was fun, right, Davey?" she said.

"Fun? That was hell!" I moaned. "Why did you do that to us?"

"Do what?"

"Why did you trick Father Aberdeen and me into going to that, that *thing*?"

"I didn't trick anybody," she scoffed.

Then I broke it to her how Father Aberdeen and I had figured out exactly what she had done. The jig was up.

"I thought you'd have a nice time," my mother said in complete denial. "You must have at least enjoyed Maureen McGovern."

"I loathe Maureen McGovern!" (Maureen, if you're reading this, I've got no beef with you. You just happened to be in the wrong place at the wrong time. We're cool.)

My mother and I ended up rehashing what had gone on repeatedly over the next few days. I was still convinced that her master plan was to get me to hang out with a priest. I was getting older, and though I wasn't entirely directionless, my path wasn't entirely clear, not even to me. Though she must have known it was too late to get me to actually become a priest, something I'm sure she would have loved, she probably figured a little priestly influence couldn't hurt. Even so, forcing Father Aberdeen and me to struggle through an afternoon of potentially fatal lunch foods, virtually every show tune ever recorded, and more senior citizens than a fiber seminar was extreme any way you slice it.

"You could have *killed* us," I pleaded with her.

"Oh, shove it."

Though she could never look me in the eye when we spoke of it, my mom continued to deny the whole thing. As for my father, he finally insisted that the case be officially closed one night after a particularly profanity-laced dinner.

Lest you think this was an isolated incident, this wasn't the first time my mother had subjected me to torture in the name of self-improvement.

"I signed you up for Typing for Beginners I and II down at Heights High this summer," my mother casually mentioned to me one day when I was thirteen.

"You *what?*" I shrieked.

I was convinced it was just some sadist plan she had come up with in her spare time. And I knew there was no getting out of it, either. Making matters worse, Heights High was just far enough away from our house that I couldn't just walk back home on my own as soon as she dropped me off.

"I'll call children's services on you!" I threatened.

"See what I care," she sighed.

My unpleasant memories of that summer aside, one recent afternoon, after watching my friend David, a successful author, hunt and peck around his laptop keyboard, typing with just his two index fingers, I remembered that miserable summer long ago and finally thought "*Oh*—so that's why she made me do that!"

Still, the idea that my mother might have wanted me to receive some guidance was a tougher pill to swallow.

A few weeks after the benefit, I ran into Father Aberdeen at the local Baskin-Robbins, where he was digging into a cup of sugar-free, fun-free sorbet. Two torture survivors, we dared not speak of that hellish day we spent together. After buying a cone for myself, I asked if he needed a ride home. It was getting late, at least by ice-cream standards, and the church was a good mile away.

"No." Father Aberdeen shuddered, barely looking up from his sorbet. "N-no, thank you."

I can't say I blame him. After everything we'd been through together, I wouldn't have gotten back into my car either.

Afterward, I went to Miriam's house to find her sitting in the living room with our sister Libby. I decided to ask them how they managed to avoid being dragged to the benefit.

"We said no," Libby explained.

Miriam nodded. "Yeah—you just gotta say no to that stuff."

I turned around and walked upstairs to my bedroom in silence, a black cloud forming over my head as if I were a character in a comic strip.

"Hey, Dave," Miriam yelled up to me a few minutes later. "You wanna come with us to get Mexican food?"

"No," I said firmly.

I was actually kind of hungry, but I figured it might not be a bad idea to start practicing.

Tasteful Nudes

It was a typical Sunday, and I was coming down from another red hot weekend of doing laundry and picking up a few things at Bed Bath & Beyond, so I decided to spend a quiet night at home, just me and the Internet. As this sort of thing often goes, it wasn't long before I started to wander. I clicked on a link on one Web site that sent me to another Web site, where I clicked on yet another link that sent me to yet another Web site and so on and so on until I found myself on a Web site that, much to my complete and utter disbelief, featured photographs of women who didn't seem too crazy about wearing clothes.

I try not to make a habit of frequenting Web sites like this, mostly because I think they pose too much of a threat to the print industry, but I figured I had come this far, so it felt weird to turn back. Also, I must stress that this Web site was not a pornographic Web site with all sorts of poking and prodding and various fluids, bodily and otherwise, flying about the room from time to time. I'm told those exist but—trust me—this was definitely not one of them—it was simply a Web site that made it its business to showcase photos of women in various states of undress, particularly that state of undress that involves not really wearing any clothes at all (which is to say the best kind). And it was on this Web site that I happened upon a photo of a woman I was pretty sure was the most beautiful woman I had seen in at least the past week. She was voluptuous, exotic, and alluring. She was also totally naked, which was a huge weight off my shoulders since it usually takes a lot of begging, bribing, and tears for me to ever get a woman to do that for me in real life.

"Hello, m'lady," I said to my computer monitor. Of course, I wasn't expecting her to answer. I just wanted her to know that I was really classy, a gentleman even.

It was the late '00s and Myspace was still the social networking site of choice. So, being a man of the times, I had my profile page open in another browser window.

"Hm," I said, stroking my chin. "I wonder if she has a Myspace page."

I typed her name into the search window and, as it turned out, this woman (whom, for matters of privacy and respect, I will simply refer to as the Hottest Naked Chick on the Internet), did indeed have a Myspace page. So I giddily sent her a friend request. I wasn't hoping to establish any real contact with her or anything—it's just there's something about becoming Internet "friends" with a woman who really seems to hate wearing clothes that somehow makes you feel more alive. Just ask those nearly four million people who had the same idea with that Tila Tequila lady.

I planned on just getting on with my life after sending the Hottest Naked Chick on the Internet a friend request, but the next day I was stunned to find a comment on *my* Myspace page from none other than—you're not gonna believe this—the Hottest Naked Chick on the Internet.

"Nice pic of you with Colbert!" she wrote. "Love him!"

As you may have just guessed, my profile picture at the time was of me with Stephen Colbert, whom I had recently met at a comedy festival. Naturally I was stunned. Not only did the Hottest Naked Chick on the Internet actually write me a note but it seemed like we also had a lot in common—like an appreciation of Stephen Colbert to give you just one example.

"This is all happening so fast," I thought.

I tried to play it cool after seeing her comment, but it was all a bit too much to handle and I couldn't restrain myself from clicking on over to her page and leaving a comment in return.

"Thanks," I wrote after a long hard think.

While I was on her page I couldn't help but notice a few updates since my last visit. Not only had she embedded one of my YouTube videos on her page, but she had also written a familiar name in the "Who I'd Like to Meet Section"—mine. That's right. Apparently the Hottest Naked Chick on the Internet wanted to meet me, Dave Hill.

Things were officially spinning out of control. And then, before I even had a chance to come back down to earth, I received a full-on Myspace message from—I guess we both saw this coming—the Hottest Naked Chick on the Internet.

"I'm a big fan," she wrote. "I'd love to come to one of your shows next time I'm in New York."[1]

"Whoa," I thought, momentarily resigning myself to never using the Internet again, as things had fully entered "be careful what you wish for" territory. I suddenly felt like Anthony Michael Hall and that other guy in *Weird Science*, where they just sit there with bras on their heads and the next thing they know Kelly LeBrock appears in her underwear asking if they want to hang out.

"I am officially in over my head," I thought. "Nay, I am officially in *way* over my head."

Eventually, however, I pulled myself together and alerted her to my upcoming performance schedule, admittedly something I do whenever someone asks, regardless of age, race, gender, sexual orientation, or whether or not they appear anywhere on the Internet with absolutely no clothes on whatsoever.

"Great, I'm going to be in New York then," she wrote. "See you soon!"

Strictly for survival purposes, I actively tried to forget the Hottest Naked Chick on the Internet was planning to come to one of my shows in the near future. I was reminded of my date with Destiny (not her real name), however, when, after the shows had come and gone, she sent me another Myspace message.

---

1 The hottest Naked Chick on the Internet lived in Nevada, a popular state for naked ladies.

"Sorry I missed your shows," she wrote. "I'm still in town. Any chance you would be up for meeting for coffee or lunch today?"

As a Z-list celebrity, I receive requests from strangers asking to meet me all the time, sometimes as many as two or three times a year. Still, it is my strictest of rules to turn down each and every one of those requests. After taking another look at some photos of the Hottest Naked Chick on the Internet, though, I decided to make an exception.

"Absolutely," I wrote back. "I would enjoy that very much."

I figured it might be a character-building experience for me, and, perhaps more important, I would get to have lunch with a woman who appears naked on the Internet, which, statistically speaking, is something that just doesn't happen to most people.

I arranged to meet the Hottest Naked Chick on the Internet at a restaurant near my apartment. I tried to get my friend Meredith, who had stopped by for a visit beforehand, to come with me as a chaperone.

"No way!" she said. "I'm not coming with you on a date."

"It's *not* a date," I stressed to her. "This is research!"

I even tried showing her a bunch of pictures of the Hottest Naked Chick on the Internet on my computer, but she still refused. Weird.

I purposely headed over to the restaurant a few minutes late in an effort to convince myself I was playing it cool, a power move, really. In reality, though, I was struggling to hold it together. Usually when I step out for lunch, I just grab a sandwich or something at the corner deli and head back to my apartment to stuff my face in solitude, not sit down with some naked superfox. There's just no training for this sort of thing.

"I wonder if she'll wear any clothes to lunch," I muttered to myself.

I was starting to feel tingly all over. Also, by this time, at least half of me was starting to think I was about to become the victim of an elaborate prank. But then I remembered I love a good prank, even when I'm the victim.

"I just can't lose on this one!" I thought.

As I walked through the front door of the restaurant, I braced myself for either outcome. But when I got inside, instead of being greeted by a gaggle of friends laughing, giving me the finger, and kicking me in the genitals (you know, prank fun), I was met by none other than the Hottest Naked Chick on the Internet, who, much to my delight, looked exactly like her photos, which I had assumed must have been pushed beyond mortal levels with Photoshop. Much to my dismay, however, she was wearing clothes—jeans and a T-shirt to be exact. It took me an extra beat to recognize her all covered up like that, but I'd like to think she didn't notice.

"Hi," I said. "I'm Dave."

"Hi," the Hottest Naked Chick on the Internet said back, shaking my hand.

It was really nice, as if suddenly I weren't some guy who's been on basic cable television a few times and she weren't a woman who hates wearing clothes, but just two totally normal people saying hello to each other in person for the very first time. So we grabbed the nearest table and began chatting.

"I love your comedy," she said.

"Thanks," I said, blushing. "I love your, um . . . you seem nice!"

"Thanks. You too."

I think I can speak for most straight men when I say this, but—with a few possible exceptions—having a gorgeous woman who regularly takes all her clothes off and lets people take pictures of her pay you a compliment is, well, is the nicest thing that could ever happen. And that alone would have been incredible, so when the Hottest Naked Chick on the Internet continued on in great detail about all the videos of mine she had seen on the Internet, I nearly soiled myself. She even seemed mildly aware that I had been on basic cable television, something not nearly enough people, naked or otherwise, ever seem to notice for some reason. Not only was she the Hottest Naked Chick on the Internet, but it kind of seemed like she was also the foremost authority on Dave Hill in North America. I was dizzy.

"What other stuff do you like about me?" I wanted to ask in an effort to keep her sitting there looking beautiful and talking about my favorite subject.

Ten or twenty minutes later, however, it occurred to me that it would be impolite not to ask her about herself, so I reluctantly changed the topic.

"So what about you?" I asked. "I, uh, notice you, uh, have those, uh, a Web site!"

I felt awkward bringing up the whole naked pictures thing like that so quickly, but it's not like I really knew anything else about her.

"Yeah," she said, rolling her eyes. "I posed for those nude photos when I was really young and naive. I regret it."

"Oh, yeah, I could see that," I said, trying to sound sympathetic. "Almost made that mistake myself back when I was a younger fella."

The truth is, I didn't regret her posing for those all-nude photos at all. How could I? After all, they were what brought us together.

"What I'd like to do is fashion modeling," she explained as our food showed up.

"Is that what brings you to town?" I asked while picturing all those naked photos of her I'd seen and reluctantly putting clothes on all of them in my head.

"Nah. There's this other job I do sometimes."

"What's that?"

She ignored that last question and turned the conversation back toward me, which I thought was really sweet. But even as much as I loved that sort of thing, I kept wondering about that other job and, what with her being the Hottest Naked Chick on the Internet and all, why she would even need it. After taking the time to field a few more questions about me, I tried to casually bring it up again.

"So, uh, what's that other job you mentioned?"

"Oh, that," she said, rolling her eyes again. "You know how some-times a businessman needs a date for lunch or dinner or something?"

"Of course," I lied.

"Well, I work for an agency that sets me up with them," she explained. "I get paid four thousand dollars per date."

"Wow! Four thousand dollars just to have lunch with someone?" I said, deciding it was best to play innocent. "That's the best job ever!"

"Sometimes it's sexual. But only if I want it to be."

"You're a straight shooter. I admire that."

I respected that she played by her own rules. But it also occurred to me that, given the close proximity of our fellow diners, everyone around us was now likely under the impression that I had arranged to meet a prostitute for lunch. She wasn't dressed like a prostitute, but it doesn't take a pimp from a *Shaft* movie to figure out that when a woman says she accepts cash in exchange for her company something might be up.

"Wait a minute," I thought after considering things for a moment. "I *did* arrange to meet a prostitute for lunch. *Awesome.*"

Naturally, the fifteen-year-old in me giggled to himself in a bizarre mixture of mild embarrassment and full-tilt excitement that only a manchild can truly understand. But a moment later, horror set in.

"Oh my gosh!" I thought. "Did the Hottest Naked Chick on the Internet/foremost authority on Dave Hill in North America want to meet me for lunch just so she could proposition me?"

I had never been so conflicted in my entire life: On the one hand, I was insulted that she might think I was the kind of guy who'd be willing to pay for sex. But on the other hand, I was completely flattered that she might think I could afford to spend four thousand dollars on it. Despite my inner turmoil, I did my best to play it cool.

"So, how often do you come to New York to see clients?" I asked now that everything was out in the open. "And how many per week?"

What I really wanted to ask, though, was how she got into it and how did it affect all those other hours in her life when she wasn't earning four thousand dollars. Did her friends or family know? Was there a special someone out there (you know, besides me) who got to have lunch with her for free whenever he wanted? And did she ever get all freaked out about it like I was?

"But you're so nice and pretty, ma'am!" I wanted to blurt out. "Why would you do that sort of thing?"

"I want to quit a lot of the time," she told me, "but the money is so good."

When I thought about my own hourly rates for my work, I couldn't disagree. Clearly she had a better agent than I did.

"They're not even trying!" I thought.

But then she explained, "What I'd really like to do is sell DVDs of me dancing around in sexy outfits."

I weighed the two options for a moment before deciding that dancing around in sexy outfits was definitely the high road, kind of classy even.

"Now *that's* an idea I can get behind!" I told her.

She seemed really nice and I felt like it was my due diligence to try to steer her away from a profession neither one of us seemed too thrilled about. Baby steps, I figured.

"Wow, I could be like Henry Higgins in *Pygmalion*!" I thought before quickly realizing I was actually just a jackass.

We chatted for a few minutes longer, mostly about me, but also about her for a couple of seconds, before we finished our food and I flagged down our waiter for the check. And even though she appeared to be the breadwinner between the two of us, I decided to pick up the tab.

"I don't have to be a john to be a gentleman," I thought as I considered some of the lessons I'd learned during our time together.

Though there wasn't any indication that things between us were anything more than platonic (nor did I want them to be, outside of my elaborate fantasy world), I was still a bit anxious as we headed back outside. After all, she was in town on business and Moneybags Hill did just spring for lunch.

"What if she got the wrong idea and still has every intention of trying to book a date with the Big Guy?"[2] I wondered.

"It was really nice to meet you," the Hottest Naked Chick on the Internet said as we stood there on the sidewalk. "Thanks for lunch."

"Any time," I replied. "Nice to meet you, too."

And it really was.

Then I braced myself for whatever might be coming next. But instead of getting down to brass tacks, the Hottest Naked Chick on

---

2 Note: I am the Big Guy.

the Internet just gave me a hug good-bye and walked away. Was I relieved? Sure. But even so, the egomaniacal and wildly insecure part of me couldn't help but get a little offended.

"What—does she think she's too good to offer me sex in exchange for money?" I whimpered to myself. "The nerve of her!"

And while, sure, it might have been exciting, titillating even, to at least have been asked, the fact is, if I ever did have a wild time with a prostitute, even a really fancy four-thousand-dollar one, I'd probably cry myself to sleep that night and try to confess the whole thing to every person, house pet, or even lamppost I saw the next day. Call me a prude, call me a cheapskate, call me a self-righteous prick—but I'm just not set up for that sort of thing.

"Let me know if I can ever help with getting that DVD together," I called out to the Hottest Naked Chick on the Internet as she continued down the street.

I don't think she heard me but it really doesn't matter. And as I watched her fade into the distance, I realized that none of it really mattered anyway. Except for one thing: the simple fact that, whenever I'm feeling down or thinking I'm some sort of pathetic and immature loser, I'll always know that there's someone somewhere out there who thinks I'm pretty darn great.

And, even better, I can see her naked on the Internet any time I want.

Rocking Me, Rocking You, and Probably Some Other People, Too

Once a year at my Catholic elementary school, they had something called "sports night" where they would play sports highlights reels in the church basement and then get someone from the Cleveland Browns or Indians to come out and tell us wide-eyed kids how getting a good education is the most important thing you could ever do, even more important than playing sports. One year some Cleveland Brown or another told us how he "put his pants on one leg at a time just like everyone else." I eventually realized he was just trying to illustrate the fact that, despite being a professional athlete, in the end he was just a regular guy like everyone else. But at the time, since I had a habit of putting my pants on two legs at a time while sitting on the edge of my bed, his words only served as further confirmation of something I already knew: I was different.

Deep down inside, in my heart, in my gut, and—perhaps most of all—in my loins, I knew I had a higher calling, one that had nothing to do with being a team player or putting pants on one leg at a time or even wearing pants at all. It was a calling of thunderous guitar riffs, explosive drumbeats, throbbing bass lines, and singers that sounded like Vikings on the goddamn warpath. It was the call of rock.

It all started when my dad bought a copy of *Led Zeppelin IV*, an anomaly in a record collection that consisted mostly of jazz and classical albums. It looked cool and different to me right away. On the cover were weird-looking symbols and some old guy with a bunch of sticks on his back for no apparent reason. By the age of seven, I had learned how to work the record player myself, so one day I dropped the needle down on the Led Zeppelin record and was instantly transformed. I could tell right away that these guys were total badasses, like no one I had ever heard before. And I was certain they could beat up any of the other bands I had been listening to. I wasn't sure I could even handle being like them, but dammit I wanted to try.

Since I was seven and all, my desire to become like the guys in Led Zeppelin was met mostly with resistance from my parents. For starters, I wasn't allowed to grow my hair like any of the guys in the band, not even like the bass player John Paul Jones, who, with his face-hugging page boy locks, seemed to have the most second-grade-friendly hairstyle of them all.

"I wanna be a guitar player!" I announced to my dad one day.

"Okay," he answered. "But you'll have to take piano lessons for three years first."

It felt like a prison sentence, but my dad's thinking was that if I could stick with piano for that long, I would have proven my interest in music was genuine and not just an excuse to get wrapped up in drugs, Satan, and other standard rock stuff. I reluctantly went along with his plan and took piano lessons from one of the neighbors for almost three years to the day, learning compositions by Bach, Beethoven, and other dead guys until my dad finally let me quit. Soon after, I began messing around on my dad's old nylon-stringed Spanish guitar, slowly figuring out how to play bits of various rock songs by ear, one string at a time. Like most people born to rock, the first thing I learned was the opening riff to "Smoke on the Water" by Deep Purple. The rocker's instinct to learn this song first is kind of like how a little baby piglet knows to start suckling on a sow's teat just moments after being born. No one knows how or why it happens—it just does.

This is the thirteen-year-old me with my first electric guitar, just moments before bringing the heat at another school mass. I just realized that I have the same hairstyle now as I did then. I can't decide whether that's sad or not.

"Check it out," I'd say to my younger sister, Katy, before unleashing my best Ritchie Blackmore[1] impression. "It's 'Smoke on the Water' by Deep Purple."

"Can you take that thing into the basement or something?" she'd say. "I'm trying to watch TV."

As awesome as I thought it was, my family got pretty sick of hearing me play "Smoke on the Water" over and over all day, so—if only to preserve their sanity—my dad arranged for me to take guitar lessons from a guy named Joe who lived a few blocks away. Joe had a Gibson Les Paul guitar just like Jimmy Page[2] and his house smelled

---

1 Ritchie Blackmore was the original guitar player for Deep Purple. If you are a rocker, you already know that. However, my publisher gave me a long talk about how this book might also be read by nonrockers (something I struggled with initially, but am now totally cool with), so I thought I should probably point that out.
2 Jimmy Page is the guitar player for Led Zeppelin, but honestly it seems ridiculous that I should have to point that out whether you are a rocker or not. Pull yourself together! I can't hold your hand through everything, dammit.

like cigarettes—a popular rock scent—so I was especially thrilled. And given my extreme rock determination, I worked hard at whatever Joe threw my way.

"Today I am going to show you how to play 'Stairway to Heaven,'" Joe told me one day. It was like I was a medieval knight being handed the coolest sword of all time or something. I almost wet my pants right there in his living room.

By the end of the summer before eighth grade, I was playing "Stairway to Heaven" and other rock anthems about as well as what could be expected from a thirteen-year-old beating on his dad's old Spanish guitar. Still, there was only one weapon suitable for doing the kind of rock damage I had in mind: an electric guitar. I was obsessed with the idea of getting one and watched MTV for hours just to see all the guitars the various bands played in their videos. It was like my own version of porn. At the time, Fleetwood Mac had a video where a couple of guys in the band happen upon dozens of electric guitars buried in the desert.

"Why couldn't they just give one of those guitars to me instead of covering them with sand like that?" I thought. It was an outrage.

Despite Fleetwood Mac basically telling me to go fuck myself in that video, I had improved enough on the guitar by the time eighth grade rolled around that my dad finally took me to buy my first electric guitar. It was shiny and black and I couldn't wait to bring it to school and start melting faces. Another kid in my grade, Tim, got an electric guitar around that time, too.

"This is 'Aqualung' by Jethro Tull," Tim said to me one day after school, before launching into the song's legendary opening riff. Even when played by a thirteen-year-old, it sounded like the gateway to Middle-earth. In that moment we both knew that our will to rock simply could not be denied. We soon became best friends and went about staking our rightful claim as guitar gods of the eighth grade.

"I can play 'Jumpin' Jack Flash,'" one of our classmates might say to us in the lunchroom.

"Yeah, right," we'd respond, though rarely with actual words.

Instead we'd just stare him down with an awesome rock look worthy of Keith Richards or someone else who lived it 24/7 like we did. Rock 'n' roll was no game to us.

It would have been great to form a band at that time, but since there wasn't much of a band scene in our elementary school, Tim and I had little choice but to play guitar with a nun named Sister Patrice at school masses instead. It wasn't exactly the relentless rock onslaught we had envisioned for ourselves, but at least it gave us the chance to play in front of an audience that wasn't allowed to leave. And once the priest was far enough down the aisle during the closing hymn, we'd usually sneak in a guitar solo or two to keep our chops up.

"Nice job, boys," Sister Patrice would tell us after mass.

"Yeah, we really nailed it. 'On Eagle's Wings'[3] was fucking sick today!"

"What?"

"Nothing, Sister."

School mass or not, it was awesome to be on stage. And if I squinted hard enough it was easy to imagine I was rocking Madison Square Garden instead of the church where I received my First Communion just a few years earlier. By the time high school rolled around, I was bringing a pretty solid amount of heat on the guitar for a fourteen-year-old, not quite face melting, but definitely hair singeing as far as I was concerned.

I ended up playing guitar at mass in high school, too, but by then it was mostly just so I could skip class to practice, which— church music or not—felt like a pretty rock 'n' roll thing to do. Outside of school, I attempted to form my first "real" rock band. Tim had already joined a group that was busy playing high school dances, pep rallies, and other events where it seemed like a good idea to have someone play Simple Minds's "Don't You (Forget About Me)" and other hits of the day. As a result, I was forced to scavenge the lower grades for hungry players to piece together a band. We called

---

3 "On Eagle's Wings" is like the "Stairway to Heaven" of the Catholic church.

ourselves the Good Ol' Boys after the scene in *The Blues Brothers* where the band plays at a country bar. It seemed like a good idea at the time. And as the self-appointed band leader, I was a taskmaster, a total bastard even, throwing temper tantrums whenever someone hit a wrong note or wasn't bringing what I felt was an acceptable amount of rock heat.

"Do you think John Bonham[4] just stopped playing in the middle of a goddamn verse like that?" I'd yell at the drummer. "Do you?"

I was a loose cannon, even scaring myself sometimes. Making matters worse, I had asked a girl I really liked to play keyboards in the band, a surefire way to get her to like me, I thought. Unfortunately, some of the other guys in the band had the same idea, so between me screaming like Buddy Rich[5] all the time and every guy in the band ogling the only girl in the band, the band broke up before ever actually playing a gig or even making stickers. I was barely sixteen and I was already learning how rock 'n' roll can be a cruel mistress.

After that two or three weeks straight of nonstop band drama, I decided to strike out on my own as a solo artist, which is to say I mostly just played guitar alone in my bedroom. Occasionally, I'd crank my amp up really loud and force the neighbors to listen.

"David, stop it!" one of my sisters would scream up the stairs. "We got a call from the neighbors again."

"Fine," I'd say reluctantly. My bedroom concerts never lasted very long, but they were still enough to satisfy my desperate need for an audience.

After high school, Tim and I decided to attend Fordham University in the Bronx together, ostensibly because it seemed like a fine

---

4 In case you actually don't know, John Bonham was the drummer for Led Zeppelin and was pretty much the greatest rock drummer of all time until he choked to death on his own vomit, which—while not in any way recommended—is historically a very rock thing to do. Just so you don't think I'm making this stuff up, Jimi Hendrix and AC/DC singer Bon Scott also choked to death on their own vomit. Look it up.

5 Buddy Rich was a legendary jazz drummer and bandleader. He is considered by many to have been the world's greatest drummer and, occasionally, a bit of a prick, which—what with his name being Buddy and all—nobody ever saw coming.

place to obtain a solid liberal arts education and equip ourselves with the necessary tools to thrive in the real world. In reality, though, we just wanted to form a band together in New York City. Our friend Pat, a drummer, was a year younger than us and still finishing high school at the time. Still, we wanted him to be in our band, so when Pat came to visit us during our freshman year, Tim and I tried to sell him on the idea of going to Fordham.

"Dude, you can buy anything you want at the liquor store off campus and they don't even ask for ID," we told him.

"Really?" Pat said in disbelief.

"Yeah, really."

"Okay, I'm in."

It worked like a charm, so the following summer back in Cleveland, Tim and I put our band together with Pat in anticipation of him going to school with us in the fall. We talked our friend Gary into being our frontman. Rather than going to the trouble of finding a bass player, Tim and I traded off on bass and guitar. Pat had some pictures of Elvis taped to his drumset, so one night Gary suggested we call ourselves Sons of Elvis. I still can't decide if it's the best or worst band name ever, but it stuck.

By the end of the summer, the newly dubbed Sons of Elvis had recorded a four-song demo tape that we were pretty sure contained some of the greatest rock music of all-time. It probably didn't, but since our plan was to take over the world, we decided not to question it. Come fall, Gary stayed behind in Cleveland. The original plan was to have him just drive to New York and play gigs with us on weekends until Sons of Elvismania kicked in enough to justify him moving. Impetuous youths that we were, however, Pat, Tim, and I ruthlessly kicked him to the curb a couple days after moving back into the dorms. Even worse, we never actually told him he was out of the band—we just assumed he'd figure it out eventually.[6]

---

6 Gary, if you're reading this now and still haven't figured things out—you're out of the band. I'm sorry it's taken me so long to be straight with you about this. We'll always have that one summer though. No one can take that away from us.

Meanwhile back at Fordham, my and Tim's friend and classmate Kevin had cool hair, was from Minneapolis, and had seen both the Replacements and Hüsker Dü more times than probably even the guys in those bands. Those seemed like good enough reasons to have him be the new singer in our band, so we started practicing with him in the basement of a pizza place near campus. Within a few weeks, we managed to get ourselves a gig on audition night at CBGB, the legendary rock club that launched the careers of the Ramones, Blondie, the Talking Heads, and just about every other New York band we liked. It felt like a huge milestone to be playing there. And, given our extreme level of both confidence and naivete, we imagined the club would be pretty excited to have us, too.

"Hi, we're Sons of Elvis," we announced proudly to the door guy upon our arrival. Rather than light up with excitement like we expected him to, he just stood there and grunted a couple of times, as door guys at clubs are wont to do. The gig itself ended up being a little anticlimactic, too. Not only was the club even darker and danker than it looked in pictures, it also reeked of stale beer and urine of various vintages. And instead of being packed with rockers, punks, dope fiends, and hipsters like we had anticipated, there were maybe two people in the crowd, including the bartender. We didn't go on until after midnight, which, being a Sunday and all, didn't seem like a prime slot. But while it might not have been exactly what we had hoped for, we still rocked with enough authority that they agreed to let us come back.

Unfortunately for Kevin, we ended up listening to a tape of the show on the drive home. And, once we were able to actually hear him sing, realized that, even with his awesome rock look, he sounded kind of like Yoko Ono with a bad cold, so we cut him loose. He was a little bummed at first, but once we explained to him that thing about how rock 'n' roll can be a cruel mistress, Kevin was cool about it and we were able to remain friends.

Shortly after we gave Kevin the boot, I was approached by a guy named John from Queens who lived in the same dorm and, since we practiced at deafening volumes in my room at the time, couldn't help but hear us.

"You're in Sons of Elvis, right?" he asked.

"Yeah," I mumbled, playing it cool.

"You should have me be your singer."

"Can you sing?" I asked him while trying to pretend that I wasn't even going to listen to his answer.

"Yeah, I can sing my balls off."

John was handsome, confident, and owned a leather jacket—three key ingredients to being a singer in a band. On top of that, he actually could sing his balls off. All of us, himself included, just assumed he was our new singer a few minutes into his audition. We even went out and bought beer and stood around drinking it together after practice, just like real rockers do. It was really, really cool.

As loud as we were, it didn't take long before school officials banned us from practicing in my dorm room anymore, so somehow we managed to talk our friends Tom and Brian into letting us practice in the kitchen of their off-campus apartment. By then, I was really getting into playing the bass, so I agreed to play it full time instead of switching instruments with Tim every few songs. I had also recently read that Bill Wyman got more chicks than anyone else in the Stones, so given the relative absence of women in my life at the time, I couldn't afford to take any more chances. We began practicing two or three times a week, writing as many songs as we could while ripping off the Replacements, Aerosmith and whomever else we considered to be gods whenever possible. Before long, we were the best band on campus as far as we were concerned (the fact that we were the only band on campus seemed entirely irrelevant), and didn't waste any time letting everyone else know we thought so. It was kind of like we were Oasis, only without any of the fame, success, or cool hair.

The new and improved Sons of Elvis played gigs in Manhattan wherever and whenever anyone would have us, usually borrowing a friend's car to take our equipment and however many band members could fit, while whoever was left after that hopped on the subway. By the time graduation neared, we knew we wanted nothing to do with anything most of our friends were planning on getting involved with after finishing school—stuff like jobs, haircuts, and other unthinkable acts.

"Where are you planning on sending your résumé?" a classmate would ask.

"Nowhere," we'd respond.

The plan was just to get a big record deal and take over the world with our unstoppable rock attack. We expected a bidding war as soon as all the big record labels in town heard even a couple notes of our music. An entertainment lawyer named Keith thought we were almost as awesome as we did and agreed to play our music for every label in town. We assumed it would probably be just a matter of weeks before we were driving cars into swimming pools, dating eighteen-year-old Brazilian models, and firing pistols at television sets (you know, stuff total rock stars do).

Unfortunately, however, none of the big record labels seemed to hear what we were hearing on that demo tape, and the bidding war we were counting on never really escalated beyond a brief misunderstanding at best. Eventually, however, we managed to get signed to a small independent record label that consisted entirely of a guy named Joe who rented a one-room office with a single telephone in SoHo. The important thing, though, was that he thought we were almost as awesome as Keith did, which made him the second biggest Sons of Elvis fan we had ever met.

"You guys are great," Joe told us.

"Yeah, we know," we responded.

With the money Joe gave us, we loaded up our equipment into a van and dragged it to a recording studio in Hoboken, New Jersey, to record what we assumed would be our multiplatinum debut. Keith's friend Doug, who had worked with bands like Nirvana, Smashing Pumpkins, and others we dreamed of becoming more popular than, flew out from Wisconsin to produce the album. Together, we worked night and day for a week and a half, sleeping only occasionally in an apartment above the studio. There was almost no time for rock 'n' roll debauchery, though one night John and I drank enough cheap red wine to think it was a really good idea to run around the block naked (for some reason, no one seemed to think it was as funny as we did, though).

We decided to name our debut album *Glodean*,[7] after Barry White's[8] wife since we listened to him constantly at the time. It was released about eight months later and we braced ourselves for the sheer pandemonium we expected to ensue. Instead, however, Joe's record label ended up going out of business a couple of months afterward and for a while we just handed out copies of our album to friends, whether they wanted it or not. Fortunately, however, Keith and Joe managed to get Priority Records, a hip-hop label best known for putting out albums by N.W.A., Ice Cube, Snoop Dogg, and other guys we didn't sound that much like, to rerelease the album a few months later.

Despite not arranging for us to hang out with gangsta rappers as much as we had hoped, Priority succeeded in getting our album into stores and our songs on the radio, especially in mine, Pat, and Tim's hometown of Cleveland. One day I was driving down the street and heard our single "Formaldehyde" playing on two different stations at the same time. I almost drove into a tree.

"This must be how the Beatles felt," I told my mom.

"Who?"

"Never mind."

Maybe even cooler than hearing our music on the radio was seeing the video we made for the song on MTV, which—being 1995 and all—still meant something. After all those years of being glued to MTV as a kid, it was awesome to actually see ourselves on the channel, even if it was almost always after midnight when our video

---

7 Like a lot of the classics, *Glodean* is now out of print. You can find it on eBay though if you've got the rock itch. I listened to it for the first time in several years recently and I gotta say we pretty much nailed it as far as rocking with authority goes.

8 Barry White was a singer/songwriter and producer who combined R&B, soul, funk, and disco into a sound that made people want to have sex, usually with him. He is perhaps the only person ever capable of singing the words "take off that brassiere, my dear" with confidence, authority, and not even a hint of irony, which was great for him and a lot of other people, too.

came on. We also got to be the musical guests on an episode of Jon Stewart's late-night, pre–*Daily Show* vehicle *The Jon Stewart Show,* where they gave us our own dressing room filled with mini candy bars and as many cold cuts as we could handle. We felt like kings.

Sons of Elvis also hit the road for our first national tour. Priority loaned us money for a van and we used it to buy a massive state-of-the-art circa 1982 black conversion van complete with a tiny television, VCR, and CB radio. We also hired a tour manager named Pete and a roadie named Mark, who both dressed in black at all times, even when they slept. Pete and Mark had also just finished working for the seemingly Satanic metal band Danzig, which made us feel like we were in really good hands.

"If you want, I'll see to it that only chicks are allowed backstage," Mark would tell us. There was rarely anyone—male or female—wanting to come backstage most nights, but we still loved his can-do attitude.

The Sons of Elvis rock assault on the United States lasted six weeks, during which we played just about everywhere east of the proverbial Mississippi. After years of playing mostly to our friends, it was great to finally play in front of a room full of strangers, even on those rare nights when there were more people on stage than in the audience. Along the way, we also managed to play a handful of huge outdoor radio festivals with bands such as Bush, Alanis Morrissette, and other people who sold several million more albums than we did. And even if most of the twenty thousand or so people in attendance might just have been waiting for the headliner to come on while we played, it was easy to pretend they were all there just to see us. We also believed it was only a matter of time before that was actually the case.

One of my favorite shows we ever played was opening up for Slash, who was doing a solo tour while the original lineup of Guns N' Roses was slowly falling apart.

"Hi, I'm Slash," he said to us before we had a chance to introduce ourselves.

"Uh, yeah, we picked up on that," I thought.

By then Slash had already long been one of the most recognizable musicians on the planet, so I thought it was cool of him to actually tell us his name rather than take it for granted that we knew exactly who the guy standing there in a top hat and shades was. As if that weren't enough, Slash let us take as many sandwiches as we wanted from his sprawling deli tray backstage, which made me feel like my bandmates and I had officially arrived. I wasn't even hungry, but I still ate a couple anyway just to celebrate. They were especially delicious, too, because they tasted of achievement.

"I'm sure I'll see you guys again soon," Slash said as we shook hands at the end of the night. I almost had a seizure. As shocking as it may seem, Slash and I haven't seen each other since, but I still loved that he made us feel like his rock 'n' roll peers, if only for one night.

Just as it seemed like things were poised to explode, the endless parade of free sandwiches, Motel 6's, and teenagers who had gotten a ride to our show from their parents began to slowly die down not long after that show we played with Slash. Our label wanted us to stop touring, ostensibly to make a new album, the one we were counting on to go platinum since the first one ended up selling about 964,578 less than needed to make that happen. Naturally, I had assumed we'd release that new album, hit the road again, probably meet up with Slash at some point, and soon enough the big bucks would start rolling in. It seemed like a solid rock 'n' roll game plan to me. However, we had been assigned a new A&R[9] guy at Priority and he didn't seem to share my band's opinion that we were writing hits.

"I, uh . . . hate it," the new A&R guy told me on the phone one day, struggling for words to accurately describe how he felt about the new tunes we'd cooked up so far.

"Oh, um, okay," I replied. "What exactly do you hate about it?"

"Mostly the guitar, bass, drums, and singing, I guess."

---

9 A&R stands for "artists and repertoire." No one knows what that means, but the A&R guy is the person at the record label in charge of making sure a band doesn't suck, overdose, or try to make a concept album.

This didn't seem necessarily good. Not long after that, I got a phone call from Tim.

"We've been dropped from the label," he told me.

Impressively confident under the circumstances, we figured some other label would snatch us up as soon as word got out that we were free agents, but that, well, never happened. We never officially broke up, but after having tasted the sweet life, we were unable to keep the rock machine running much longer under those grim and entirely unglamorous circumstances. And since my parents had started hiding their wallets from me by then, I eventually had to break down and get one of those jobs my mom kept talking about.

To avoid actually giving in and working for the man (a very non-rock thing to do), I ended up starting my own one-man house-painting business (a very rock thing for the broke rocker to do, you know, as far as actually getting a job goes). Most days, I drove myself to work in Sons of Elvis's nearly broken-down touring van, the symbolism of which was completely lost on me at the time.

One day I was hired to paint a fifteen-year-old girl's bedroom while she was away at summer camp.

"Would you like a radio to listen to while you work?" the girl's mother asked as I stood there in my paint-spattered work clothes, bracing myself for the task at hand.

"Sure," I said.

She returned a few minutes later with a large portable CD player. It was hard not to notice that there was a giant Sons of Elvis sticker plastered to the side of it.

"Ouch," I thought. "That's gonna leave a mark."

It seemed like just a few months ago I was playing with my band in front of tens of thousands of people at huge, outdoor music festivals where everyone wanted our autographs and sometimes even more.[10] Now here I was painting butterflies, flowers, and whatever other girly

---

10 The "more" I am suggesting here, of course, is sex and other stuff usually offered by groupie types. Since I was the bass player in the band, however, I have no way of knowing for sure if this was the case. I'm just going on assumptions here.

stuff I could come up with on some teenager's bedroom wall, my once luxurious, post-grunge rock 'n' roll mane now encrusted in dried paint and spackling paste. As I stood there letting all that sink in, it dawned on me that rock 'n' roll can not only be a cruel mistress, it can also be a total fucking bitch when it wants to. But then I thought about it a little more and chose to look at the situation a little differently.

"Whoa," I suddenly mused. "This girl is away at summer camp and has absolutely no idea that her favorite member of her favorite rock band of all time is painting her bedroom right now. She's gotta be the luckiest kid in the whole wide world. If she only knew, if she only knew."

Sometimes it really is all about perspective.[11]

---

11 And, needless to say, I painted the fuck out of that bedroom.

A Funny Feeling

Being "in the arts" is never easy. In addition to all the clove cigarettes, scented candles, and ultimately regrettable haircuts, the artist is almost guaranteed to experience firsthand either clinical depression or addiction, or maybe even both at some point in his or her creative life. To its credit, though, addiction has plenty of plus sides—addicts often have great parties and even better outfits, for example. But, aside from rapid weight loss and enhanced cheekbone definition, depression just kind of sucks. I learned that for myself shortly after college, a popular time, statistically speaking, for that sort of thing to kick in whether you are thinking of forming a band or going to school for graphic design or not.

Looking back on it, depression had likely been plotting its attack on me for a while. Not only was I a fairly anxious and worrisome kid, but I also come from a long line of people who furrow their brow and grit their teeth for no apparent reason. For the most part, though, it seemed like depression just decided to show up one day like an annoying relative I never even knew I had.

It was a Saturday morning and I had spent the night before—as I did most Fridays—loading up on all-you-can-drink wine and assorted fried things with friends at a Chinese restaurant on the Upper West Side and then stumbling around Manhattan until we were either no longer certain we were going to live forever or one of us passed out on the sidewalk, whichever came first. I don't blame any of those things for what happened next (though the gallon of wine probably didn't help much), but when I woke up the following morning I felt extremely off. Sure, I had a hangover—those had been business as usual since college (high-five!). But, in addition to that familiar headache, grogginess, and begging of one of my roommates to buy me a burrito, a tidal wave of paranoia, panic, and despair had also shown up for brunch.

"Whoa," I thought. "Must have gotten ahold of some bad Kung Pao last night."

I figured it was nothing a nap couldn't fix, so I tried to go back to sleep for a bit, only to find it impossible. In fact, lying in bed without my roommates or Saturday morning cartoons to distract me from my brain only made things worse.

"I am seriously calling that Chinese restaurant and demanding a refund just as soon as I find my pants," I said to myself, groaning. "The Mai Fun is no fun."[1]

As the day wore on, I started to feel like I'd been sucker punched in the gut by a prizefighter, the wind permanently knocked out of me. I spent the next few days puking—or at least trying to—even though I ate next to nothing, convincing myself I probably had just about every disease I could pronounce. And suddenly every aspect of my life, even the stuff I was normally pretty psyched about, seemed to suck beyond repair, a perspective that felt extreme even for me and my already dark, twenty-something world view.

Not exactly sure what to do about the situation, I decided to hop a plane to Cleveland to visit my parents for a long weekend that ended up lasting several years. I figured I'd probably still feel pretty crazy back home, but at least then I could just blame my parents for everything. And if these awful feelings persisted, worst-case scenario I could always just move back into my childhood bedroom and spend my days working at the grocery store up the street from my parents' house and my nights watching *Golden Girls* reruns on television for the next couple of decades until the fog lifted.

---

1 I guess you could mentally add a rimshot sound effect here if you feel like it.

"The way I see it, I put in my time as a bagboy, work my way up to stockboy, then produce guy, and next thing you know—bam!—your brother is a goddamn part-time assistant manager," I told my sister Miriam. "I'll never have to pay for cole slaw again. None of us will! Can't you just taste it already?"

"Are you feeling okay?" she asked, recognizing something besides my often questionable career aspirations might be afoot.

Despite feeling absolutely awful, I was oblivious enough to reality that I still wasn't sure what she was getting at. Even so, I promised Miriam I would go see a doctor before combing my hair, putting on a clean shirt, and heading up to the grocery store to show off my people skills.

Unfortunately, the psychology department at the local hospital was booked solid for the next two weeks, which might as well have been two years as far as I was concerned.

"I'm not sure I'm going to be around in two weeks," I told the lady on the phone. I don't think either one of us really knew what I meant by that. Was I just going out of town or possibly doing something really negative by comparison? Either way, it worked like a charm and I went in for an appointment the next morning, which was a massive relief.

As I sat in the waiting room, I looked around at the other people sitting there with me. It was hard not to wonder what kind of crazy shit might be going on inside their heads. And I wondered if they had similar thoughts about me. Ditto for the cute girl at reception who seemed to grab her pen back from me a lot more quickly than seemed reasonable.

After a few minutes, I was greeted by Mark, a warm and friendly guy in his mid-thirties, who would become my therapist.

"How can I help you today?" he asked, sounding more like an oddly laid-back car salesman than a guy about to analyze me.

"I'm really not sure," I answered.

Mark had a mullet, which I thought was refreshing given his profession, kind of cool even. Still, it didn't exactly fit with the Sigmund Freud clone I'd expected. Also, his office looked like a regular doctor's office instead of being outfitted with overstuffed leather chairs, Oriental rugs, and richly stained woodwork like I'd hoped.

"So much for this being just like a Woody Allen movie," I thought.

Still, I knew this was a time when I really needed to pick my battles, so I decided to let it all slide.

"Tell me what's on your mind, Dave," Mark said, wrinkling his brow a bit in an effort to suggest genuine concern.

"Do you ever get the feeling you might die at any moment and it actually doesn't sound like such a bad idea?" I asked.

"And what kinds of things might cause you to suddenly die, Dave?"

"All of them."

"I see."

Mark and I continued our chat for about an hour before he gave me his diagnosis. As it turned out, I wasn't crazy (at least not in a way recognized by modern medicine), but instead had a combination of clinical depression and anxiety with a dose of obsessive-compulsive disorder (OCD) thrown in for good measure, an assortment of garden-variety mental illness.

"Is this your way of telling me I'm a wuss?" I wanted to ask him.

Like a lot of people, I had always dismissed the things he'd just told me I had as forms of weakness, the kind of stuff that could be sorted out simply by telling the afflicted to pull themselves together. "Crazy" at least gets you invited to a fun party every once in a while. But "mental illness" doesn't pack quite the same punch. "I saw that dude drink ten shots in a row, break a bottle over his own head, drop his pants, and then barricade himself in the bathroom with a goat—he totally suffers from mental illness." You never really hear that sort of thing.

Mark also arranged for me to get a prescription for the antidepressant Zoloft.

"You might find it causes vomiting, diarrhea, fainting, decreased bladder control, dizziness, hives, peeling of the skin, swelling of the tongue, and, perhaps most of all, erectile dysfunction," he explained. "But other than that you might find it quite helpful."

"Sounds fun. Thanks."

While I popped my pills and met with Mark each week to discuss whatever was pummelling my psyche that day, hour, or minute, I tried to make sense of it all. Like skydiving, colonic irrigation, and intimate hair removal, mental illness is unfortunately the sort of thing one has to experience firsthand to truly understand, regardless of whether or not you've ever shit your pants or spent three hours in the shower trying to induce an erection. Depression, for example, is a misnomer, if you ask me. It has little to do with just being sad—that would make it almost charming by comparison. It's more like swallowing a small bomb that is perpetually threatening to go off in five minutes, five hours, or maybe even five days—you're not sure—and not being able to mention it to anyone. I've also heard it described as feeling completely alone in a crowded room, but to me it felt more like not even being in the room at all.

Adding to all this weirdness, of course, was my mother, who struggled to understand what was going on with me. Hoping to knock out the problem, she showed up in my room one day with a rosary in her hand, a not entirely surprising Catholic-lady move.

"This will help," she assured me before pressing it in my hand and patting my head.

"But Mom, my therapist says I have OCD," I told her. "I really don't think reciting a bunch of Hail Marys and Our Fathers over and over again is a good move for me right now. It'd be like throwing water on a drowning man."

"Says who?"

"Says me mostly. But I bet my therapist would agree."

"Just hang on to it anyway."

I appreciated the gesture, but at the time the only thing the rosary definitely helped with was confusing the cops when they pulled me over a few days later ostensibly for running a stop sign but ultimately to search my car for drugs. My hair was long and I looked like hell so I guess they decided to just roll the dice and hope they found something to bust me for. (In case you're wondering, aside from the rosary, they did find plenty of drugs, but that's only because I had started taking my Zoloft prescription with me everywhere.)

Run-ins with the cops aside, I slowly began to settle into my new life as a mentally ill person living with his parents. On the surface, it didn't seem all that bad. I dragged myself out of bed at five thirty each morning, unable to stare at the ceiling any longer, and sat in the kitchen waiting for my parents to finally come downstairs by seven o'clock or so, which felt like an eternity. Then I'd watch them eat breakfast and I'd pretend to do the same with an old piece of toast or whatever they happened to push in front me. After that, I'd usually go back to staring at the ceiling in my room for a few hours before retiring to the Barcalounger in the family room to watch television until midnight. Then I'd go upstairs to toss and turn for a few hours before starting it all over again the next morning. From a distance, it probably just looked like I was on a shitty vacation.

"Blanche was up to her old tricks again last night," I'd say to my mom in passing.

"Yeah, well she's nothing but a tramp if you ask me," she'd respond.

"The biggest, Mom. The biggest."

Aside from my steadily dropping weight (a bonus in my case as I had been on a strict Ben & Jerry's diet in the months prior), the only outward sign that something was seriously wrong was my clothing. Depression, anxiety, and OCD had rendered me a sartorially challenged individual. Suddenly, an old button-down shirt and a moth-eaten sweater vest I'd found in a garbage bag in the attic seemed like a perfectly reasonable ensemble to not only wear every day, but also to sleep in at night. My mother capitalized on my compromised state by talking me into wearing almost every article of clothing she'd gotten me for Christmas over the past ten years or so.

"David, remember those gray and tan wool slacks I got on sale for you last year?" she'd ask. "I bet they'd look great with that maroon turtleneck and your high school letterman jacket."

"Anything you say, Mom," I'd mumble.

I was so defenseless, she probably could have talked me into putting on clown makeup. Still, I was so caught up with my own thoughts I no longer recognized the importance of personal flair. As a result, photos of me from this period remain perhaps the greatest tragedy of all.

Meanwhile, my therapist, Mark, had given me some homework to do. As he explained it, my OCD had kicked in as a way to deal with my anxiety. OCD and anxiety teamed up to cause my depression. To help me better understand things, Mark wanted me to pick up a book on OCD called *Stop Obsessing!* and read a few chapters before we met again.

"Do you have a book called *Stop Obsessing!*?" I asked an employee at the local bookstore.

"I'm sorry," he told me. "We don't have it at the moment."

"Do you have a book a called *Stop Obsessing!*?" I asked him again two seconds later.

I don't think the guy at the store found it very funny, but at the time I thought it was pure gold. And possibly a sign that the regular me was still in there somewhere.

I had also begun to subject myself to daily "worry periods," something both Mark and that OCD book I finally got strongly recommended. The worry periods were designed to help me gain some control over my obsessive thoughts, the nature of which seemed to change on an almost daily basis. One day I might be convinced I'd gotten mad cow disease from a corn dog, the next I'd worry that I might accidentally stab my entire family with a wayward butter knife at the next holiday gathering[2] or perhaps do something else that would make it so there was no way in hell anyone would ever give me that bagboy job I still hadn't entirely ruled out. And while I never developed physical compulsions, I had a habit of creating mind exercises to try to distract myself from my obsessions. One of my favorites was to type out the lyrics to classic rock songs in my

---

2 Note to my family: I have since learned that the odds of this ever happening really aren't very good at all. Seriously, I wouldn't worry about it too much. Except for you, Rob.

head. I'd picture the keystrokes on the typewriter and everything. Ridiculous maybe, but that's the name of the game when it comes to OCD.

Each worry period consisted of locking myself in a room at the same time each day for between twenty minutes and an hour— depending on what I thought I could handle—and attempting to do nothing but sit there and think the darkest, most apocalyptic thoughts possible about whatever was terrorizing me the most that day.

"I am definitely going to be kidnapped by Shriners," I might tell myself one day. "In fact, I'm pretty sure I heard one of those tiny little cars pull into the driveway just now. There is no escape. And I *will* be forced to wear one of those weird hats."

No one suggested I pull my hair, send everything on top of my dresser crashing to the floor, or scream "Mommy! Mommy! Mommy!" the whole time, but some days I would throw that stuff in anyway just to make it my own.

The idea behind the worry periods was to embrace the hopelessness, to really let it make me its bitch for a while. And, by assigning a designated time to freak out about something and then try to do nothing but freak out about that one thing only during that designated time, I would eventually get to the point where I would no longer get so worked up over some bullshit or another that I'd find myself rushing to puke in the bathroom of a Jewish deli down the street from my parents' house before my corned beef and latkes had even shown up to the table. It's just hitting me now that it was all a bit weird. Even so, the worry periods were surpisingly helpful. Supposedly brain scans of people who have undergone such therapy have shown that you can actually change the physical makeup of your brain if you do it long enough. Sometimes I wonder if I could use similar techniques to physically alter myself in other ways. The possibilities are endless.

After a few weeks of pills, therapy, and worry periods, I decided to take my own additional steps toward a better, less deranged tomorrow, the biggest of which was to get a job. Mental illness or not, the thought of working for the man had always given me reason enough to be depressed. But—given my druthers at the time—I would have just lain in bed all day biting my toenails, drooling on my pillow, and practicing my heavy breathing, so I figured having to show up for a job might keep me from doing that so much.

Partly out of convenience and partly so I would feel extra bad about ever calling in "sick," I gave up my part-time-assistant-manager-at-the-grocery-store dreams and instead took a job working for my friend Tony's dad's landscaping company. I never thought of myself as a wimp, but I also wasn't the first guy you should call if you needed a giant wheelbarrow full of gravel pushed up the side of a steep hill. I figured struggling with that sort of thing as well as any lawncare equipment I'd be asked to handle would help distract me from whatever was happening in my head. After all, it's hard to give neurosis the attention it screams for when one false move could send your big toe flying into the pachysandra. My plan worked, too. Never underestimate the healing power of a Weedwhacker. And don't even get me started on a leaf blower—it is the hammer of the gods.

Despite all the therapy, the Zoloft, and even the leaf blower, it was still a long time before I felt like I was no longer at risk of changing my name to Sparkles and moving into a group home where I'd be required to wear pajamas, mittens, and a helmet at all times. Fortunately, I never really felt suicidal. Sure, there were plenty of days when being dead had its appeal, but when depression is at its worst, suicide, for many people (including me thankfully), just feels like it would take way too much time and energy. Getting yourself to change the channel on the television is hard enough. Who has time to go to the hardware store or CVS for death supplies? It's just too much of a scheduling hassle.

Gradually, however, as promised by the medical community, I started to experience tiny windows of seminormalcy where I'd not only have renewed interest in things like ice hockey, girls, and heavy metal but, perhaps more important, restored hatred of things like jam bands, people who wear sweatpants on airplanes, and the unpredictable coming and going of the McRib.[3] These windows got bigger and bigger over time, too. And while I would occasionally find myself seemingly back at batshit crazy square one, it didn't take quite as long to start feeling better again. It was kind of like being the pilot of a shitty airplane—the ride never quite felt smooth, but as long as I kept the engine running it seemed like I might be able to keep the thing in the air awhile longer, even if it meant coughing from fumes the whole way. My outfits slowly began to improve, too.

I was also able to get my OCD under control in a few months and all these years later it seems to only really make itself known in the form of me checking to make sure I locked my apartment door a little more often than I would like. But it took a good five or six years before I felt like I really had much of a handle on any of that anxiety or depression bullshit. It still pays me a visit every once in a while, usually after a perfect storm of stress, travel, lack of sleep, and a few too many open bars knocks me on my ass just long enough for it to show up like that annoying relative all over again. And, as unwelcome as it is, at least it comes with the surprising side effect of making real life problems like death, restraining orders, or the advance I got to write this book not necessarily any less upsetting, but, by comparison, refreshing in their tangibility. Also, like most things in life, it doesn't take long to find others familiar with experiencing an occasional case of the crazies. After all, Norman Bates was right: "We all go a little mad sometimes." It's nice to have someone you can call to talk you down from the proverbial or literal ledge and for you to be able to do the same for them.

"Hey, it's Dave," I'll say over the phone to a similarly afflicted friend or relative.

"Hey, Dave. How's it going?"

"Not too good. I think I caught herpes from the StairMaster yesterday."

---

3 Seriously, McDonald's, this has gone on long enough, so for chrissakes please stop toying with our emotions. You know everyone loves the McRib. It's delicious and the fake rib impressions on the "meat" only add to the fun. Just leave it on the menu for good already. What—do you hate money?

"Again?"

Despite what all those made-for-TV movies, sappy commercials, and other things that don't skimp on having sad piano music in the background might tell you, I don't think dealing with depression makes someone a "survivor." There's only two groups of people in the world deserving of that title and one of them is Beyoncé. People dealing with clinical depression don't deserve any special treatment, either, at least not any more than someone with a bad case of the flu, chronic back pain, or even two broken hips and a third testicle. But they do deserve the same acknowledgment and insurance coverage that all those other people get, no questions asked. (Even the three testicle guy. You'd think he'd be bragging instead of complaining but whatever.)

What the person suffering from depression doesn't deserve, however, is pity. Not now, not ever. Unless, of course, that pity ends up leading to sex, in which case I'm all for it. In fact, I'm sitting here right now and I feel absolutely worse than ever.

. . . .

Northeastern Ohio Velvet

When I was a kid growing up in Cleveland, Ohio, my favorite thing about Christmas was Santa Claus, that mysterious and bearded old man who traveled the entire globe in a single evening, breaking into people's homes in the middle of the night, eating whatever food might have been lying around, and leaving behind gifts of all shapes and sizes, some of which weren't exactly what the recipient had asked for,[1] but whatever. And despite his on-the-go lifestyle, Santa still found time to sit in a big armchair and pose for pictures for hours at a time at the department store down the street from my house. I could go there, sit on his lap, and tell him exactly what I wanted for Christmas each year until he pushed me off his lap and signaled for the next kid in line to come over.

I realize my affection for Santa Claus didn't make me unique. Still, I was pretty sure I was the only kid who really "got" Santa Claus. Even so, as eventually happens to us all, one day I found out that Santa Claus wasn't "real." Rumors already had been percolating for a few months in the second grade when I happened upon my sister Libby in my parents' bedroom. Libby was just three years older but for some reason was allowed unsupervised access to the Scotch tape and scissors, wrapping a gift I had very specifically asked Santa for

---

1 A three-pack of underwear? Really, Santa? Who the hell do you think you're dealing with here? Pull that crap again and I'll stab you!

that year. Libby seemed to have her mitts in just about everything, so it didn't raise that much of a red flag with me at first. I just assumed Santa had farmed out some of his busy work locally and my sister, an overachiever, seemed as likely a candidate as any. (My mom did that sort of thing with Libby all the time. Why should Santa be any different?) Libby, however, gave me too much credit, and assumed the jig was up.

"Sorry, David," she said while putting the finishing touches on wrapping up an Evel Knievel stunt cycle. "There's no Santa Claus."

She tried to soften the blow by telling me that what really mattered was the spirit of Christmas and also some of the Jesus stuff we learned in school. It was a lot to take in, but in the end I figured, whatever—I'd still get all the presents and sit on the lap of some guy dressed as Santa Claus once a year. Everything would be just fine.[2]

But regardless of whether or not Santa Claus was real, I eventually learned that there comes a day when some people think you're "too old" to be sitting on Santa's lap. (The reasons for which I struggle to comprehend even as I type this years later.) And it was at this point, I guess by the time I hit my twenties or so, that I realized if I still wanted to experience the magic of Santa Claus each holiday season, my only choice was to simply *become* Santa Claus. To let the student become the goddamn master.

And so I made that my goal. Unfortunately becoming Santa Claus wasn't as easy as I thought it would be. Most of the guys playing Santa at the mall, for example, hold on to that job like it's a pair of season tickets to the Yankees behind home plate. But my time finally came during the holiday season of 1996 when I was living in Cleveland. Some friends were organizing a Christmas fund-raiser for the local public theater and insisted that I come. That's when a lightbulb turned on in my head.

---

2 Also, a small part of me still refused to discount the possibility that Santa simply employed stunt doubles and other seasonal help to fulfill the demand, which went a long way toward poking holes in Libby's "Santa isn't real" theory. I let go of it eventually, but at the time it helped soften the blow.

"Sure, I'll come to your party," I told them, "but only if I can be Santa Claus."

"We already have a Santa Claus," they replied.

"I *said* I'll come to your party, but *only* if I can be Santa Claus," I repeated while staring straight ahead into the distance.

It was a bit harsh, maybe, but playing hardball paid off because, as fate would have it, my friends had just replaced the theater's Santa suit and the old costume was still lying around somewhere. So they eventually gave in and suggested that I could wear the old Santa suit, and be more of a roving Santa, the kind that just gives people a quick Santa fix on their way to the bar or restroom, while the jerk in the new suit would sit and pose for pictures and stuff. It wasn't exactly the Santa debut I had hoped for but I knew this was my shot, so I accepted.

"You won't regret this," I told them as I marched away.

I swung by the theater a few days before the party to pick up the costume. It didn't take long to figure out why they had decided to replace it. It was an old, red velvet suit with white trim that was so soiled and matted you'd swear it had been ripped from a corpse, a World War II bunker, or both. There were innumerable holes in it—presumably caused by an attack of some sort—and the beard had turned a urine yellow, seemingly half from age and half from whatever Santa got up to on break. And the smell—it told a story, a story I never wanted to know. It could kill crops.

Despite its compromised state, the Santa suit instantly transformed me as soon as I tried it on. No longer was I just some guy from Cleveland named Dave who might still live with his parents. Instead I was this magical, jolly, glowing Santa Claus, the kind of Santa everyone would want to be around, the kind of Santa that lady had absolutely no good reason to yell at for changing his clothes in the parking lot.

The big fund-raiser was still a couple of days away but I had a few Christmas parties to swing by before then, so I figured it might not be a bad idea to take the Santa suit for a little test drive. And I was glad I did because here's what I learned pretty much instantly: being

Santa Claus is *awesome*. I felt dashing, bold, and really, really warm all over. As I got into my mom's car with the suit on, I could only imagine the kind of electricity Santa, the actual Santa, must feel every time he hops into his sleigh, grabs those reins, and tells those reindeer to hit it. And don't even get me started on what it's like to watch a fellow driver slowly discover Saint Nick sitting there next to him at a stoplight. I've never gotten around to smoking crack, but I doubt it could be much better.

My first stop was the house party of my friend Pat's brother. I parked my car out front and slowly walked up the driveway, bracing myself with each ice-crunching step for the awesomeness of what was about to happen.

"Merry Christmas, everybody!" I bellowed as I walked through the front door.

"Santa!" they all cheered.

Every man, woman, and child in the place lit up with excitement at the very sight of me and it felt great. Really, really great. It was like I was Superman, Big Bird, and Barbra Streisand all rolled into one— everyone wanted to be around me, pose for pictures with me, and even sit on my lap. The rush was incredible, like getting a prostate exam in the middle of a roller-coaster ride at a women's prison—the kind of thrill you never see coming in a million, trillion years.

But there's another side to this sparkly little coin. As electrifying as it was when Santa first hit the scene, I quickly learned that the unparalleled rapture and pandemonium begins to slowly fade after about five minutes. Next thing you know you're just some creepy guy shuffling around the house in a skanky old velvet suit, like you just stepped off a bus from Atlantic City. No one wants to make eye contact with you, everyone starts keeping tabs on exactly how much you've had to drink and how much time you've spent in the bathroom, and you can pretty much forget about holding anyone's baby. Even the dog lost interest once he realized the urine scent on Santa's pants wasn't fresh.

Of course, my only choice after that was to move on to the next party. And so I did. And when that euphoria died down, well, I just kept moving on, party after party, as many as it took, to get my fix once more. Sometimes I'd barely make it past the front door before jumping back into my car and disappearing into the night.

By the night of the big fund-raiser, both the Santa suit and I had put on a few extra miles, but I still pulled on the velvet and headed down to the theater with my new girlfriend.

"You must be pretty psyched to be rolling into the party with Santa Claus," I said to her.

She was speechless. And who could blame her? I'm sure some of you ladies reading this right now can guess how pumped she must have been. Walking in with Santa is pretty much the best way to go to a Christmas party, like going to a planetarium with Stephen Hawking. She was one lucky gal.

Since I needed to focus on being Saint Nick, and also because I didn't own a car, my girlfriend drove us to the theater. We parked on the street out front and headed inside, which was just plain explosive. The rush I had been experiencing in the week prior was nothing compared to the rush I felt walking into that theater. There were at least two hundred people in the place and—even though there was already another Santa Claus on the scene—people still seemed really psyched to see this Santa, the roving Santa, the one that could not and would not be confined to an armchair, the people's Santa. It was like I was Elvis casually dropping by the Flamingo for a quick round of blackjack.

"It's Santa!" everyone predictably screamed.

"You're damn right it's Santa," I replied.

Adding to the excitement was the fact that with a few nights of being Kris Kringle already under my belt, I was pretty much a pro. I told all the kids I'd get them whatever they wanted and sometimes even stuff they had never even thought of before, I bought shots for the men, and I flirted with all the ladies in that mostly harmless, Saint Nick kind of way that no one can make a big deal about in court. I even brought a paper bag with the word "naughty" written on the side and filled with charcoal briquettes.

"Merry Christmas!" I'd say as I pressed a lump of coal into people's hands. "Santa knows you've been baaaaad this year!"

Then I'd give them a sexy wink that suggested I knew exactly what sort of mischief they had been up to lately. Other than the annoyance of having to find some place to dispose of the charcoal, they seemed to love it. It was an awesome night and Kris Kringle—yup, that's me—was on top of the world. It was like I was starring in my very own Christmas movie, one in which a lot of chicks totally wanted to make out with Father Christmas.

Unlike my previous outings, there didn't seem to be an end to that Santa Claus high to which I'd so quickly become addicted. If one cluster of people tired of my antics, I'd just move through the crowd until I found a new group eager to receive the biggest thrill of their holiday season. But it all ground to a halt when my girlfriend informed me that some guy had made lewd comments to her. I can't remember his exact words but it was something along the lines of how he enjoyed her appearance so much that it was having some sort of impact on the situation in his trousers. He also seemed to be under the impression that if my girlfriend were to have sex with him, his prowess would impress her so much that she would struggle to maintain any sort of physical relationship with me in the aftermath. There might have been some profanity in there as well. In short, he was being a major a-hole.

As you can probably imagine, my girlfriend was an attractive woman,[3] smoking hot even. And, sure, the drinks were flowing, but I couldn't help but think that this guy was just jealous that I was Santa Claus and he wasn't. It was quite simply unacceptable. My girlfriend was upset, and I couldn't help but get really angry about the whole situation because, well, you don't just go making lewd remarks to Santa Claus's girlfriend. It's like trying to grope Minnie Mouse at Disneyland right in front of Mickey. Why would anyone do that? Especially during the Christmas season!

"Looks like Santa's got some ass to kick," I told her. "No one talks to Santa's woman like that but Santa!"

Not wanting me to cause a scene, my girlfriend begged me to

3 Ask anyone.

drop the whole thing and just focus on being awesome at being Santa Claus. In fact, she warned me that if I said anything to this jerk, she was going to leave the party without me (something I really couldn't risk because, as mentioned previously, I didn't have a car and my parents probably wouldn't be willing to pick me up).

"Fine," I said before getting back to being the greatest Santa of all time.

But here's the thing about being the greatest Santa of all-time— when you're the greatest Santa of all-time, people love to buy you drinks. So, after another hour or so of doing the polite thing and knocking back free drink after free drink, my mind drifted to that guy who had said all those awful things to my girlfriend, and I somehow forgot about how good ol' Saint Nick wasn't going to say anything to him.

"You know what?" I thought as I struggled for balance. "I'm definitely, definitely gonna have to say something to that prick. Nobody talks to Santa's girl like that! Nobody!"

The next thing I knew, I was pushing my way through the crowd in search of the bastard, totally forgetting about the spirit of Christmas, good will toward men, or any of that crap. People noted the fire in Kris Kringle's eyes and jumped the hell out of the way.

"Santa will you—" an oblivious little girl with pigtails said.

"Not now!" I barked. "Not! Now!"

I continued on my mission and, after a couple of minutes, finally found the dude in question. He was standing by himself, drinking a beer, clueless to the fact that he was about to have his ass handed to him by the king of the North Pole.

"Hey, man," I grunted.

"Santa Claus!" He smiled.

I thought my tone very clearly implied, "You are so close to death right now it's not even fucking funny!" But that's the thing about being Saint Nick, people usually misinterpret your blind rage as jolliness.

"I know what you said to my girlfriend," I snarled through clenched teeth and beer-soaked beard.

"What are you talking about?"

"You know what I'm talking about!"

"Huh?"

"Why'd you go talking like that to my woman, you prick!"

It was at this point that it would have been hard not to notice that Santa Claus was seriously pissed off. But as is often the case when one really drunk guy accuses another really drunk guy of something, the defendant denied having said anything to my girlfriend and even went on to say something about how I was "really drunk" and also "crazy." Regardless, I persisted with my accusations and he persisted with his denials until we were right up in each other's faces, the stray hairs of my Santa beard tickling his nose in an entirely unpleasant way.

"You're a fucking asshole," I informed him.

"You're the fucking asshole, dude," he replied.

We continued in our volley of insults and accusations until I was pretty sure one of us was going to throw a punch. I was even more sure that one of us was going to be me. And I liked it. A lot. So I slowly clenched my fist, studying the guy's face to decide exactly where I was going to land the deathblow, the first punch I had ever thrown in my entire life, which was going to be a really great one, the kind people end up talking about for a long, long time. Then I cocked my arm back, hoping the guy somehow wouldn't notice. And, finally, there I was—about to swing, about to demolish the guy—when I happened to catch my reflection in a nearby window. And that's when it hit me all over again: I'm Santa Claus.

"Santa can't go beating up someone at a Christmas party!" I thought as I stood there squinting at my reflection. "And Santa definitely can't get his ass kicked at a Christmas party! Sure, the outfit is already red so it won't really show the blood that much. But still, that's just pathetic."

Recognizing there was no alternative, I lowered my arm back to my side and slowly backed away from the guy as he did the same. Apparently, he didn't want to fight, either, though as we studied each other's retreats we gave each other our best "You might be the luckiest motherfucker on the planet right now because I've just decided not to kill you" kind of look.

As my would-be opponent disappeared back into the crowd, I stumbled to the bar area in search of my girlfriend. Sadly, she was nowhere in sight. Because of my near brawl, I was already crashing from that huge Santa rush pretty hard. But once I realized that my girlfriend had made good on her threat, I hit zero altogether. The harsh reality of my situation settling in, I barrelled through the crowd of onlookers, sending their festive drinks flying in the process.

"What's up with Santa?" the looks on their faces seemed to say.

Meanwhile, the other Santa, that bastard sitting in a chair with a brand-new red velvet suit on, just looked at me with disgust.

"You're all naughty!" I screamed as I made my way toward the exit.

I flung open the doors and stumbled into the night, where the familiar cold Cleveland rain began to soak my beard further and bring many of my Santa suit's long-dormant scents back to life. I scanned the block and found the only signs of life coming from a small bar directly across the street.

"Maybe she went in that bar," I thought, my detective skills momentarily kicking in.

Then I ran across the street, oblivious to any upcoming traffic, my pain too great and my blood alcohol level too high to notice. I flung open the door to the bar to find it was packed, a whole other Christmas party raging without mercy. And guess who just walked in—Santa Claus! Predictably, everyone started to freak out and, since I was pretty much a full-on junkie by that point, I was instantly back on top again.

"Santa!" they all screamed.

"You're damn right it's Santa!" I screamed back.

Even when the chips were down, that high came rushing back and I drank it in like a man tasting cool water for the first time after forty days in the desert. I posed for more pictures, high-fived everyone in sight, and even let a couple of fully grown men sit on my lap.

I was quite simply on top of the world until I finally worked my way to the other end of the bar and there, sitting silently on the very last stool, was my girlfriend, chewing on a straw and looking positively furious.

"Don't worry—I didn't kill that guy," I said. "You know, because I'm Santa Claus."

"You asshole!" she replied.

Somehow my explanation seemed to just enrage her further, so I began apologizing and trying to calm her down every way I knew how. Still, my Santa powers were useless on her and she started saying all sorts of crazy things a woman might say to a guy from Cleveland who still lives with his parents and doesn't have a car or a job or any of that stuff: how she wanted to "break up with me," how she "wasn't going to give me a ride home," and even how I was, in fact, a "horrible Santa." It was bad, really bad, the last kind of stuff a guy dressed as Santa ever wants to hear. Right then and there I realized I really didn't like the kind of person Santa Claus had turned me into—this power-mad, belligerent, and completely hammered narcissist. I also realized that this was one situation Santa couldn't make all better. The only person who could make this situation better was me, Dave, the guy with a fake beard on. So I pulled down that beard and took off my damp and dusty velvet hat and told my girlfriend how I really felt, how she was the greatest girl I'd ever met and how I really didn't want to lose her. And, perhaps most of all, how I was so sorry about almost trying to beat up some guy who, all these years later, I still think absolutely deserved it.

It took some doing; I begged, I pleaded, I even offered to chip in some money for gas—but eventually I won her back. And, for the record, yes, she did end up giving me a ride home *and* I got to control the radio and she even refused to accept any of the cash I half-heartedly offered for gas.

And on that ride home I realized one more thing. I realized that the real reason Santa Claus doesn't actually exist is not because there's no way just one guy could deliver all those toys in a single evening. And it's not because he probably would have been shot a long time ago for even trying. It's because there's no way anyone could handle that kind of power. It's just way too much for one person. I had experiênced it for not even a week and it turned me into an utter monster.

I decided from that Christmas forward, I was just going to be Dave, the guy I was before I became Santa Claus, the guy that didn't get invited to nearly as many Christmas parties, the guy that could barely get anyone to sit on his lap without someone threatening to call the cops, the guy that didn't get even half the Christmas gifts he asked for no matter how many times he threatened to never come out of his room again. And even though that Santa suit is still somewhere out there in my parents' garage, I can say with, like, 75–85 percent certainty that I will never, *ever* put it on again.

Pedicab Shmedicab

If I ever needed money as a kid, I'd just "borrow" it from my parents. My mother always left her purse on the kitchen counter so, as soon as she left the room, I'd help myself to loose change. It was a "Don't ask, don't tell" scenario; I didn't ask for the money and I didn't tell her I took it. As long as her purse weighed about the same when she picked it up next time, it never seemed to be an issue.

By the time I hit my thirties, however, "loans" both big and small were harder to come by. And simply asking family members for their bank account information was usually met with either silence or profanity, which I eventually took to mean that, if I needed money, I had to "earn" it by "working." Before I became the show business phenomenon I am today, I had to do that the hard way—by getting an actual job. The problem was, there weren't many out there that really spoke to me. That all changed, however, in 2003, when I returned to New York after a prolonged detour back to Cleveland and laid eyes on a pedicab for the first time. Enchanted, I vowed right then and there that I, Dave Hill, would one day become a pedicab driver and there wasn't a damn thing anyone could do to stop me.

To the uninitiated, a pedicab is like an adult-size tricycle with a cart on the back for passengers. If you're looking for a way to get around town that offers neither the convenience of a cab nor the glamour of a horse-drawn carriage, you could do a lot worse. As for me, I never wanted to ride in the back of one. I just wanted to be the guy doing the pedaling. Big time.

As awesome as being a pedicab driver seemed, it took awhile before I had both the spare time and the confidence to put my other life pursuits on hold to really give it my all. The stars finally aligned one day when I was wandering around midtown Manhattan thinking about how I didn't have a job or money or any of that other stuff that tends to be helpful when you are a grown man living all by yourself in one of the most expensive cities in the world. It was in that moment that a pedicab driver stopped right in my path, as if on cue from the gods. Right then and there I knew it was time to stop making excuses and start living the dream.

There was a number on the side of the pedicab, practically begging me to call. Still, I hesitated to grab my phone and start dialing.

"Certainly there are plenty of guys out there with the exact same dream as me," I thought. "Who am I to think I might actually be one of the chosen?"

But then I decided to just take a deep breath and embrace my destiny. After a couple of rings, a guy with a thick Brooklyn accent answered. "This is Terry," he said.

"This is Dave, Terry," I told him. "Are you the pedicab guy?"

"Uh-huh."

"Well, I'm the guy you're looking for, then."

Since this was fate, I assumed he would know exactly what I was talking about. He didn't, but after some clarification, Terry said I could come in the next day to discuss becoming the pedicab champion I was born to be. I was so pumped I almost wrestled the driver off the very next pedicab I saw.

"I'll take over from here!" I'd say.

On the rare occasions when I'd had job interviews before, I usually took it easy the previous night so I could make a good impression. But this time, in the spirit of the very freedom that being a pedicab driver represented to me, I decided to get really drunk with my cousin Kieran. I got so drunk, in fact, that I threw up not only on the sidewalk as we left the bar, but also the following morning and again in a midtown Starbucks across from Terry's office immediately before my interview

"Can I get a venti decaf skim latte with four shots of espresso, extra foam, and hazelnut syrup please?" I asked the barista, patting my brow. "Oh, and the key to the restroom, too?"[1]

"Ninety percent of success is just showing up," I reminded myself as I walked out of America's caffeine station-cum-public restroom, wiping drool from my mouth.

Terry's "office" ended up being just a bunch of pedicabs pushed together in the corner of a parking garage. I actually got to sit in a pedicab during the interview, which made me feel like the luckiest guy in the world.

"I'm not gonna lie to you, this is a tough job and it sure as hell ain't for everybody," Terry told me as I hung on his every pedicab-based word. "Most guys never make it past a couple of shifts."

"What a pack of losers!" I thought as visions of myself twenty or thirty years into the future and still driving a pedicab danced in my head. My hair would be a salt-and-pepper gray and the lines in my face would tell a story, the story of a guy who is so awesome at driving a pedicab that it's not even funny. Everyone would know my name and I'd probably know most of theirs, too. I couldn't wait.

Terry told me all about what it's like to be a pedicab driver: the ins and outs, the highs and lows, the thrill of victory (i.e., successfully picking up a customer), and the agony of defeat (i.e., failing to pick up a customer). The more he talked, the more I had to fight the urge to just take to the streets in a pedicab right then and there.

"So you want the job?" he finally asked.

"Do I 'want the job'?" I thought. "I *am* the fucking job!"

My training would begin the following morning. I couldn't wait to see the look on Terry's face when he realized what a natural I was.

---

1 This is an old trick to circumvent that whole "restrooms are for customers only" thing. Works like a charm. You just have to make sure there's an exit you can easily slip out of that won't require you to pass the register once you're done with your business. Otherwise you're stuck paying for that cup of overpriced hot bullshit I just mentioned.

It would be like in all those movies where the last guy anybody in school expects to be good at football ends up being so good that everyone else on the team feels like quitting altogether. Also, a lot of otherwise unattainable girls want to have intercourse with him, which is awesome.

"You're good, kid," I imagined Terry reluctantly admitting once he saw me pedaling away. "Real good."

I also imagined rolling back to Terry's "office" at the end of each shift with piles of money spilling out of the back of my pedicab like I was a goddamn pirate.

"Before long, that son of a bitch will probably be working for me," I thought.

I showed up at the garage the next morning sober and alert, my mind a sponge and my body a weapon. I assumed I'd hit the streets right away, but instead I just pedaled around the garage as Terry showed me the ropes.

"You have to remain aware of the cart at all times," Terry kept telling me as I attempted to pedal in a circle, figure eight, or whatever other shape Terry seemed to think I better know how to pedal in if I ever expected to make anything of myself.

As I sat on top of the bike taking orders, I felt like Elizabeth Taylor riding that horse in *National Velvet*—perhaps in a bit over my head but ultimately determined to win. Even so, despite Terry's warnings, I ended up banging into so many cars, cement columns, parking attendants, and other stuff in the garage you would have thought it was in the job description.

"Let the pedicab do the work for you," Terry kept telling me in between bouts of groaning and shielding his eyes.

Even now I'm not sure what he meant by that. Maybe it was some Zen Buddhist thing since he seemed kind of deep. Terry also kept telling me how I didn't "look confident on the bike," as if he were some sort of wild animal capable of smelling fear. The more he said it, though, the more I became convinced what he really meant was I "look like a moron on the bike." Terry also seemed like a real jerk sometimes.

My lesson lasted about an hour. And, despite my cavalier attitude toward not crashing into things, Terry agreed to let me take my first shift the following afternoon. Even so, there were plenty more rules he wanted me to follow.

"Do not, under any circumstances, ride into oncoming traffic," he kept saying.

Apparently, this is a bad idea for several reasons. If you ask me, though, the more Terry mentioned it, the more he just sounded uptight.

As I rolled my pedicab out of the garage the next day, a profound feeling of freedom washed over me. Not only was the pedicab mine to pedal anywhere I wanted, but Terry had no idea where I lived. The fact that I could probably just keep on pedaling until I reached home, never to be seen again, had me vibrating with excitement. As if that weren't enough, the weather was crisp yet pleasant, perfect pedicab weather, it seemed.

"I'll probably have to beat people off with a stick," I thought.

As I began pedaling up 6th Avenue, the first thing I realized is that Manhattan is far from the flat landscape I'd always perceived it to be. As it turns out, it's more like a urine-and-exhaust-scented version of the Himalayas, full of impossibly steep inclines and dips in the road so severe you feel like you could fly over the handlebars at any moment. Add to that the fact it seems as if most cabs would actually be delighted to hit you, and suddenly you've got quite a ride on your hands.

"Holy shit!" I screamed half a dozen times before considering the fact that this sort of behavior might be bad for business.

Once I managed to chill out a bit, I decided to head for Times Square, a place I'd had little use for since they cleaned it up, but I figured I'd find the greatest density of people hell-bent on jumping in the back of my pedicab. Along the way, I spotted a handful of other pedicab drivers. Assuming we were brethren, I tried to give them a knowing look, the kind that said "Hey, pal, just another day in the life of an awesome pedicab driver—am I right or am I right?" But none of them seemed too interested in sharing a moment of solidarity with me. It suddenly occurred to me that maybe us pedicab drivers weren't brothers at all. Maybe we were outlaws, each looking out for number one. Once that idea settled in, I decided I wanted each and every one of them dead. Ditto for the hot dog vendors, fake Rolex salesmen, street musicians, and anyone else vying for the cold hard cash of unsuspecting pedestrians. It's funny how quickly the streets can change you.

As I continued my journey, I tried to shift my focus away from murder and toward getting people in the back of my pedicab, that place where they would suddenly owe me money. Terry gave me all sorts of tips on how to make that happen.

"Try to look like you're having a really good time," Terry suggested.

That was easy because I *was* having a really good time, maybe a little too good a time. In fact, I was giggling like a mental patient. If anything, I probably needed to tone it down.

Terry also suggested I try raising my eyebrows, gesturing toward my pedicab's spacious and comfortable backseat, and repeatedly asking people if they wanted to ride in my pedicab while somehow giving the impression that I was the type of guy who could pedal super fast. Eventually, the power of suggestion would hopefully win over, they'd climb in the back, and I'd start rolling into traffic before they had a chance to change their mind.

"Want to ride in my pedicab?" I'd ask anyone willing to make eye contact. "It's fun and efficient. And I can pedal faster than a goddamn cheetah!"

No matter how excited I am, I struggle to be very assertive without the assistance of alcohol, so I could only get myself to offer someone a ride a couple of times before I found myself sheepishly pedaling away. Still, like prostitution, drugs, or Girl Scout cookies, the pedicab business is a numbers game. If you want to succeed, you've got to hit up as many people as possible.[2]

---

2 Actually, scratch that about the Girl Scout cookies—everyone likes those. Especially those Samoas. They're so good, sometimes I can't decide if the person who invented them is a god or just an asshole.

Even so, it only took a handful of rejections before I started to get lost in the metaphysical realities of driving a pedicab. I wondered where all the people who might actually want to ride in my pedicab might be hanging out; I wondered if a cab would actually stop if it hit me; and I wondered how I was doing compared to all those other pedicab drivers out there.

I snapped out of it, however, when I heard a voice coming from behind me. "Take us to 53rd and Madison," it said.

I turned around to discover a couple in their forties already sitting in the back of my pedicab. Apparently they had jumped in during my mental business meeting.

"You got it!" I beamed.

Game on!

I began pedaling like the wind while weaving in and out of traffic just like one of those cabs that seemed to want me dead. My every move became fueled by the look of exhilaration I presumed to be on my passengers' faces as they held on for dear life.

"So, what part of the city do you kids live in?" I yelled over my shoulder.

I knew they were tourists by their matching Times Square sweatshirts, "I Love New York" fanny packs, and foam Statue of Liberty crowns. But I also knew that tourists love it when you mistake them for locals.

"This will be reflected in the tip," I thought.

After a few blocks into charioting my first official passengers, the physical challenges of the game began to further reveal themselves. With two fully grown humans in the back, that cart felt like I was dragging a dead rhinoceros behind me.

"Terry wasn't lying," I thought. "This really is a tough job."

I suddenly understood why those wusses he mentioned at our first meeting quit after just two shifts. I was still confident I wasn't one of them, yet there was no denying that my legs felt like they might snap like popsicle sticks any second. And my lungs felt like they were about to pop like airbags in a head-on collision. Before long, I even felt a dampness I recognized as sweat on my neck. Still, I had a job to do—pedal those last two blocks to 53rd and Madison, a familiar intersection that suddenly sounded a world away—so I powered through like the pedicab king I'd set out to be.

The couple tipped me generously for my hard work, giving me three dollars on top of the ten they owed—a 30 percent tip to you and me. Between that and the wave of endorphins I felt from pedaling two average-size adults almost six blocks, I began to experience something I quickly came to think of as "pedicab driver's high." It's similar to runner's high, only you mostly feel like you're dying. But you just made over ten bucks so it's not so bad really.

As I took it all in, I thought about just basking in the glory of a job well done for the remaining seven and a half hours of my shift But like a killer shark having tasted blood for the very first time, I found myself wanting more just as soon as I caught my breath, so I resumed the hunt.

"Come to papa," I thought, merging with traffic once more. "Daddy's hungry."

Unfortunately, the pedicab driver's appetite isn't always quickly satisfied and—for all the reasons mentioned previously—I spent the next forty-five minutes pedaling around slowly, getting lost in thought while occasionally trying and failing to convince someone hailing a cab that getting into the back of my pedicab was a much better idea.

"One of us gives off almost no deadly carbon monoxide," I'd brag. "Guess which one!"

As I continued down Broadway, enraging cab drivers every inch of the way, I heard a familiar voice call out to me.

"What the fuck are you doing?" it said.

I looked over my shoulder to find my friend Matt, whom I had worked with as a writer on a failed television show a few months earlier, chuckling incredulously in my direction.

"Living the dream, my friend," I yelled back. "Living the motherfucking dream."

"Seriously, what are you doing?" he persisted.

"I'm honestly not sure anymore," I said, caving. "Want a ride?"

Matt had originally planned to walk into the subway station he'd been standing next to, but—friend that he is—he agreed to let me take him free of charge to the next stop instead, so I might feel the exhilaration of having someone ride in the back of my pedicab again and he might better understand what it's like to have a friend on the edge.

"You learn a lot about people on one of these things," I told Matt as I took him in the direction of 42nd Street. "And a lot about yourself."

"I don't doubt it," he laughed.

I dropped Matt off a couple of minutes and a few close calls later. My plan was to get back out there and chase after my fortune some more right after that, but as nice as it was giving a friend a glimpse into my new life, seeing Matt also reminded me of the life I used to have, the one that didn't involve telling people I could pedal faster than a cheetah or exerting myself almost to the point of having an aneurysm. Exhausted, I decided to bring my pedicab back to the garage for the night. Fortunately, Terry wasn't there to see me roll into the garage in defeat. But he did call me the next morning to see how my maiden voyage had gone.

"So, how was your first day on the bike?" he asked.

"Awesome," I lied. "Really, really awesome."

"How much money did you make?"

"About a hundred and fifty bucks, give or take," I lied again.

"Not too bad," he mused.

I doubt he actually bought my $137 exaggeration, but I was grateful he went along with it.

I showed up for my second shift the next afternoon, sore yet determined to reach new heights, which—given my earnings from the day before—seemed kind of doable. The night before, as I tried to recuperate, I'd done some Internet research and learned that pedicab drivers can earn as much as $40,000 a year. The discovery made me hopeful, but I was also starting to doubt whether I had the physical, mental, or emotional goods to pull in even a fraction of that amount.

As I hit the streets on my pedicab once more, that feeling of freedom I had felt the day before was still there, but it was coupled with the feeling that maybe I was starting to lose my mind as my friend Matt seemed to suggest with a mere raise of his eyebrows. On the one hand, I really wanted this whole pedicab thing to work out. Maybe I really could make $40,000 on this bike and, who knows, maybe I'd even grow some dreadlocks and start getting into jam bands, too. You know, really get into the whole lifestyle. But on the other hand, I was starting to panic. I had been back in New York just a few months and in that time managed to go from being a decently paid television writer to a guy trying to pedal a bike with a big cart attached to it through rush hour traffic.

True to the pedicab game, however, I was only able to freak out for a few minutes before another fare hopped into the back of my pedicab without warning. This time it was a plus-size businessman, rushing to a late afternoon appointment across town.

"It's impossible to catch a cab this time of day," the guy said, wiping his forehead with his tie.

"You know what's not impossible to catch this time of day?" I wanted to ask. "The ride of a fucking lifetime!"

I felt on top of the world again as I rose from my seat in an effort to send my pedicab's wheels spinning faster than they'd ever had before. The plus-size businessman wanted to go from 46th Street and 7th Avenue to Columbus Circle and I intended to blow his mind with just how quickly that shit was about to happen.

"Hold on tight, my friend," I said over my shoulder to him with a wink and a nod.

I don't know if it was the afternoon heat or residual exhaustion from the day before, but I got about a half a block before I felt that familiar strain again. Determined, I pedaled on. But by the time I got to 57th Street, exhaustion had turned to genuine concern as I could feel my every resource rapidly depleting. Fifty-seventh Street suddenly felt like Mount Everest. And it was hard to tell if the bright light blinding me from the west was the sun or something much more profound. Had I been lying in a hospital emergency room, this would have been the moment when the machines started beeping like crazy and all the doctors and nurses started flying around the room in a controlled panic.

"Save yourself!" I wanted to yell back to my passenger as I struggled to keep my wheels turning.

Still, the desire to not look like some damn milquetoast was ultimately greater than my desire to not die, so somehow a force greater than any I had known before took over and guided me what felt like the remaining 85 miles or so to Columbus Circle.

"Thanks, pal," the businessman said as he pressed a crisp bill into my palm.

It turned out I had just made twenty bucks and, apparently, a friend.

After the euphoria from having just earned twenty bucks while not having to be pulled onto a gurney in the middle of 57th Street subsided, I crashed hard. And I had to take a good look inside myself to figure out if I had what it took to pedal on. I also had to take a good look inside my wallet to make sure I had my health insurance card with me in case any other three-hundred-pound businessman thought a pedicab was a good way to get around town. After that, I began to slowly pedal east, doing my best to keep the bike moving and my lungs filling up with air. Then, I rolled shamefully back to Terry's garage for the second day in a row. Once again, Terry wasn't there, so I just parked my pedicab, gave the finger to the couple of other pedicab drivers in the garage while they weren't looking, and packed it in for the night.

I woke up early the next morning feeling what I thought might be phantom leg pains, the kind people get after an amputation. But I was disappointed to find my legs still intact, making me still theoretically capable of going through with yet another pedicab shift. And with two shifts (sort of) already under my belt, it was time for my moment of truth, when both Terry and I would find out whether I was in the majority of those guys who never make it past a second shift or if I was one of the chosen after all.

Before I had a chance to decide which category I was in, my phone rang. The caller ID told me it was Terry on the other end. And I was just about to answer it, too, when I instead threw it on the bed and let it go to voice mail. Then I sat down in front my computer, pulled up my resume, cleared my throat, and slowly began to type.

"August 15, 2003–August 18, 2003—Pedicab Driver . . ."

· · · · · · · · ·

Witness the Fitness

Note: If you've taken even a quick glance at my author photo in this book, I'm guessing it's pretty obvious that I work out. A lot. Okay, fine, maybe it's not that obvious or really even apparent at all when you get right down to it. And—who knows—since I'm writing this before the author photo has even been taken, I can't guarantee that it's the full body shot I was promised by the guy who swore to me he was the publisher of St. Martin's Press in the bus station men's room that day. My point, however, remains the same: I work out, maybe not a lot, but definitely more than I used to, which is great for me and—I'd like to think—a lot of other people, too.

I should be clear that I never planned on becoming the absolutely captivating physical specimen I am today; I was forced into it. I would also like to stress that I'm not one of those people who thinks that everyone has to work out around the clock and starve themselves to death just so they can look like the stars of Hollywood or those fair-skinned little waifs in all the fashion magazines. Unless, of course, you think it might lead to sex, in which case I say go for it. Anyway, this is the story of how I became one of the greatest fitness experts of all-time. I think you'll find it very instructive, perhaps even inspirational.

I was driving back to my parents' house during one of my visits to Cleveland a few years ago when I turned to my mother and said, "Mind if we stop at the grocery store on the way home? I wanna pick up some ice cream."

"You don't look like you need ice cream," she replied, staring at the road ahead.

"What's that supposed to mean?"

"Nothing. It just seems like you might not need ice cream. That's all."

At the time I figured my mom was just being a jerk for some reason, maybe even for the fun of it, so I really didn't give her words much thought beyond that. Shortly after the ice-cream incident, however, I began paying closer attention to the comments section of some videos I had posted on YouTube.

"Who is this fucking fatass?" one read.

"This guy is a fat fucking douchenozzle," read another. "LOL!"

"Shut up, you stupid fat shit," read a third. "Also, are you an asshole? Because you seem like you might totally be a major asshole. Oh, and one more thing: suck it."

There wasn't much I could do about the YouTube commenters' opinions about my being an asshole aside from maybe showing up at their homes and doing something inexplicably nice for them, like mowing their lawn or presenting them with a Bundt cake, two things I both have no time for and also refuse to do. Still, I realized that when it comes to the truth, there is almost no one you should trust more than your own mother and a handful of totally anonymous Internet commenters, so I decided it was time to examine the situation a bit more closely.

I headed into the bathroom, stripped myself as bare as I could talk myself into, let the fluorescent light have its way with me for a moment, and then took a good hard look at myself in the mirror. As it turned out, my mother and all those Internet people were right. I seemed to have settled into what I like to think of as a "festive build," the kind that comes not necessarily from eating fast food every single meal of the day or anything, but just from simply saying yes to life and also just about any food or drink that is set in front of you any time ever and never really getting around to working it off.

I couldn't remember the last time I'd weighed myself, but stepping on the scale and seeing the little arrow race past 190 seemed like uncharted territory and significantly more than when I'd last done it. I remember my grandfather telling me when I was a kid that he weighed a rock-solid 190 pounds when he was in the Army. But as I stood in front of the mirror, my pale and freckled flab bathed in harsh light, the phrase "military build" didn't come to mind. To be fair, "fat fucking douchenozzle" didn't come to mind, either, but if I had to go with one of the two, I guess that would have been it.

Despite confirming both my mother's and the YouTube commenters' suggestion that I had officially become plus-size, the real wake-up call came when I put on one of my suits and found that it was much more formfitting than I remembered. As I stood there in what had somehow become a tiny little suit with buttons threatening to shoot across the room like bullets, blinding any and all in their path, it occurred to me that a lot of my other clothes seemed to be shrinking lately, too. I crunched the numbers and realized I simply couldn't afford to update my wardrobe to accommodate my good-times-all-the-time lifestyle. It would be much cheaper to just lose a few pounds.

Despite the harsh realization that it was time to lose some weight, I also knew that quitting beer, ice cream, cookies, and other things I like to keep on the nightstand was out of the question. I'm not a goddamn crazy person. And some days I feel like that stuff is all I really have in life, so I decided I would instead just try to eat healthy when the sun was out, sort of a vampire diet, I suppose, only, instead of human blood, any food I happened upon after dark was fair game. It seemed like a solid plan.

"This is going to be right up there with the Atkins Diet once word gets around," I thought proudly.

With my new, really strict diet in place, I began to address what I was told the other key ingredient to weight loss was—exercise, something I had done my best to avoid since the late '80s. Since I knew I couldn't count on myself to be disciplined enough on my own, I went all out and joined a gym. Not only would it make me commit to actually showing up somewhere and working out a couple of times a week, but it would also give other people the chance to see a man without limits in fucking action. It seemed selfish to keep that sort of thing to myself, and I couldn't wait to inspire everyone around me with my awesome commitment to fitness. To gear up for things, I bought some of those athletic pants that make that swishy sound when you walk around in them. I wasn't messing around. I looked pretty cool in them, too.

"Enjoy your workout," the lady at the front desk told me at the gym after I checked in for the first time.

"No, *you* enjoy my workout," I felt like telling her.

This shit was going to be epic. No muscle group would be left unattended. I figured I'd probably get asked to do my own instructional fitness video before long.

"Hi, I'm Dave Hill, and if you want to look as incredible in really tight pants as I do, then let's get to work!" I imagined myself saying to the camera as a half dozen superfoxes in skimpy spandex stood behind me, bracing themselves for the killer yet sexy workout ahead.

As it turned out, however, the only thing I could really get myself to do with any frequency was use the elliptical machine. It's a little on the dainty side as far as gym equipment goes, but it does promise a full-body workout right there on the machine and, perhaps more important, I once read that Jennifer Aniston uses it.

I made the elliptical machine my bitch a couple of times a week like clockwork for several months and largely credit it for helping me achieve the just slightly less doughy look I was totally going for. It's a highly effective tool and if you don't believe me you can ask Jennifer Aniston, a major Hollywood star who knows what it's like to look great all the time, just like this guy.[1] The only thing I don't like about it is at the end when it gives you a "workout summary." Instead of giving me a bunch of numbers I don't understand, I wish it would instead make me feel good about myself by telling me how bangable I am or something. Or maybe it could just be straight with me for a change. Just once when the workout summary comes up, I'd like to see it say, "Look, Dave, clearly you had a lot to drink last

---

1 Note: I am "this guy."

night. But don't worry, no one is judging you. There's only so many hours of the day you can sit around in your underwear before you start to feel like having eight or ten drinks and then maybe eating a pint of ice cream and staying up until 2:00 A.M. looking at pictures of largely unattainable women on the Internet. In fact, if you factor in all of that stuff, the fact that you even showed up here today is pretty impressive. Now go hit the showers, you gorgeous and totally unpathetic man!" The technology to make that sort of thing possible is probably decades away, but I can still dream.

As fond as I was of the elliptical machine, however, it wasn't long before I started to find going to the gym to be more annoying than going to the post office, then going to the DMV, and then having to go back to the post office because you forgot to mail a couple of things the first time. For starters, as best I can tell gyms are legally required to play the Black Eyed Peas at all times, which, despite the fact that I am sometimes genuinely looking to get a party of some sort started, is more than I can bear. Also, there's too many damn rules at the gym: no cell phones, no cameras in the showers, no incorporating glitter into my workout.

"If they're going to be dicks like that, why even show up?" I thought.

Lucky for me, I found a solution to my gym problem a couple of years ago when my friend Walter asked me to play guitar on a two-week tour of Europe with his band. Since I am even more incredible at playing the guitar than I am at the elliptical machine, I said yes. And while two weeks isn't a particularly long time to be on the road rocking people in America, in Europe it can be a lot to handle, mostly because of the catering. As opposed to America, where you're lucky if you get a six-pack and an already opened bag of pretzels, European clubs usually have a bounty of food worthy of ten Thanksgivings laid out for you as soon as you show up for sound check, and then a whole other spread of food, so big you'd think you were crashing a Russian wedding, served later for dinner. As if all that's not enough, the dressing room is usually stocked with enough alcohol to satisfy Andre the Giant on a week-long bender. It's as if they are actually happy to have the bands come play at their club or something. Seriously, it's kind of weird.

After just a few days of eating, drinking, and rocking Europe into what I was pretty sure was total oblivion, I realized my bandmates would probably find my lifeless body one morning during the tour if I didn't do something to counter the effects of all those cheese plates, mini chocolate bars, and other stuff us rockers tend to ingest in massive doses because we think we're going to live forever. But with my gym having no branches in the area, I figured I was screwed (albeit screwed in that way that's kind of a relief because you know you have an excuse to not work out at all). Then one day while in St. Gallen, Switzerland, Walter, a much thinner and handsomer man than I will ever be, even with the help of the medical community, got an idea.

"Hey, Dave," he said. "You want to go for a run with me after sound check?"

Generally speaking, I had tried to avoid running most of my life unless I was being chased by Nazis or something, which—to be fair—has yet to happen. I've always found running to be hard, boring, and just really sucky in general—three things I am generally opposed to in life. Still, nothing sucks entirely when you're doing it in Switzerland, one of the few places I've ever been that turned out to be just as adorable and idyllic as it looks on postcards and those little packets of hot chocolate mix. There are little gingerbread-looking houses everywhere, goats running around, little flower patches I can barely keep myself from diving right into—it pretty much has everything.

Since I had a pair of running shoes with me (mostly just for the look) and I'm incapable of turning down either physical challenges or shots of whiskey despite my utter disdain for both, I decided to meet Walter in front of the club for what I was told was going to be a "light jog."

We began our "light jog" by making our way first through the cobblestone streets of St. Gallen and then up into the hills that surround the town. I was ready to stop after the first few hundred yards, but whatever pride I have wouldn't let me, so I kept running alongside Walter while doing my best to not look like I might die at any second. By the time we had run about a mile, however, I was ready to drop. But I realized I could never find my way back to the club on my own, so I had no choice but to just keep running with Walter despite the fact that I was certain I'd be riding in the back of a Swiss ambulance if all of this went on much longer. Still, I figured if anything really bad happened, Walter would have to take care of it—I was quite simply too good at guitar for him to let me die in the hills of Switzerland.

Much to my and his surprise, I managed to complete what ended up being about an hour-long run. And by the time we got back to the club, I felt like a champion, a really pathetic, beaten down champion who was about to lose control of all his bodily functions, but a champion nonetheless. If one of those low-budget movies where they use a raggedy old dummy to simulate throwing a human body off the top of a building happened to be filming in the area, I probably would have been kidnapped.

"Thanks, Walter," I told him. "This was really great."

At least the run had me sweating profusely for the next several hours, so I was still completely drenched by the time we hit the stage, which made even my guitar solos on the very first song look extra cool.

Against my better judgment, I went running with Walter again the next day and then the next couple of days after that through cities like Vienna, Munich, Berlin, and some of the other ones they have over there in Europe. At each new city I knew I had to keep running with Walter if I ever wanted to make it back in time to play the show. So my survival instinct kicked in and I would run through whatever pain, tears, and occasional blood loss came my way. I think you're probably supposed to build up a bit more slowly than I did, but I decided to just run each day as far as Walter felt like dragging me. I have no idea how far we went each day, but I do know it usually lasted about an hour. And when we were done—despite still being worried that someone might try to throw me off the top of a building—I felt

This is me in the hills of St. Gallen, Switzerland, going for a run for the very first time in my adult life. This is early in the run, before the tears.

pretty great. Sometimes it was just because I was so relieved to simply not be running anymore, but I felt great nonetheless.

Thanks to all that running I was doing, I felt better equipped to become the one-man Oktoberfest I had originally set out to be on the tour. I ate and drank as much as I wanted each night. And while all that eating and drinking definitely made it harder to go running, I knew I'd feel great once the run was over, so I just powered through. Plus, if I didn't go running, I wouldn't be able to fit into any of my stage outfits, so I had no choice by then.

When the tour was finally over, I was pretty destroyed. I could sleep off all that alcohol and maybe even some of the bratwurst, but after going from never running at all to running an hour each day for two weeks straight I could barely walk. I decided I had to take a break for a couple of weeks or my legs might have snapped in two. Eventually, however, I was ready to rise like a Phoenix and take to the streets again.

Having regained use of my legs, I went to one of those fancy running stores where they videotape you running and tell you how you need to spend a couple of hundred dollars in their store if you ever expect to be able to run properly.

"Yeah, you're gonna need some prrrretty special shoes if you hope to keep this up," the guy at the running store told me.

Since I already had the swishy pants, I figured I might as well throw down on some decent running shoes, maybe even magical ones, and bought a really fancy pair that made me look like I was even better at running than I actually was.

Since I bought my super professional, space-age running shoes, I have gone running several times each week. Without Walter there to convince me that I might die or at least get beaten up by a roving street gang if I even stopped for a breather every once in a while, it was a little hard at first, especially since I live in New York City and tend not to get lost very often, even when I'm several blocks from my home. But eventually I just decided that every time someone on the street yelled for some reason or a car horn went off in the vicinity, that it was people cheering me on, and that was enough to keep me going as I high-fived anyone who would let me.

As it turns out, running is even better than the elliptical machine as far as making me feel great afterward and helping me get rid of that doughy flab even faster. A nice run seems to release a level of endorphins (the science behind "runner's high" I'm told). And making my way through the streets of wherever I happen to be at the moment provides much better stimulus than watching some exercise machine's LED display mock my every move until I finally give it the finger and head for the door. It's also a good time to do some thinking about, I dunno, whatever you want really.[2]

Aside from all the stuff I just mentioned though, I have to admit that I absolutely hate everything else about running. I hate the outfits (cool swishy pants aside), I hate the amount of time it eats up out of my day, and, most of all, I hate the actual act of running, the part

---

2 Especially weird shit that you don't want anyone else to know about.

where you have to put one foot in front of the other over and over and over again.

A very close second, however, is other runners. Unfortunately they are impossible to avoid. Even during a rainstorm or a blizzard or even the middle of the night, there always seems to be at least one other bastard out there who's got the same idea as I do. I see them from afar, panting and padding their way down the street, easily recognizable by their ridiculous attire (none of them dress as cool as I do). They usually go with some combination of criminally short shorts, an absurdly tight spandex garment, and a hat that makes them look like they've accepted a dare. They usually spot me from about fifty yards away as we come toward each other. At about fifty feet, they start to try to make eye contact and then, when they're finally right upon me, they give me the look, the one that says, "Hey, look at us! We're both running! You and me! We have something in common! We're part of the same club! We're runners! Yeah! Let's keep on running! It's what guys like us do!"

And to that I just think, "Calm the fuck down, sunshine! It's great that you're running and all, but let's get something straight— you are not my buddy, mister! I hate running and, the more I think about it, I hate you. I am completely miserable right now, and I'm not looking to bond with you over the fact that we're both hurdling down the street, barely hanging on for life. I'm just trying to get this over with, not revel in the experience with some bastard in quasi-athletic hot pants."

Trying to bond with someone over running, to me, is like trying to bond with someone in a truck stop restroom. Imagine I'm making a mad dash for the toilet, about to lose control of all of my bodily functions, and—just as I'm about to sequester myself inside the nearest stall—I stop and try to make some sort of brotherly connection with another guy who's about to redecorate the place with the contents of his intestines if he doesn't keep it together.

"Hey, buddy," I'd grunt. "I couldn't help but notice you're all red in the face and rushing toward a bathroom stall, too. I mean, I'm not a detective or anything, but, uh, are you about to shit your pants

like me? Because I'm totally about to shit my pants. In fact, wait—
yup, there it is—I've actually started to shit my pants. I should probably get into that bathroom stall already. Ha! Ha! Did you go to that
Cracker Barrel a few exits back? Because I did and, while I hate to
point fingers, well, anyway, you get the picture. Ha! Ha!"

I apologize for the graphic detour, but hopefully you see my point.
That's just not how I operate. When I'm doing my business, whether
it be in a restroom or on the street, I am an island. Still, the threat of
making eye contact with other runners can't stop me from running.
I'm probably still at least a couple of weeks away from being a candidate for the cover of *Men's Fitness*, *Men's Health*, or any of the other
magazines in which I plan on showcasing my hot, hot bod, but running is still the thing that makes me feel like I still might one day be
able to get those goddamn Wheaties people to finally come to their
senses and slap me on the box after all. It also keeps me consistently
looking like I probably won't die of a heart attack for at least a few
weeks, maybe even months. I'm not the only one who's noticed,
either.

"You fucking dork," one of my recent YouTube video comments
read.

"You are such a douchebag! LMAO! Suck it," read another.

"Fuck you, you fucking jerkoff," read a third.

I might be reading into things, but I think it's pretty clear that
all my hard work is really paying off. And I gotta admit—it feels
pretty nice.

I Kind of Remember You in the Chelsea Hotel

It was 2003 and, after showing up in New York City with just a duffle bag for what was supposed to be "a long weekend," I got an offer to write for a cable television show and decided to stick around for a while. I was doing the usual new-guy-in-town couch surfing for a few weeks until one day my friend Brad suggested I check out the Chelsea Hotel, the legendary (or infamous, depending on how you look at it) residence of more writers, artists, actors, and musicians over the years than you can shake a stick at. People like Mark Twain, William S. Burroughs, Jimi Hendrix, Jean-Paul Sartre, Patti Smith, Stanley Kubrick, Frida Kahlo, Robert Crumb, Iggy Pop, Jasper Johns, Tom Waits, Robert Mapplethorpe, Madonna, Dylan Thomas, William de Kooning, and so many more I could probably fulfill my contractually obligated word count for this book simply by listing them all here. Since I exhibited signs or at least delusions of being a creative type myself, Brad thought it might be a good address for me.

Like most rock devotees, I was already a bit familiar with the Chelsea. It's where Sid Vicious stabbed Nancy Spungen, Leonard Cohen banged Janis Joplin,[1] and—at least according to his song "Sara" anyway—where Bob Dylan wrote "Sad-eyed Lady of the Lowlands."

---

1 If you've ever wondered what it might be like to get busy with Janis Joplin, check out Cohen's "Chelsea Hotel #2." He goes into pretty good detail about it. Maybe even a little too much detail. Oh, and the title of this essay is a bastardization of the first line of that song.

I'm guessing he did a fair amount of banging while he was there, too—it just stands to reason. Either way, I couldn't wait to put my stamp on the place, assuming I didn't have to actually kill anybody, that is. More important, though, I just needed a place to live.

I swung by the Chelsea on a rainy weekday morning and asked for Stanley, the hotel manager, part owner, and guy largely responsible for curating the myth surrounding the place. I felt like I was meeting an icon. With his cardigan sweater and reading glasses hanging around his neck, Stanley appeared nebbish at first but quickly assumed a relatively large-and-in-charge presence.

"Go get yourself a cup of coffee and wait in the lobby," he told me, barely looking up from whatever he was doing. "I'll come talk to you in a little bit."

I headed down the block to grab a coffee just like Stanley told me and returned a couple of minutes later to take a seat on a bench in the lobby. The place oozed history.[2]

"Wow, this is where Dylan Thomas stumbled home to after drinking himself silly[3] at the White Horse Tavern!" I thought. "And where Andy Warhol shot *Chelsea Girls,* including the naked parts!"

Paintings by dozens of the hotel's current and former residents lined the walls, as they did just about every other inch of common space in the building[4] and it seemed like just about every person who walked by me was, at the very least, thinking about something really cool.

As I took it all in, Stanley stood just a few feet away at the front desk, sorting through stacks of mail and seemingly observing me for a bit. It occurred to me that having me sit and wait was a power move or maybe even a test to make sure I was really interested in living at the hotel.

---

2 It was also a little musty, but I didn't let that get to me.
3 Legend has it he died there, but he didn't. He died at the Chelsea. So there.
4 I later learned that many of the paintings had been given to Stanley in lieu of actual rent checks. It was a friendly system, I thought, but I couldn't help but wonder what options the dancers and poets had when funds were low. "Stand back, Stanley. This is a sexy dance about how I'll jump in front of a bus if you ever kick me out of here."

"You can't break me, Stanley," I thought. "I'm already in too deep!"[5]

Finally, as if he were responding to some imaginary timer that had just gone off, he walked over to me.

"Tell me about yourself," Stanley said.

I told him how I was mostly a writer and a musician.[6] I also told him that part about how I had come to New York for the weekend and never left. He mostly just listened before waving over a concierge standing nearby.

"This is Dave," Stanley told him. "Show him what rooms we have for him."

Without saying a word, the concierge motioned for me to follow him onto the elevator. Over the next few minutes, we got off at a few of the hotel's twelve floors as he unlocked a handful of single rooms and waved me inside. Most of them were cramped and appeared as if they hadn't been renovated in decades (which they probably hadn't). Each room was completely different, too, seemingly decorated with whatever midcentury rugs, curtains, and other odds and ends might have been lying around, but still looking pretty great to my impressionable eyes nonetheless.

"Here you go," the concierge said as he unlocked each door.

He didn't say much else and, if I lingered in any room for more than a few seconds, he just stood in front of the nearest mirror adjusting and readjusting his Kangol as if he'd been planning on coming up to the room to do that anyway whether I was there or not. It was an undeniably cool move, so I made a mental note to get one of those hats as soon as possible.

"So which room did you like best?" Stanley asked me once I got back down to the lobby.

"The room with the double bed and floral wallpaper was nice," I told him.

"And it's only three thousand dollars a month. Can I assume you'll take it?"

---

5 You know, because I had already bought the coffee.
6 I had yet to go into show business at this point in my life.

I had to stifle my laughter after that one and most of the rental prices he mentioned (you know, cuz I was broke) but there was one room I thought I could handle. It was the smallest room in the place and would cost me $1275 a month, three times what I had been paying in Cleveland for a four-room apartment with a deck. Location, location, location—am I right?

"Suit yourself." Stanley sighed.

I was expecting all sorts of questions about my finances, or—even worse—proof that they actually existed, before I'd be allowed to take the place, but Stanley just told me to show up tomorrow with a check and the keys would be mine.

"These are my kind of people," I thought.

I hurried back to my friend Victoria's place, where I'd been crashing while she was out of town, after work the next day to gather my few belongings and head over to the Chelsea. I had been staying at her place for a few days already, so it occurred to me that—whether I could pick up on the scent myself or not—the place probably smelled like a guy who rarely changed his socks and also liked to sit around in his underwear, drink beer, and eat Chinese food whenever possible. As I tidied up a bit, I figured it might not be a bad idea to let some fresh air into the place even though it was early March and still freezing outside. I decided to crack a window and, as the cold winter air rushed into the room, heard a slow, creaking sound coming from the window. For reasons I still can't comprehend, I failed to notice that the window I'd just opened also happened to be housing a large air conditioner.

"This seems bad," I thought.

I rushed back over to the window but it was too late. The air conditioner had already become gravity's bitch. But I managed to get there quickly enough to grab the cord to the air conditioner as it slithered out the window. I yanked it as hard as I could, certain that crisis had totally been averted, only to find myself holding nothing but a fistful of frayed wires, like I was a cartoon character. Next, I heard a stentorian thud. I pitched myself out the window to see the air conditioner in pieces on someone's backyard patio four storeys below. I gasped at the sight of it and cringed at the thought of what might have happened if the window I opened had been in the front of the building. I could see the cover of the *New York Post* already: "Cleveland Moron Cools Off Avenue C Pedestrians . . . Permanently!" I figured the only way I'd be staying in New York City after that would be for court appearances. The whole episode took about three seconds, but at the time it felt like it had played out over several pants-shitting minutes.

It occurred to me that I should probably own up to my careless-ness (okay, it might have been flat-out stupidity) to whoever lived on the first floor, but with no one dead or even injured, I figured it might be better to just take the low road and get the hell out of there as quickly as possible.

"222 West 23rd Street between 7th and 8th," I told a cab driver as I hopped in the back. I thought it would sound cooler that way. And I still think it did.

When I got to the Chelsea, I flung open the front doors and ex-citedly dashed inside.

"I'm moving in!" I said to the front desk guy, waving my key in the air as I headed for the elevator with nothing but a duffel bag.

Moments later I let myself into my new home, room 732. It wasn't much bigger than a freight elevator and only slightly cozier with just a twin bed, a mini fridge, and an old TV to comfort me. Hinting at the fun ahead, the room also came with an old upright piano against one wall. I could have used the extra space it occupied, but I felt like it gave the room a touch of class. And while I could actually play a little, it seemed cruel to subject my neighbors to the opening chords of Billy Joel's "Only the Good Die Young" more than a couple of times a week, so I rarely touched it when sober.

Perhaps most noticeable about my new place was the fact that it lacked its own bathroom. Instead, I had a second key that would get me into a bathroom with a toilet and a shower at the end of the hall that I'd be sharing with three other tenants. I was told that was the European style, which sounded glamorous, so I just went with it. Besides, as small as my room was, having my bathroom in a whole other part of the building was a blessing in a way as it allowed me to distance myself from the crime scene should I ever have any gastrointestinal issues. However, having the bathroom entirely separate from my room presented its own set of challenges. Given the Chelsea's frequent film appearances, it wasn't unusual for me to stumble out of my room in the morning wearing just a towel, only to find the hallway lined with craft service tables and production assistants puffing on Marlboro Lights.

"I'm sorry," some guy with a clipboard and headset might tell me. "We're filming a movie so we're asking people to try and stay out of the hallway."

"Sure thing," I'd say, helping myself to what I assumed were free bagels and all-you-can-eat Reese's peanut butter cups. "Just as soon as I get done taking a shit."

I didn't like to talk that way, but I was now officially an artist and—sorry—but artists don't censor themselves.

My room did have a small sink and a mirror in one corner, presumably for brushing teeth and performing other last minute cosmetic wonders before hitting the town. I knew myself too well, though, and immediately laid down the law with the only guy in the room—me— that that sink would never, ever do double duty as a urinal as long as I lived there. Sadly, however, I only lasted four hours before I found myself coyly shuffling over to the sink with my pants unzipped. Sorry, but sometimes artists don't have time to walk all the way to the end of the hall to use the toilet, either.

Despite my lax in-room urination policy, I quickly learned that my new status as a resident of the Chelsea Hotel was something to take pride in as long as I gave the sink a good rinse every once in a while.

"This is Dave," a friend would say while introducing me to someone or another at a bar. "He lives at the Chelsea Hotel."

"Cool!" they'd invariably respond.

It was as if people were giving me partial credit for all the great writing, music, and art that had been spawned there over the years. It felt a bit silly, but being new in town and all, it was nice to have an icebreaker other than just saying "I'm new in town" over and over again like I was some kind of she-male advertising my reasonably priced in- and outcall services in the back of *The Village Voice*. Besides, I chose to believe it was only a matter of time before I whipped up something of important cultural significance back in room 732.

Once the initial thrill of my new address wore off, though, it was hard to deny that my room itself was pretty depressing. The walls were dirty, the carpet even dirtier, and my presence wasn't helping matters with either. Though I had a window, it was covered in steel bars and the view was only good if you're into bricks. I'd never made plans to kill myself before, but among the many reasons I hadn't was the fact that I had never lived anywhere I would have ever been comfortable having someone find my body. Room 732, however, was a different story. I could totally, totally see it. It was almost like a dead body would have completed the decor. I could practically hear my friends' hearts sink the first time they swung by for a visit.

"There's a darkness to this place," my friend Fred said upon seeing the place for the first time. "You have to get out of here before it swallows you whole."

It might have been a little melodramatic, but he definitely had a point. And while I certainly didn't want to over-romanticize the place, I quickly realized that if I didn't, Fred's assessment might eventually prove correct.

To that end, I decided to actively try to turn things around. On the interior decorating front, I bought a bunch of plastic flowers from the dollar store downstairs, some Christmas lights from a nearby hardware store, and a tapestry from an Indian gift shop across the street. Then I pulled some posters for a Spanish radio station featuring buxom girls in bikinis off a few lampposts along 23rd Street and hung them up in my room with the help of some duct tape. Within minutes, the place was so festive you could barely even smell the pee anymore. It was less shabby-chic than just plain shithole-chic, but still an improvement and still in keeping with the mildly suicidal vibe of the place.

"It looks like a real artist lives here," I thought as I took in my

Room 732: My room at the Chelsea Hotel that I decorated all by myself. If you blur your eyes a little bit, it's really not so bad.

handiwork. "All I have to do now is create something, anything, and my work is done here."

My neighbors at the Chelsea were as eclectic as my decorating skills. Next door was a part-time drag queen who held New Age meditation sessions in his room twice a week. Across from me was a Swiss club promoter who was so awesomely rude and unfriendly whenever I encountered her that I almost looked forward to it. Down the dimly lit hall was a movie star, a surf guitarist, and a retired dancer with a penchant for using a garbage bag as a purse.

But my favorite person on the floor—and the only one I ever really became friends with—lived in a room just two doors down at the end of my hallway. He was an old man with whom I shared the bathroom. The first time I ran into him was early one morning when I was just getting in from a long night out. As unlike me as it was, I had decided to use the bathroom in the hall before heading back to my room and, when I came out, discovered my new neighbor standing there impatiently in a pair of old Army pants, unlaced hiking boots, a baggy sweatshirt, and a winter hat over close-cropped gray hair.

"Hi," I said. "Sorry for taking so long."

The man said nothing in return, instead just sighed and rolled his eyes as if to show his disdain for having to share his bathroom with yet another random bastard. I ran into the old man in the hallway several times over the next couple of weeks. I said hello each time and eventually graduated from receiving a blank stare in return to an indifferent nod to a friendly nod to an actual hello. After about three weeks, however, when I spotted the old man in the hallway wearing just a tank top, I noticed something different about him. He had breasts and was, it turned out, actually a woman.

"My name is Dave," I told her, finally officially introducing myself.

"I'm Storme," she replied, shaking my hand.

In retrospect, it kind of made sense that I had mistaken Storme for a man all that time. Though she was retired by that point, she was a legendary drag king (the female version of a drag queen, just like it sounds) who used to tour the country performing in a show with a group of female impersonators. She also worked security at a number of lesbian bars around town over the years. And, perhaps most famously, she is credited with helping to spearhead the Stonewall riots in 1969. Some say she threw the first punch. She was a total badass and knew it.

"It's nice to have you as a neighbor," Storme told me. "The girl in there before you would sit there on her bed naked with the door wide open all the time. I hated it."

"Yeah, I'm not really planning on doing that sort of thing very much," I assured her.

Over time, Storme and I became more and more friendly, often stopping outside each others' doors to chat, especially if one or both of us had had a few drinks. Equally tough and sweet, she seemed to pride herself on being the eyes and ears of the hotel. And she wasn't shy about the fact that she owned a gun—or at least used to—and knew how to use it.

"Honey, if anyone in this hotel ever gives you any trouble, you just let me know and I'll take care of it," she said to me one day without prompting. "In fact, if anyone anywhere ever gives you any trouble, you just let me know where I can find them and I'll see to it that they never bother you again."

God, I loved that woman. She was like my eighty-something bodyguard, confidant, and surrogate grandmother all rolled into one, willing to lend me a shoulder to cry on or a shoulder to take a bullet for me whenever I might need it. And though it turned out I didn't have occasion for either, it was always nice to know she was just a few feet away should my circumstances ever change.

Meanwhile, I had been waiting for some of the magic of the Chelsea's walls to rub off on me so I could start cranking out some sort of art or another that was guided by the ghosts of all the legends that had come before me. But, with the television show I had been writing for suddenly canceled and me suddenly unemployed, the only part of any of that romantic picture that seemed to come easily was being a starving artist. And since I didn't even have a stove in my room, I couldn't even eat ramen noodles every meal of the day like artists are supposed to do. Instead I ate whatever room temperature stuff was on sale.

I knew I had to discipline myself if I ever wanted to stay in the hotel long enough to create anything lasting and important, so, in an effort to make that happen, I decided to lay down a second law with myself, one I actually intended to obey.

"There will be absolutely no unnecessary spending!" I promised myself. "This is about survival!"

As I stepped outside to face the world with my new, second really important law in place, I discovered a street fair was going on right in front of the hotel. There, amid all the cheese-covered corn on the cob, discount Peruvian sweaters, and other things that seem like a good idea at the time, I spotted a guy selling marionettes of stuffed farm animals. I had to have one. Not only was the guy making them walk around and everything, but in them I saw an opportunity for myself to become the world's preeminent stuffed goat marionettist, something I was certain no Chelsea Hotel resident past, present, or future could possibly compete with.

"How much for the goat?" I asked excitedly.

"Forty bucks," he told me.

"I'll give you thirty-nine!" I said, playing hardball.

"Uh, sure," the guy said, handing me the goat.

I was halfway down the block and a bit embarrassed when I realized it only took about ten minutes for me to break another one of my "rules." But then I just focused on how awesome I was about to become at stuffed goat puppetry and everything was cool.

"From this day forward, I shall illustrate the human condition with this stuffed goat," I thought.

Needless to say, I was feeling pretty good about myself. So with the "art" part of "artist" now officially covered, I decided to focus on that other key ingredient of being an artist—a decadent lifestyle.

To that end, I starting having friends over for parties on weekends. I dubbed them "miniraves," a term I borrowed from my friend Johnny. And though they never involved any actual raving, I'd like to think the miniraves embraced the same sort of joie de vivre (if not all the drugs and ridiculous outfits) as their namesake. I would invite as many people over as could fit somewhat comfortably on the floor and on my bed (usually about six or seven), they'd all bring a six-pack, bottle of wine, or some kind of whiskey, and we'd sit there for hours talking, drinking, and listening to music on a CD player I'd picked up for thirty dollars at Kmart once I decided to take this artist thing more seriously. It was kind of like a college dorm room party, only there was no chance in hell that we would ever get busted for it.

"People have been murdered in this hotel," I reasoned. "So what if I have a few friends over every once in a while?"

When I wasn't entertaining friends in my room, I still never strayed too far from the Chelsea. A couple of nights a week, I'd see how many margaritas I could handle at El Quijote, the stopped-in-time Spanish restaurant in the ground floor of the hotel. I had heard that Patti Smith and Robert Mapplethorpe used to hang out there when they lived at the Chelsea, so—as a fellow icon in the making—it felt important to do the same whenever possible.

When I wasn't getting drunk at El Quijote, I'd sit in the lobby and watch people wander in and out. On any given night, I'd see famous actors, teenage models, wide-eyed tourists, total nutjobs, and even Arthur Miller pass in front of me as I sat on a couch eating an ice-cream bar I bought from the deli next door. Being 2003 and all, I'm sure it wasn't anything near the wild scene it had been in past decades, but, seeing as how I had been living above a hair salon in Cleveland only weeks before, I felt like I was living Warhol's *Chelsea Girls* anyway.

One night, as I stood talking to one of the front desk guys, a drunken woman visiting from Italy stumbled up to the reception area.

"I would like to live in this hotel next time I come here to New York City," she slurred in a sexy, English-as-a-second-language sort of way.

The front desk guy said nothing, instead just smiled politely as she pressed on like a wasted Sophia Loren.

"How much does it cost to live here?" she asked.

"The rooms are all different prices," he answered as if he were simply repeating lines being whispered to him by someone crouching under his desk.

"Tell me how much. I can afford it; I have plenty of money. You don't need to worry so much, meeester."

"You could have all the money in the world," he replied, stepping forward a bit for emphasis. "That doesn't mean you can live here."

"What is that supposed to mean?" the drunken Italian lady asked, insulted. "Why you say that to me? Why?"

The madder she got, the sexier (and drunker) she seemed to me. I thought I might be falling in love.

"Living here is like being in a real-life play," the front desk guy began to explain. "You have to come here and audition for the manager, Stanley. And then he decides if he wants to cast you."

Dumbfounded, the drunken Italian lady shook off the entire conversation as if she were spitting out an ice cube before stumbling back into the street. To me, however, the place was finally starting to make sense. Despite its history, the Chelsea Hotel wasn't some sort of cool kids' club or hipster residence, as people (myself occasionally included) often mistook it for. It was more like a Tennessee Williams play come to life, with a hodgepodge of characters all thrown in the mix to see what might happen next, one of whom was a little more into peeing in the sink than most people but whatever—everyone knows Williams was out of his mind toward the end anyway.

As much as I was certain I had become a key player in the "real-life play" that front desk guy was talking about, I reluctantly decided it might be time to move on after nine months of calling the Chelsea Hotel home. It was mostly because I had yet to find steady employment and could no longer afford it. But it was also because there didn't seem to be any end in sight to my peeing in the sink, and I felt like it might do me some good to go somewhere where that sort of thing simply would not be tolerated.

When I told my friends I was moving on, the same ones who initially begged me to leave the Chelsea, they offered to take up a monthly collection so I might be able to stay, if only to keep the miniraves going. Still, I knew it was unfortunately time to go, so I packed up my duffel bag, Christmas lights, plastic flowers, and whatever else I had accumulated over the past few months, and moved in with some friends who had a spare room in Brooklyn.

"Holy fucking shit, I'm in Brooklyn," I thought as I woke up for the very first time at my new outerborough address, tears practically forming in the corners of my eyes.

Don't get me wrong—I love Brooklyn. But when you've been living history, getting hammered with the ghost of Mapplethorpe, and peeing in the sink whenever you goddamn well feel like it at the Chelsea Hotel, waking up on the other side of the East River is a bit of a blow. Still, I'll always know I experienced that rare Chelsea Hotel magic firsthand, if only for a little while.[7]

If you look up the Chelsea Hotel on Wikipedia, you'll see a long list of all the legends who have called the place home, some for just a few nights, some for a few weeks or months, and some for many, many years. Charles Bukowski, Allen Ginsberg, Johnny Thunders, Nico, Dennis Hopper—the list is endless. I'm proud to say that my name is also a part of that list, but not because of my vast body of work, my mastery of goat puppetry, or even the fact that I actually did end up stabbing someone while I was there. (Don't worry, it was only with a pen and it was an accident.) It's mostly because Wikipedia lets anybody with Internet access edit its pages. They really gotta start regulating that stuff. It's hard to know what to think or believe anymore.

---

7 And, as it turned out, it was probably good I left when I did. Not long after, the hotel was sold, Stanley was ousted, and, by most accounts, the place was never the same. I'm glad I missed that part.

The Streets Are Hell

If there's one thing I pride myself on, it's my crime-fighting skills. Wherever there is violence, villainy, or even just garden-variety shenanigans, nine times out of ten (assuming I'm already in the area) you will find me righting wrongs, wagging my finger, and handing out my own swift brand of justice. And, naturally, the criminals in question end up wishing they'd made other plans that day.

Unfortunately, just about all of my crime fighting tends to go unrecognized by the authorities.[1] And the fact that the crime rate in New York City seems to be at an all-time low doesn't help matters much. I just read on the Internet that the murder rate in this town hasn't been this low since 1963. It's like people aren't even trying anymore.

Fortunately, there's a place I can always go when I need a taste of the action, the mean streets of Cleveland, Ohio, my hometown. Thanks to a perpetually struggling economy, general urban decay, and basketball asshole LeBron James skipping town for Miami, Cleveland manages to rest comfortably on the list of America's top-ten most crime-riddled cities with more murdering, burglarizing, and other negative behavior per capita than you can shake a stick at. In 2010, Cleveland's neighborhoods even made it onto the ABC News list of "America's 25 Most Dangerous Neighborhoods." Twice. Not too

---

1 The cops won't even give me an honorary badge, cool hat, or anything. It sucks and it's also really lame. To be honest, I've just about had it with their bullshit.

shabby. Say what you want about the Indians, but when it comes to crime, Cleveland is hitting it out of the park.

I managed to get the lowdown on all this from my friend Travis, a kindred spirit in giving the finger to crime. Travis has been on the Cleveland police force since shortly after college. He was always good at giving orders. His dad was a cop. And he could grow a fuller mustache than anyone else I knew in high school. It was pretty much his destiny to wind up "on the job."[2]

Travis and I met when we were sixteen. Our mutual friend John's parents had gone out of town for a few days and, as these things often go, John decided he should probably throw a party. Given Travis's natural air of menace, John asked Travis to guard the front door and decide who should and shouldn't be let inside to drink warm Miller from a keg in the basement, and see if they could talk anyone into giving them a handjob in one of the upstairs bedrooms. An ideas man, Travis saw an opportunity and decided to charge an entrance fee as long as he was at it.

"Five bucks," Travis said to me stone-faced as our eyes met for the very first time.

"No," I told him, somehow sensing he was on the grift. Between the mustache and his size (Travis was already a foot taller and a hundred pounds heavier than everyone else in our class), I'm guessing I was the first person of the night to challenge him on the cover charge. Despite, or perhaps because of, my insolence, Travis and I have been friends ever since.

Travis and I hadn't seen each other in about five years when we decided to get together for lunch during one of my regular visits back

---

2 Cop talk for "being a cop." According to Travis, it can also mean "carrying a gun." For example, if an on-duty cop asks an off-duty cop if he is "on the job" and the off-duty cop says yes, it means that—despite the fact that he's wearing a pair of Dockers, a Hawaiian shirt, and a promotional Newport Lights golf visor—he's still packing heat. Travis taught me all this because he thought it would help keep me from getting shot on wing night and stuff like that.

home to Cleveland. I'd heard he'd been assigned to the motorcycle unit, so I made a point to meet with him while he was on patrol. It seemed crazy not to try to get a ride out of him, especially if he had a sidecar like I hoped.

Travis asked me to meet him at noon in a parking lot inside his district—a cool, coplike thing to do. So I borrowed my parents' Buick and rolled out of relatively crime-free suburban Cleveland and into the bedlam of downtown. When I arrived, I was disappointed to find that Travis had shown up in a regular police car.

"We don't ride the bikes much in the winter," he explained.

"This is bullshit," I protested.

"Just get in."

Shaking off my dismay, I hopped in the front passenger seat of his squad car, where there were extra guns and a really cool radio.

"Don't touch anything," Travis warned.

"Fine," I huffed.

Despite the rough start, Travis and I hit the ground running, easily settling into the familiar camaraderie we'd established back in high school.

"How awesome is it that David Lee Roth is back in Van Halen?" he asked.

"It's totally awesome."

"Totally."

As Travis rattled off various food options, a call came in on his police radio. After we settled on Italian, he picked up the receiver and began speaking in undecipherable police code—lots of numbers, abbreviations, and other gibberish. Sitting next to him, I felt like a dog watching television—plenty intrigued but not taking that much away.

"Code two, ten-four," Travis said before dropping the receiver and flooring it.

Within seconds, we were flying down a residential street at double the speed limit.

"What's going on?" I asked while scrambling to pull my seat belt across my chest.

"B and E," Travis said, staring intensely at the road ahead.

"What's that stand for again?" I asked like I had somehow just forgotten.

"Breaking and entering," Travis answered in a tone that suggested anyone, even I, might be a suspect.

"Does this mean we're not getting lunch?" I asked.

If the answer was yes, then I'd be this crime's first auxiliary victim, which was bullshit. My parents rarely got around to picking up any groceries before my visits, so I was pretty hungry.

"We'll get lunch, but I gotta deal with this shit first," Travis answered, this time more irritated than wary, before screeching around a corner.

Being a civilian, it was hard not to worry that we were going to be pulled over by the cops for going so fast. But then I remembered that we were the cops and it was intoxicating. As Travis's driving became increasingly erratic, however, I started to worry again, this time for my safety. The fact that we were the cops and, as a result, no longer had the cops to call for help, made things even worse. All I could do was hold on tight and hope for the best. I calmed down, though, when we pulled up to a ranch house in a run-down section of town. The place was so beat-up it was hard not to wonder who would have thought it was a good idea to pull a B and E there in the first place.

"What should I do?" I asked nervously as Travis cut off the ignition and jumped out of the squad car.

"I don't care." He smiled.

I took the smile to mean that if I decided to join him, he wasn't going to do a damn thing about it, so I giddily unbuckled myself, hopped out of the passenger seat, and scurried after him as he walked toward the house.

"This is my friend Dave," Travis said to Jim, a mustachioed cop who was already in the driveway breathing in the crime scene.

"Nice to meet you," Jim said in a joyless, coplike way before the two of them turned and headed for the front door. I followed gingerly behind them. It's not always good to move gingerly or even to use words like that when you're fighting crime, but I didn't want to take any chances.

At the door, we were met by a man of about sixty who wore glasses and a plaid hunting jacket. He shook with the kind of nervousness one tends to get after having just become a victim of a B and E.

"Thanks for getting here so fast," he said.

"Not a problem. I'm Officer Mitchell, this is Officer Kozlowski," Travis said, nodding toward Jim. "And this is Officer Hill."

Nice. In the span of about forty feet I'd morphed from lunch date to full-fledged police officer. And given that I was wearing a down ski jacket and a pair of jeans, I was apparently working undercover, too, which was great for me.

"So what happened?" Travis nonchalantly asked the older man while I began sniffing around for clues.

"I'll show you," the man said, leading us to the kitchen.

There we were met by his wife, also about sixty and also shaking. As we all filed into the cramped kitchen in the back of the house, the man hit PLAY on a VCR sitting on top of an old refrigerator.

"I got a surveillance camera trained on my backyard," he explained while pointing at a small black-and-white television hanging from the ceiling. "Some kids came along and tried to steal some car parts I had sitting back there and then they took off over that fence."

"Did they take anything?" Jim asked in a way that seemed to imply something more along the lines of "Goddammit, we came here for nothing!"

"Yeah, they took my gun," the man exclaimed. Things suddenly got a lot more interesting for Officer Hill.

"What gun?" Travis pressed, not nearly as excited as I was.

"Yeah, what gun?" I chimed in.

"I'll handle this, Officer Hill," Travis said firmly.

What with him being a veteran, I understood his thinking, but even so it was hard to contain myself. Just a few minutes earlier, the most exciting thing in my immediate future had been a chicken Parmesan sandwich or maybe some spaghetti, and now here I was, investigating the case of a missing gun. I felt tingly all over.

"When I saw them up on the monitor there, I ran out after them with my gun," the man said.

"And then what happened?" Travis smirked in that way that cops do when they're pretty sure a story is about to get really good.

"I went around to the back of the house and the two kids were rooting through my stuff."

"Yeah?"

"They saw me and my gun and came at me."

"And then?"

"Then they tried to take my gun from me and the damn thing went off."

"Holy fucking shit—someone got shot!" I thought while spinning around the room looking for a body.

Travis and Jim remained composed, though, probably because this seemed like the part of town where people having and even shooting guns is business as usual.

"Did anyone get hurt?" Travis asked, as if there might be a dead body somewhere that the guy had for whatever reason forgot to mention.

"My finger got cut while they were wrestling me for the gun," the man explained, holding up his left hand. I felt bad for him—it must have stung a little.

"What happened after that?" Jim pressed.

"Yeah—what happened after that?" I followed excitedly, prompting sidelong glances from both Travis and Jim that suggested my talking privileges were in serious danger of being officially revoked.

"Watch the tape," the man said, gesturing back to the television. "It's all on there. They took my gun, hopped over the fence, and then ran into the house right behind mine over there."

"Officer Hill, take notes," Travis told me. "I want to know exactly when you see the perpetrators on the screen."

I realized he was just throwing me a bone, but even so I struggled not to appear too giddy as I rifled through my pockets for a pen and paper. My pen poised, we all stood in silence watching the monitor for a minute or so before two boys who seemed to be in their late teens appeared on the tiny screen.

"There they are! It's the perpetrators! It's the perpetrators!" I squealed, doing my best to act like I'd seen this sort of thing a million times before.

After another few seconds, the man with the bloody finger appeared on screen waving a pistol around like he was in a Spaghetti Western.

"And there you are," I screamed. "And there's your gun that those perpetrators are totally about to take from you like candy from a goddamn baby!"

To their credit, Travis, Jim, and even the man all acted like they really needed me to give the play-by-play to understand what was happening on the screen. As a rookie, I appreciated the gesture.

Once the video finished, Travis and Jim did some paperwork and the man gave them the tape to take back to the station for further review. Meanwhile, I gave one last "Goddamn if this doesn't get any easier!" kind of look around the man's living room—always a good cop move.

Back in the driveway, Jim agreed to head back to the station with the videotape while Travis and I went to check out the house the two kids had supposedly run into.

"Things just keep getting better and better," I thought.

But as excited as I was to finally fight some crime at the professional level, I was also starting to get a bit nervous about the possibility of getting shot.

"Are we still gonna get lunch?" I asked Travis as we climbed back into the squad car, in hopes of distracting myself from the prospect of death.

"Yeah," Travis said. "But you gotta remember I'm at work right now, and I gotta take care of shit, so just chill out for a second!"

"Sorry!" I responded in a manner that suggested I wasn't going to put up with Travis turning his tough cop talk on me for much longer. Just because I was a rookie didn't mean I didn't deserve to be treated with dignity.

A minute later we pulled into the driveway of the modest two-storey house behind the house of the man with the bloody finger. As we hopped out of the car, it began to rain, which served as just another reminder of the fact that police work is never easy. Then Travis began to make his way up the driveway, slowly removing his pistol from his belt holster as he walked. Despite my taste for action, I was starting to get officially scared. I figured a cop doesn't take his gun out unless he thinks he might have to use it.

"What should I do now?" I whispered nervously as the rain slowly made a mess of my hair.

Travis said nothing and instead just waved with his gun for me to follow him toward the back of the house, hopefully because he wanted the backup, but maybe just because he wanted to make sure I stayed out of trouble. I tried to keep it together but suddenly felt in way over my head. Not only did it seem like someone might very well get shot, but I was also totally starving. I could feel my blood sugar dropping and everything. It was really unpleasant.

As I followed Travis back behind the house, he waved at me again with his pistol, this time in a way that seemed to say, "You gotta stay back now because this is the part where someone might answer the door with a gun and try to shoot us." I crept slowly back to the side of the house while giving Travis an "Oopsie!" gesture—palms up, arms bent, face adorable yet confused.

"If one of us actually ends up getting shot, this will definitely go down as just about the worst lunch date of all time," I whispered. Travis just looked at me.

As I stood there anxiously, I saw a woman in her early twenties walk up the driveway then quickly turn around and head back down the street.

"There is a woman in her early twenties who just walked up the driveway then quickly turned around and headed back down the street," I whispered to Travis in an effort to settle back into my police work.

"Stop her!" Travis whispered sternly. "Ask her what the hell she's doing."

"What the hell are you doing?" I yelled at the woman as I shuffled down the driveway. I didn't even let my voice crack, not even a little. It felt good, empowering even, to be so manly like that. Even so, the woman just kept walking. She didn't even look over her shoulder. Not only was it kind of rude, but it also hurt my feelings.

"Pure balls on that one," I thought.

Then I yelled, "You, in the pink jacket," which totally stopped her in her tracks. Then she turned and looked right at me, Officer Dave Hill, a young rookie thrown into the goddamn mess of these city streets for the very first fucking time in his career.

"What . . . the hell . . . are you doing?" I asked through clenched teeth.[3]

"I was just gonna see if my friend was home, but I don't think she is 'cause her car's not in the driveway," she told me.

Suddenly she was singing like a goddamn canary.

"And now what are you doing?" I asked her, not even close to fucking satisfied.

"I was just gonna go home, I guess."

"Good!" I said, doing my best to stare a hole right through her. "You can just get the hell out of here and don't ever come back as far as I'm concerned."

She had already turned away by the time I said that last part, but I'm pretty sure she heard every word of it. And as she faded out of sight, I headed back up to the side of the house where Travis was still standing at the back door with his gun drawn. A total pro, Travis seemed to sense my presence without even looking at me.

"What did she say?" he whispered.

"She said she had just come to see if her friend was home but she didn't think she was because her car's not in the driveway," I whispered back.

"Where is she now?"

---

3 When you clench your teeth, throw the word hell into a sentence, and then space it all out for emphasis, people know you mean business and the woman in the pink jacket was no different. Try it sometime. It's great.

"She left because I told her she could just get the hell out of here and never come back as far as I was concerned."

Travis just looked at me after that, before finally lowering his weapon.

"I don't think anyone is home, either." Travis sighed. "Let's get some lunch."

Just in case Travis and the lady in the pink jacket were wrong, though, we headed back toward the squad car with one eye on the house at all times. I felt like a kid in a water balloon fight, quickly retreating from the opposition while looking over his shoulder, only instead of being afraid of getting hit by a water balloon I was afraid someone might pull out a gun and shoot me in the face, which is different. The odds of that happening probably weren't very good at all, but—again—given our original plan (sandwiches), all the non-sandwich-related action seemed extra intense.

"Are you sure it's okay for us to just leave like that?" I asked.

"You want me to just break down the door and barge right in?"

"Yeah!"

You probably saw this coming, but Travis just looked at me after that, too. It was honestly getting kind of annoying.

As we drove away, Travis suggested we go to a diner around the corner.

"What happened to Italian?" I asked.

"They're closed by now." Travis sighed in a manner that suggested that I better get used to making sacrifices pretty darn quickly if I ever hoped to make anything of myself on the force.

Adding insult to injury, we didn't make it ten more feet before a voice came on Travis's police radio again. It was Jim. He wanted Travis (and me, I took it) to get back to the station and pronto. Apparently he had watched the videotape again, this time with the sound on, and the old man's story didn't exactly wash.

"Well, there goes lunch," Travis said.

"Are you kidding?" I asked. "I'm about to faint from starvation!"

"Sorry, Dave, duty calls," Travis said before rerouting.

I couldn't argue with him. Besides, it was more his loss anyway because little did Travis know that I'd planned on picking up the tab at lunch in a bold act of self-imposed rookie hazing.

"I'm gonna have to take you with me to the station first because the parking lot we left your parents' car in is in the other direction," Travis told me. Whatever. I still say it was because he wanted me to finish the case I'd helped crack wide fucking open.

A few minutes later, we were back at the precinct where we were greeted by Jim and another cop who looked just like him: same mustache, same dark world view, everything.

"Pete, this is my friend Dave," Travis told him. "He's visiting from New York City."

"New York City, eh?" Pete said in a manner that suggested he hoped I spent most of my time running from a bunch of street gangs just like in that *Warriors* movie but realized I probably didn't.

Before we got down to business, Travis, Pete, and Jim all lit up cigarettes. I decided to bum one from Travis as long I was standing there. Up until that point in my life, I'd kept a strict rule to only smoke when really, really drunk, but I decided to make an exception in the name of crime-fighting solidarity. Plus, as any decent cop movie will tell you, it's never a bad idea to take a big drag of a cigarette and exhale slowly right before bringing the fucking hammer down.

"So what's the story?" Travis asked Jim as a thick haze of smoke began to fill the air.

"Well, it seems the old man's gun went off long before he made it around to the back of his house," Tom explained between drags. "Here, have a look for yourself."

Jim hit PLAY on a nearby VCR and we watched the surveillance video again, this time with the sound on. Sure enough, we heard a gun go off about ten seconds before the man with the bloody finger ever showed up behind the house, which, of course, suggested to us crime-solving types that maybe the old coot was a bit more trigger-happy than he had originally led us to believe. Jim, Pete, and Travis all smirked at one another as the tape finished and the monitor went back to playing static. I smirked, too, though I wasn't exactly sure why.

"Looks like someone's gonna have to talk to the old man about getting his story straight." Travis groaned.

"Yep," Jim said.

"Yep," I agreed.

All three of them looked at me after that; I guess it was just a cop thing. Then we all snuffed out our smokes and headed out back to where the squad cars were parked. As Travis and I took to the streets again, I began to wonder if I'd get to do the questioning once we got back to the old man's house. I was surprised, however, when, just a few minutes later, Travis drove into the parking lot where I'd left my parents' car instead.

"What are we doing here?" I asked. "What about the man with the bloody finger? What about the goddamn B and E? What about *us*?"

"You're off the force," Travis told me, offering his hand and a smile.

"Huh?"

"It was good seeing you, Dave. Let me know when you're back in town next."

"Yeah, sure," I told him, my throat a little dry from that crime-solving cigarette I'd smoked earlier. "I'll do that."

On the drive back home, it was hard not to question what had really happened that day. How many shots were actually fired and who pulled the trigger? Was the whole thing an inside job? Did the man with the bloody finger know the two boys on the videotape a lot better than he had let on? And did that woman in the pink jacket think it was maybe just a little bit sexy when I yelled at her in my manly cop voice? But on top of all these unanswered mysteries, I felt exhilarated. Even though neither Travis nor I found ourselves in a haze of gunfire or wrestling some perp to the ground before carting him off to jail or anything cool like that, there's just something about being a lawman that makes you feel way more alive than, say, sitting around in your underwear eating room-temperature soup.

Part of me wanted to ignore that thing Travis said about my be-ing "off the force." But waiting at a stoplight on the way home, I couldn't help but notice I was no longer sitting in a squad car. And suddenly my jeans and down jacket didn't make me look so much like a guy working undercover as they did a guy who had just borrowed his parents' Buick for a few hours. Even so, when the light turned green, I stepped on the gas pedal extra hard in an act of rogue defiance. Yeah, I knew I was in a 35 mph zone, but I gunned it right on up to 37 mph before turning on the cruise control anyway. I might have been a civilian again, but I was a civilian playing by his own goddamn set of rules.

About twenty minutes later and a world away from the crime-riddled streets of Cleveland, I pulled into my parents' suburban driveway. After parking the car out back, I walked through the side door into the kitchen and threw the keys on the counter.

"How was lunch?" my dad asked, looking up from the newspaper.

"Who's asking?" I said, still in cop mode.

"Your father."

"Oh, yeah, sorry. It was fine."

I tried to just head up to my room after that, but my dad stopped me before I managed to get out of the kitchen.

"Have you been smoking?" he asked. "You smell like cigarettes."

"No I don't."

"Yes you do. Were you smoking or not?"

"Look, dammit, you don't ask me any more questions because asking questions is *my* job, you got me?" I told him.

My dad refused to let me borrow his car for the rest of my visit for talking to him like that, but whatever—it's not like you can expect a totally regular civilian to understand us goddamn lawmen anyway.

· · · · · · · · ·

Big in Japan

If there's anything I've learned about myself in this life, it's that I can't stop rocking. But here's the thing about rocking and playing in bands: when you're a young man, playing in a band is cool. Other guys think you're cool, girls want to make out with you (or at least you think they do, which is what really matters), and you yourself are convinced that the only possible outcome of your rock 'n' roll exploits is that you will one day go on to become the greatest rock god of all-time.

But then the years start to roll by and you get older, and maybe a little fatter. And suddenly you find yourself at an age where playing in a band can be kind of sad, maybe even downright pathetic. And it's at exactly that age that some friends and I decided to form our brand-new rock band.

We called ourselves Valley Lodge[1] and we knew it was all over before we had even started. We knew there weren't going to be any platinum albums or stadium tours or groupies hell-bent on licking us from head-to-toe and maybe even making plaster replicas of our genitals. But none of that mattered because, when you're rocking out, you don't care about anything else. You don't care about problems with money or women. Or even the fact that you've suddenly

---

1 Like most not-exactly-great band names, it seemed like a good idea that one day at practice.

become that sad, old rocker dude you'd always swore you'd never be. All you care about is rocking out and then rocking out some more.

To that end, we rocked out whenever possible, which admittedly wasn't that often since all the other guys in the band had wives and jobs and babies and other bullshit that tends to get in the way of things when you're trying to rock the fuck out of people. As a result, we'd play every couple months or so. Usually about fifteen or twenty of our friends would show up, mostly because they felt sorry for us or pitied our unwillingness to let the dream die.

"You, um, er . . . looked like you were having a lot of fun up there," they'd tell us after shows. "And it's so great how you just don't care how it looks."

That was pretty much the deal for a while. Then one day everything changed. I woke up and—like most days—the first thing I did was check my e-mail. And aside from the usual spam about how I might learn to better please a woman and a couple of replies from some of the many "missed connections" ads I'd placed on Craigslist, there was another e-mail.

"Hello, Valley Lodge," it read. "We are a record label based in Tokyo. We think you are so very great and would like to release your album in Japan."

"Finally someone who gets it," I thought. "Finally someone who gets how unstoppable we are at rocking people."

"Fuck yeah, motherfucker, you can release the fuck out of that album!" I wanted to respond before instead writing, "Thank you. My bandmates and I would like that very much."

Releasing an album in Japan would have already been way beyond my wildest, most delusional dreams. If those old pictures of Cheap Trick and Kiss playing over there are any indication, it's the ultimate place for rock. So after I received another e-mail from the guy at the Japanese record label a few days later, I almost had a seizure.

"Hello, Valley Lodge," it read. "We were wondering if you might be willing to do a tour of Japan in support of your album."

"Hell yeah, we would. We'll rock every man, woman, and child over there so hard you're gonna have to mop down the entire country when we're done!" I wanted to respond before instead writing, "Sure. That sounds like a lot of fun."

Then I immediately called up the other guys in the band and told them how we needed to get on a plane with our guitars, our tightest pants, and our cocks and balls as soon as humanly possible. In my mind, we'd fly over there and, wherever the people of Japan needed their asses handed to them by our gravity-defying hot rock action, we'd just show up and kick them in the nuts with the handful of compositions we'd managed to write on those rare occasions when all three of the other bandmembers' wives let them come to practice.

In reality, however, we were scheduled to do a four-city tour starting in Osaka.[2] We arrived after a sixteen-hour flight, instantly finding ourselves delirious with jetlag because apparently the time difference between America and Japan is like six-to-eight weeks or something. By the time we actually got on stage, we were just plain hallucinating.

"Hello, Osaka," I said, testing the microphone. "We are Valley Lodge from New York City and we have come to rock you!"

Most of the people in the audience just stood there in silence after I said that, presumably because they didn't understand a word of it, but maybe also because we looked like we were about to die. My bandmates and I were a little confused, too, because even though the club in Osaka was a lot like the ones we'd played in New York, there were actually people at this one. Lots of them. In fact, the place was packed.

"Are these people here to get their asses handed to them by our gravity-defying hot rock action?" I wondered. "Or are they just here to watch a bunch of old dudes muddle their way through a couple songs before they start pelting us with beer bottles, ashtrays, and whatever else they can send sailing at our heads?"

There was only one way to find out. So I gave my bandmates one of those hot rock nods that signifies the start of a hot rock show and

---

2 Osaka is pretty much the Chicago of Japan. It's an awesome city, but you can tell most of the people living there would really like to move to Tokyo someday.

we launched into our first hot rock jam. And that's when something crazy happened, the people in the audience actually knew the song. They even sang along.

"That's weird," I thought.

In my fragile state, a part of me worried we had just become the victim of some elaborate prank where some wily bastard convinced a bunch of Japanese people to show up to the club and pretend to like our band. But then I realized that would take too much planning[3] and instead decided we should probably just play another song and see if it happened again.

And it did.

As we powered our way through our second number, I looked out into the crowd of people packed in there like, um, whatever those little salty fish that come in a can are called, and saw them once again bobbing their heads along with the music. Pretty Japanese girls were mouthing along with every word I sang and leather-clad Japanese rocker dudes were pumping their fists in approval. It was electrifying to finally play for a crowd of people who were there not because they were afraid we might blow off their wedding if they failed to show, but because they actually thought we were good at rock, maybe even kind of awesome at rock.

"Do you think you can handle some more, Osaka?" I screamed, basking in the adulation.

Adding to the relative insanity of it all was that it was all taking place in Japan, the most mind-blowing place I'd ever seen in my whole life. None of us had ever been there before and we found everything we encountered to be completely fascinating.

"Look, a vending machine that dispenses beer right in the middle of the street!" I said to my friend Carl, whom we brought along to give the appearance of an entourage, before insisting he take a picture of me pounding a can of Asahi right next to a police officer's head.

"The soap dispenser in this men's room is remarkably well-designed

---

3 Or would it? My friend Charlie Todd actually did this to a band from Vermont playing their very first show in New York City.

and efficient," my friend and Valley Lodge guitar player John would tell me.

"Not to mention completely adorable!" I'd respond.

"I know, right?"

"Heeheeheeheeheehee!"

As awesome as everything was, though, it didn't take long for us to realize that the reason Japanese tourists took so many pictures when they come to America isn't because they were culture shocked like us. They just think Americans are total morons. We couldn't disagree, either. We felt like pantsless cavemen compared to these people.

From Osaka we continued on to Kyoto[4] for not only the second show of the tour, but what would also mark the very first time we'd just played a show and then actually had another show to play right afterward. Prior to then, we'd always played every show like it was our last—not because that's what you're supposed to do, but because—between the jobs, babies, and other stuff I mentioned earlier—we truly didn't know if all four of us would even wind up in the same room together again. To actually have another show lined up made us feel like a real band.

"How was the club last night compared to the venues you play in America?" Ryo, a translator assigned to help us survive the tour, asked me in the van.

"It was much, much smaller than what we're used to," I lied. "But we really enjoy playing intimate shows like that. Really gets us back to our roots, you know?"

---

4 If you ever want to just plain shit your pants, go to Kyoto, as it's quite possibly the most beautiful place on the entire planet, full of centuries-old temples, strolling geishas, and so much natural beauty your camera will explode trying to document it. A bit of history: During World War II, when America decided it might be a good idea to blow up Japan completely, the U.S. government was especially keen on dropping an atomic bomb on Kyoto because, as one of the country's intellectual strongholds, they figured its residents would be "better able to appreciate the significance of the weapon," which is to say they thought the people of Kyoto were smart enough to really "get it" when their entire city was torched. In the end, though, Secretary of War Henry L. Stimson insisted Kyoto be the one place spared of U.S. crosshairs because he'd gone there for his honeymoon and, presumably, shit his pants, too, something one can only hope Mrs. Stimson was cool with.

Embrace the fantasy, I figured.

Our show in Kyoto was another stunner, simply because it once again resembled a show in which a real rock band gets on stage and there are a lot of people there to not only see them, but actually to enjoy them, and—who knows?—maybe even secretly fantasize about passing each band member around like a goddamn rag doll as they take turns licking him from head-to-toe.

"We did it again!" I said to my bandmates as I leaned up against our van and guzzled one of those beers you can drink right there on the street and no one can say a damn thing about it.

And that's when our expectations were once again exceeded.

As my bandmates and I stood there patting ourselves on the back for what we were certain was another successful rock assault, five uniformed college girls stumbled out of the club we'd just decimated. Four of them were hammered and one of them was really, really hammered, so much in fact that she couldn't help but collapse on the ground and immediately start hosing down the streets of Kyoto with what appeared to be roughly five gallons of beer, nine pounds of noodles, and an unquantifiable mass of unidentifiable pink stuff.

"Maybe we're not so different after all," I thought.

But then something just plain insane happened. Two of the hammered girls peeled the really, really hammered girl off the sidewalk and carried her off into the blurry (at least to her anyway) night. Then the other two hammered girls got down on their hands and knees and began cleaning up all the puke. As my bandmates and I watched this all go down, our heads practically exploded. Needless to say, we got some pretty great pictures of that, too.

From Kyoto we soldiered on to Nagoya[5], high-fiving, whipping off our shirts and twirling them over our heads every inch of the way. The Nagoya show was yet another scorcher, a super blast even. And I should probably tell you all about it someday. But the fact is, we've got more important things to discuss here: Tokyo, the main

---

5 Nagoya is pretty much the Philadelphia of Japan. You can take that however you want.

This is me roaming the streets of Tokyo in my spare time. I'm
pretty sure that is a doctor's office of some sort behind me.
(photo credit: Dale May)

event, the final stop of the tour, and the culmination of our fantastic rock 'n' roll journey.

I had expected Tokyo to be the Japanese equivalent of New York
City. In fact, as we approached the city limits, I almost felt like we
were coming home. But I soon realized that comparing Tokyo to New
York is a total insult. To Tokyo, that is. In fact, if Tokyo and New
York were in prison together, New York would be Tokyo's bitch, with
Tokyo buying New York for a carton of cigarettes and having inter-
course with its face for weeks on end just to show it who's boss. I
mean that, of course, in the nicest of ways. It's just that Tokyo has so

much to offer.[6] It's like New York times ten but still crammed into the same amount of space and then popped into the microwave at full heat for ten minutes. You must go.

As we pulled up to the hotel in Tokyo, my bandmates had a little surprise for me.

"The guys and I have been talking," John said. "And we've decided that you really ought to have your own hotel room for a change."

"That's so sweet," I thought.

Naturally, I assumed the guys wanted to reward me for all the hot rocking I'd been doing, but it turned out that they just didn't want to put up with my snoring anymore. I was a little hurt, but I couldn't blame them. I do snore a lot, like a bear even.[7] And while I might have felt a bit shunned, I was actually kind of psyched, too, because my Tokyo hotel room had a very special feature.

Over the course of the tour, I'd become increasingly fascinated with Japanese toilets, you might even say obsessed. I'd use them wherever and whenever possible and then document them in blushing. sometimes even excruciating detail on my blog—what they looked like, their most exhilarating features and, perhaps most importantly, how they made me feel both "down there" and deep down inside my heart of hearts. And my hotel room in Tokyo just happened to have what I consider to be the Holy Grail of Japanese toilets. Sure, I'd seen it before, but up until then I never thought I had the level of privacy or intimacy required to really go to town, to really become one with it.

To the naked eye, the Holy Grail looks pretty much like a regular toilet. But then on the side there's this command center, like it might instantly transform into a jet fighter at any moment. And I had seen a bidet—those European ass-blasting machines—before, but I had never bothered to use one because I figured if I wanted my ass to be all wet and drippy like that, I never would have gone to the bathroom in the first place.

---

6 And I assure you 99.99999 percent of it has nothing to do with prison sex.
7 I'm hoping some of the more attractive readers of this book get to find that out for themselves in the very near future.

Upping the ante on things, the Japanese have managed to combine the toilet and the bidet into one futuristic machine that's probably illegal in most countries. So, with our final show of the tour, the climax of our rock 'n' roll odyssey, just a couple of hours away, I decided to shift my priorities and take the Holy Grail for a little test drive.

I walked into the bathroom and shut the door behind me. Sure, I was alone, but I wanted to make sure I was really, really alone. Then I sat down on the toilet and used it to the best of my gastrointestinal abilities, which—considering the fact that I'd spent the past week ingesting nothing but beer, sushi, and whatever else I could possibly lather in wasabi and chili oil—was pretty impressive.[8]

The initial transaction concluded, I began to inspect the command center. There, I saw a button emblazoned with what looked like the letter "m" being sprinkled with water droplets.

"Ladies and gentleman, I give you the butt button," I thought.

In front of the butt button was a volume knob of sorts, so I just cranked it up as high as it would go because I figured "Fuck it, I'm on vacation."

Then I closed my eyes, took a deep breath, and pressed the butt button. Suddenly, a jet stream came out. And I don't know if there was an electronic eye on this thing or what, but when I hit the butt button, somehow it just . . . found me right where I needed to be found. And up until that point in my life, I had never given much thought to if I got blasted in the anus with water at what temperature and water pressure I would want it to be. But it didn't matter because the Japanese had figured that out for me, too. As it turns out, it's exactly 72 degrees and sort of like being gently tapped in the anus over and over again. It's beautiful. So I began repeatedly hitting the butt button as fast as the futuristic apparatus would let me.

After about forty-five minutes of this, I was drenched in sweat and slowly fading in and out of consciousness. Then I looked down

---

8 Apologies for the graphic details here, but, among other things, I am a journalist and am obligated to present the facts as I see them.

at the command center again. This time I saw another button, which had a silhoutte of a woman on it.

"The lady-parts button," I presumed.

It felt like forbidden territory. I know I'm not a lady and I wasn't even sure how the electronic eye would assess the situation. And I certainly didn't want to confuse the technology. But then I just thought "When am I going to start living my life?"

Then I closed my eyes again, took another deep breath, threw in the sign of the cross for good measure, and pressed the lady-parts button. This time another jet stream came out, only this time it hit me in what some people, including me, like to call the taint.[9] Like most people, I had spent my whole life trying to avoid letting exactly this sort of thing ever happen to me. But once it did, I couldn't imagine how I managed to go all those years without being blasted in the taint with water every single day of life. It was intoxicating. So then I started hitting the taint button as fast as it would let me. Then I went back to the butt button. Then I went back to the taint button. Then I went back to the butt button. And then I went back to the taint button again. And again.

After about two hours of this, I felt as if I were floating over my own body as I looked down on it. I'm also pretty sure I saw that bright light that people who've had near-death experiences always talk about. And I was about to go back for more when John burst into my room screaming "Come on, we gotta go rock the fuck out of Tokyo!"

Ripped from another dimension, I pulled up my pants, marched out of there with my head held high, and rocked the fuck out of Tokyo with a cleaner ass and taint area[10] than anyone who's ever rocked the fuck out of Tokyo before.

---

9 I'd like to think I don't need to tell you this, but—in case you don't already know—the taint is that little patch of skin between the anus and whatever you've got up front. My doctor told me this bit of anatomy is actually called the perineum. But what fun is that? If you ask me, that guy just needs to get over himself already.

10 I know what you're thinking. Does having an especially clean ass and taint area really make that much of a difference? And to that I say: you bet your ass and taint it does.

Our show in Tokyo that night was the stuff of legend (well, to me anyway). Not only was the club four times the size of all the clubs we'd played in Japan thus far, but there was also four times as many people there and they seemed even more into it than all those other people I already told you about. We got a second encore and everything. I was so pumped I even got the courage to finally test out some of the Japanese I'd been practicing in the van on a gorgeous girl who'd spent the entire show standing right in front me, singing along with every word and seemingly getting lost in my bloodshot eyes.

"*Odori ga sugoku umai des ne,*" I told her. "*Koko o so wa te.*"

She ran away pretty quickly after that. But I guess if a total stranger told me I was a fantastic dancer, and then followed up by instructing me to "touch him here," I probably would have done the same. Oh, well, they seemed like the perfect words at the time.

Still coming down from what felt like the greatest rock show of all-time, I woke up the following morning confronted by the sobering actuality that it was time to go home—back to America, back to reality, back to waiting two weeks to hear whether or not one of my bandmates was able to play a gig or it turned out his wife was really counting on him to go to that engagement party with her after all.

Before I came crashing down to earth just like the mighty Icarus, however, there was still a matter of unfinished business to attend to. Because of my Z-list celebrity, the Gibson guitar company had loaned us a few guitars to use on the tour. And also because of my Z-list celebrity, we had to return the guitars to their office in Tokyo before we left the country. The original plan was to slow down to about ten miles per hour and just toss them out the side of the van to whomever was standing out front so that we might be able to squeeze in a bit more sightseeing before heading to the airport. But when we got there, a Gibson employee was outside waiting for us and—because he is Japanese—[11] insisted that we come inside, meet

---

11 The Japanese are a delightfully hospitable people.

the whole staff, tour the entire facility, and drink some tea with everybody.

"Let's make it quick," I muttered to my bandmates as we reluctantly followed behind.

Once we got inside, however, I immediately changed my tune. There, standing to greet us, was Tomoko, a preternaturally beautiful Japanese woman who appeared to have subtle track lighting around her entire impossibly bewitching frame. The fact that she also happened to work at my favorite guitar company only added to her allure. And the fact that I absolutely didn't want to leave Japan at all had me officially thinking crazy.

"Maybe I don't need get on that plane with the guys," I thought. "Maybe I could just stay here in Japan and keep being a huge rock star. And maybe Tomoko and I could move in someplace together, settle down, start filling the place up with half-Japanese babies, and maybe even get three or four of those life-affirming toilets."

The more I thought about it, the less it sounded crazy and the more it sounded like a fucking plan. That all changed, however, when the head of Gibson Japan walked into the room, shook my hand, and said, "So, Dave, we understand you really enjoy the toilets here in Japan."

"Really?" I asked, trying to act like I had no idea what he was talking about. "What would ever make you think that?"

"We read your blog," he said. "We *all* read your blog."

"You what?" I thought, my skin turning even paler than usual.

As I looked around, I noticed that every Gibson employee in the room had their hands politely pressed to their lips as they quietly snickered to themselves. Except for one, however—Tomoko. Instead, she just stood there giving me one of those looks that people tend to give you when they know you've traveled all the way to other side of the earth and the only thing you really seem to care about is the fact that the toilets there are designed so you could probably go without changing your underwear the entire trip next time.

It was in that moment that I realized maybe it was time to go back home after all, back to my old life, the one where I wasn't a huge rock star, I was just some old guy with a guitar who, if he wanted to get his taint cleaned, had to do it the old-fashioned way.[12]

"Thanks, everybody," I said.

"You're welcome," they replied.

"And thank you, Tomoko," I said.

She just kind of nodded and got back to her paperwork after that. Hey, I tried.

As sad as I was to get on the plane home, it gave me a lot of time to reflect about things—Japan, the tour, Tomoko, rock 'n' roll, and just life in general. And somewhere over Siberia it finally hit me.

"It doesn't matter that I'm not some huge rock star," I thought. "And it also doesn't matter if I never make it back to Japan again."

The only thing that mattered was that simple act of rocking out, of finding that one thing you love doing more than anything else in the world and doing it to the point where people worry you have some kind of medical condition. And rocking out doesn't have to mean playing guitar in a band, either. It can be whatever you want it to be, whether it be stamp collecting, gardening, mechanical bull riding, accounting, or maybe even knitting to the point where people can't stop themselves from gathering around you to bear witness to your unstoppable wefting and warping ways.[13]

As it turns, however, rocking out for me means actually strapping on a guitar, plugging it into a huge amplifier, and then strangling that thing like it was a goddamn wild animal hellbent on killing me, which, as it turns out, is actually a lot cooler than any of that other stuff I just mentioned.

Unless, of course, to you rocking out means parking yourself on a Japanese toilet, holding on for dear life, and claiming your destiny at long last.

In that case, we're pretty much neck and neck.

---

12 You know, with the liquid soap, the sponge, the cowboy hat, the disco ball, and whatever else I think might really help take things to the next level.
13 This is knitting lingo. I looked it up.

The Time I Went to Prison

The joint, the hoosegow, the gray bar hotel. Call it what you want, but I've always held a fascination for correctional facilities and the incarcerated in general. Otis,[1] for example, was my favorite character on *The Andy Griffith Show*. He was a man with a story to tell.

This is my story.

I was drinking with my friends Carl and Clark one night at a bar in Hell's Kitchen when suddenly, from out of nowhere, I got an idea.

"Wouldn't it be funny if I did a comedy show in prison?" I slurred.

"That would be hilarious!" Clark said, choking on his beer. "You'd die!"

"Yeah, they'd totally kill you!" Carl agreed with a smile. "It would be so great!"

"I know, right?" I agreed back for some reason.

We spent the next few minutes busting our guts over how my comedy routine might go over in prison, the various ways in which the inmates would torture, then kill me, all the nonconsensual intercourse I would be subjected to both before and after my death,

---

1 In case you haven't seen it, Otis was the town drunk on the show. He'd sleep all his benders off in one of Mayberry's two jail cells, letting and then locking himself in with the sheriff's key as he did it. It was funny every time.

and who would have to call my parents to tell them where to pick up the body. We were having a really nice time.

When I woke up the next afternoon, though I struggled to remember exactly why I'd brought up the topic of prison in the first place, I thought, "You know what would be *really* funny? If I went ahead and called an actual prison to set up a show."

As I sat on the edge of my bed giggling uncontrollably to myself in my underwear, I was pretty sure it was one of the best ideas I'd had in a really long time. I decided to hop on the Internet and research what prisons were convenient to my apartment. And, as it turned out, there was a place called Sing Sing about thirty miles north of New York City in Ossining, New York, just a train ride away. It is a very popular, very prisony prison. I decided I should probably give them a call right away.

"Sing Sing Correctional Facility," a voice on the other end grunted after a couple rings.

"Hello," I said. "I'd like to speak to the comedy booker."

The line got quiet. As it turned out, Sing Sing didn't have a comedy booker. Undaunted, I pressed on and, after a few seconds of hushed conversation on the other end, was connected with the "deputy of programs."

"Hi, this is Dave Hill . . . from show business," I said.

"Of course, Dave!" the deputy replied. "How can I help you today?"

"I'd like to come up there and give your inmates the show of a lifetime!"[2]

After a few minutes of back and forth, I succeeded in booking myself a show at Sing Sing, a place I was determined to make every bit as fun as its name suggests, if only for a little while. I had hoped the deputy would have just said, "How soon can you get here?" But apparently they had a pretty action-packed schedule already and the show had to be slated for about six weeks out. It was a little frus-

---

2 Alright, our conversation might not have gone down exactly like that, but it's my book and that's how I choose to remember it.

trating, but I was still thrilled and immediately called Carl and Clark to tell them the good news.

"Sing Sing here I come!" I screamed.

Carl and Clark seemed just as excited about things as I was and, just as I had hoped, found my booking a show in a prison even funnier than our hypothetical conversation the night before.

"This is the greatest thing ever!" Carl said. "You'll be killed instantly!"

"I know!" I laughed. "I know!"

In the weeks leading up to my Sing Sing debut, Carl, Clark, and I found the idea of me going to prison to be increasingly funny every time we discussed it. We even told all our friends about it, and it was funny every time then, too. About a week before my prison debut, when the reality of my situation finally kicked in, I suddenly didn't find it quite as funny anymore. Instead, it seemed more like some sort of horrible prank I was inexplicably about to play on myself.

"What's to stop a murderer who's behind bars for life from killing again, maybe even just to break up the day a little bit?" I wondered.

I came up empty.

"I'm a dead man," I moaned to myself.

Suddenly, all I could think about were the innumerable ways my show could go horribly wrong. I saw myself bombing, with microphone feedback filling the airspace where I'd hoped laughter would go. A lone inmate would approach the stage, slow-clapping at me before removing a shank[3] from his waistband and driving it straight through my ribs, causing the inmates to laugh for the first time of the night. Then he'd call all his friends over to take turns shanking me, playing soccer with my head, calling me names, and having sex with my face. As I faded in and out of consciousness, I'd make eye contact with a corrections officer standing just a few feet away.

---

3 A shank—or shiv, as it is also sometimes called—is a makeshift knife. Inmates use them because, as you might imagine, their access to actual knives in prison isn't great. The fun thing is you can make a shank out of whatever you want—a screwdriver, an old toothbrush, or whatever. As long as you can somehow get it sharp enough to puncture flesh, you're in business.

"Sorry, buddy," his eyes would say. "I got a wife and kids and six weeks until I reach my pension—you're on your own. Oh, and you need to work on your comedic timing."

In the week leading up to the show, I watched this movie in my mind repeatedly. Sometimes I'd see it from my own perspective and sometimes I'd see it on one of those grainy security camera monitors I'd seen on those cable television prison shows.

"An auditorium full of furious and violent felons is no laughing matter," the narrator would say. "Funnyman Dave Hill found out the hard way."

Then they'd zoom in and freeze on my face and add some dramatic piano music to let the viewer know that I was pretty much the deadest guy ever.

There were no two ways about it—I had to get out of this mess. To that end, I decided I would simply write an e-mail to the deputy at Sing Sing explaining that, as it turned out, I had been implanted with a baboon heart at birth and—while it had served me well for most of my life—it was now acting up and if I didn't have surgery on it right away, I'd be dead by the weekend, which meant that I regretfully had no choice but to cancel the show. I'd even throw in something about how upset I was that I couldn't just head on over to prison immediately after surgery because my uptight cardiothoracic surgeon was being a total dick about it.

Just as I was about to compose that e-mail, however, I saw there was another e-mail already waiting for me in my inbox. It was from the deputy at Sing Sing.

"I was just checking in to see if you were all set for your big show next week," the deputy wrote. "The inmates are *so* excited to see you."

"'*So* excited to see me'?" I thought. "What the hell is that supposed to mean?"

And then I remembered: when I arranged the show, the deputy had asked me to send him a photo of myself so he could make a poster to hang around the prison. I had intentionally sent him the

COMEDY NIGHT AT SING SING

Presenting Comedian

Dave Hill

As seen on HBO Cinemax, MTV, VH1, Comedy Central, Court TV, Sundance Channel

Thursday, July 9, 2009
Evening Module
Auditorium

If you are interested
and have one year
clean disciplinary
write to John Mahoney,
Special Subjects
First come first served

Brilliant."
-New York Magazine

"Hill's loose jabs and affable, nice-guy demeanor are what make his gently absurdist comedy so enjoyable."
-The Onion

"I saw a great young guy last named Dave Hill who is really funny."
-Robin Williams, MoviesOnline.ca

"Hill's deadpan delivery as a talk show host who has severely overestimated his own coolness is priceless."
-AM New York

"Like watching a self-important teenager strut around his bedroom, a fantasy world of his own fame complete with nunchucks and all that is 'totally sweet'."
-The Aspen Times

"Thanks to his quirky humor and knack for attention-getting, Dave Hill has shot to the stop in a surprisingly short period of time."
-Time Out New York

Ok. To Post
D. Brown Act Sgt 6/17/9

This flyer helped convince three hundred Sing Sing inmates to come to my comedy show instead of whatever else might have been going on that night in prison. I was pumped.

most effeminate looking photo of myself[4] I could find because I thought that would be just one more funny thing in this whole scenario. And maybe it was, for a time, but now the men of Sing Sing knew exactly what I looked like. And, since convicts are historically irritable people and some of them might have been getting out soon, I realized I had no choice but to accept my fate.

"I'm really looking forward to coming," I wrote back to the deputy, tears gathering in the corners of my eyes. "Oh, and, you know, just so I might better prepare myself, can you tell me exactly what sort of guys are '*so* excited to see me'?"

"So far about two hundred and fifty inmates have signed up for your show," the deputy later replied. "They are all maximum-security violent felons and they really like jokes about being in jail. They will no doubt be your 'toughest' crowd." Then, just to fuck with me, he put in one of those smiley face emoticons.

"That sick bastard!" I thought before slamming my laptop shut.

Despite my constant terror in the week prior, when the day of the show finally arrived, a sort of peaceful resolve washed over me, kind of like how the death row inmates always seem on those cable prison shows I was just talking about. Sure, I might get shanked or made someone's bitch but—dammit—these guys were gonna get one hell of a show!

"Maybe I can just pretend I'm Bob Hope doing a USO show, only instead of soldiers I'll be performing for murderers, rapists, and other guys who hate rules," I thought. "Everything will be just fine."

I had originally planned to head up to Sing Sing alone, but in the end I decided to bring Carl, Clark, and my friend Laura with me. If anything actually did go horribly wrong, I wanted someone to be able to tell my story. And since Carl and Laura were comedians, too, I had the option to push them on stage at any moment if I got too lonely out there by myself.

To help get into the spirit of things, on the drive up we took turns

---

4 There are plenty to choose from. What can I say? I look a lot like my mother. And sometimes I dress like her, too.

reading aloud from a dictionary of prison slang I'd found on the Internet. As it turned out, they have fun words for just about everything in prison. There was, of course, "keister," a verb meaning to hide something in your ass, and "eye fucking," which means to stare at someone aggressively for much longer than he'd normally be comfortable with. "Feed the warden" means to use a toilet,[5] "jack shack" refers to the cell of a frequent masturbator, and "quit swinging on these nuts" is what you might say to someone who is being a sycophant.[6] But our hands-down favorite was "fifi," a fun word used to describe an artificial vagina made from a hand towel, a plastic bag, some hand lotion, a few rubberbands, and, presumably, lots and lots of tears.

Sing Sing itself occupies a stretch of land along the banks of the Hudson River that would likely be prime real estate if it weren't for its current residents. As soon as we pulled onto the grounds, a corrections officer rolled up to us in an unmarked van.

"Hi." I gulped. "We're here to do a comedy show."

The corrections officer stared at us blankly for a few seconds before directing us to the main entrance on the other side of the building. As we pulled away, he shook his head in the way those weary townspeople always do in horror movies after they've just reluctantly given directions to that wooded area where all those people were mysteriously killed that one summer to a carload of wayward and oversexed youth who think they're gonna live forever.

After parking the car, we nervously made our way through Sing Sing's massive front doors, where we were met by a handful of surprisingly upbeat corrections officers who guided us through airport-level security procedures. Unfortunately, they made us ditch the cameras we'd hoped to use to take all sorts of really fun "Let me outta here!" pictures to show friends and family around Thanksgiving and other holiday gatherings. Once we finally proved we weren't

---

5 You know, for number two. Think about it.
6 This is in case you don't feel like just calling him a sycophant, which admittedly doesn't sound nearly as prisony.

trying to smuggle in one of those birthday cakes with the big file baked inside, we finally received hand stamps visible only under the ultraviolet lights that hung beside each of the gates that separated the inmates from freedom.

"No glow, no go!" the corrections officer bellowed not-so-jokingly as he pounded our hands with the stamp a bit harder than seemed necessary.

Apparently, the otherwise invisible stamps are used to prevent inmates from doing that thing that always happens in movies where someone clubs some other guy over the head with a pillowcase full of loose change, drags him into a supply closet, strips him naked, changes into his clothes, and then walks out of prison like he was just visiting or something. In light of this, I made a mental note not to wash my hands too aggressively at any point during our visit so I wouldn't end up dating someone named Rollo by the end of the day.

As we passed through the ancient and ominous brick and steel corridors on the way to the auditorium where the show would be taking place, I felt as if we were suddenly in some old prison movie.

"This is so cool!" I said to the corrections officer leading the way.

He didn't seem to agree, so I decided to just keep my mouth shut and stop pretending I was James Cagney in the role of Cody Jarrett, the ruthless, deranged leader of a criminal gang who winds up behind bars in the movie *White Heat*, something I was really enjoying but whatever.

When we arrived at the auditorium, a small sign at the entrance announced that my show would preempt that week's movie night, a screening of *How to Lose Friends & Alienate People*.

"No biggie," I thought. " These guys probably know plenty about that subject already."

Shortly after we got settled backstage, the inmates began to file in. And as much as I'd promised myself I wouldn't, I still found myself trying to guess what each guy did to wind up there.

"The guy with the mustache and glasses looks kind of rapey," I thought. "And that guy over there with the shaved head and hairy knuckles? Strangler all the way. A bit stabby, too, I guess."

Still others looked like they just might be into dumping bodies into a river or maybe setting buildings on fire while people they didn't like all that much were still inside. As their numbers grew, however, it became hard to focus on any of that stuff. Before long, they just seemed like a bunch of guys who all happen to work out a lot, have the exact same taste in clothes, and like to get face tattoos when the mood strikes. There ended up being about three hundred inmates in attendance, which—being in show business and all—I was happy to see.

"Maybe that sexy poster wasn't such a bad idea after all," I thought.

In the event that I needed to stall for time, I'd brought along a small guitar and amp combo.[7] So I decided to get the show started by playing overly animated heavy metal guitar solos, a skill I picked up in my lonely teen years. I'm not suggesting these guys were savage beasts or anything, but, not entirely ruling out that possibility, I figured a little music couldn't hurt. And much to my relief, it actually seemed to work. By the time I stepped up to the microphone, the inmates appeared to be willing to hold off on shanking me or even hurting my feelings for at least a few minutes.

"I never thought I'd have the chance to say this, but it's really great to be here in prison with all you guys," I said to kick things off.

I don't normally like to cater to a specific audience when writing my material, but I decided to make an exception this time and come up with a set just for the guys at Sing Sing. Most of it had to do with whether or not I'd end up being anyone's bitch should I ever wind up in prison. It was hard to make out exactly what they were saying amid all the clapping, laughing, and hollering, but the general consensus seemed to be that, if that ever did happen, I would be passed from cell to cell quicker than the latest issue of *Juggs* magazine. It was a little unsettling at first, but then the part of me that just wants to be loved more than anything else won out and I was flattered. A lot.

---

7 Also, I figured it couldn't hurt to have a long piece of wood between me and any outraged attacker should things go south right out of the gate.

"Who here is from out of town?" I asked the inmates once I got a bit more comfortable.

They seemed to enjoy that one.

"And who came from farthest away today?" I continued.

That line sort of confused them. As it turned out, most of the Sing Sing population hails from the New York City area. Still, they laughed politely until a guy in the front row slowly looked around, raised his arm, and yelled, "I'm from Kansas City!"

"So, did you always want to live on the East Coast?" I asked. "Or did it just work out that way?"

I thought I had hit it out of the park with that line, but instead of convulsing with laughter the inmates just groaned in unison while slumping in their chairs.

"I guess even violent felons have feelings," I thought. "All right, noted."

Despite that momentary bump in the road, I was having a really nice time in prison and decided to hand over the mic to Carl and Laura. Carl did a short set about his fictional workout regimen and the inmates ate it up, particularly after he decided to remove his shirt and blind them with his pasty flab.

Then it was Laura's turn.

Being an entertainer and all, Laura decided to wear a lovely red dress to prison to enhance her already striking beauty, something the inmates seemed to appreciate a little more than she had anticipated. Her set was going well, but at some point she started to feel like one of those characters in a Bugs Bunny cartoon who turns into a giant lamb chop or turkey leg in front of some other character who hasn't eaten in a really long time. Only she felt that way times three hundred.

"Thank you and good night!" Laura said, ending her set early as Big House vibes won out.

As Laura took shelter backstage where the inmates could no longer drool over her, a gargantuan corrections officer who had been assigned to prevent anyone from doing anything really prisony to us during our visit walked over to her.

"Are you okay?" he asked.

"Yeah." Laura shrugged. "I guess I just got a little scared out there."

"You know why you got scared, don't you?" the officer asked.

"No. Why?" Laura asked hopefully, thinking the officer might perhaps offer her a little insight into the human psyche.

"See those guys out there?" the officer said, gesturing to my new buddies. "Those guys are all murderers and rapists."

Laura didn't appreciate his answer too much, but—having the emotional maturity of a fifteen-year-old and all—I sure got a kick out of it. Things were getting better by the second in prison as far as I was concerned. So, with Laura on close watch, I took the stage to wrap things up.

"Thanks for coming, guys," I said. "And I just want you to know I think Sing Sing is the best prison ever!"

"You're a fucking moron!" one of the inmates yelled in response.

"Is that you, Dad?" I shot back and immediately said good night. Go out on a high note, I figured.

To my sheer and unbridled delight, the inmates gave me a standing ovation before the officers began urging them back to their cells. And as we passed the cell blocks on our way back to the outside world, the sweet adulation continued.

"Dave! Dave! Dave!" they chanted in unison.

I'll be the first to admit I sometimes seek approval in the wrong places, but it was still awesome. I felt like the lord of the fucking underworld.

Before we passed through the final set of prison doors, the warden handed me a copy of the poster used to advertise my show. It looked pretty much like a typical comedy show poster with the exception of one bold block of text in the corner that read "Must have one year clean disciplinary to attend."

"Next time let's make it one month clean disciplinary!" I told him. "I wanna pack the place!"

He just looked at me after that, so I decided to focus back on all that clapping and cheering in the distance as we headed back to our car. I couldn't get enough of it, so I made sure to keep a leisurely pace.

"Would you come on?" Laura groaned at me. "I wanna get out of here."

"Look, just because you're not having a good time in prison doesn't mean I have to be miserable, too!" I scolded her before basking in the adoration of my Big House buddies some more. I felt like Tim Robbins in *The Shawshank Redemption* only I couldn't wait to come back.

"See you next year, Dave!" one of the inmates called out to me from his cell window, waving between the bars.

"Yup, see you next year," I thought, waving back. "I guess I'll just go do whatever the fuck I want now."

It was hard not to consider how wildly the inmates' lives and mine were about to diverge after all the good times we had just had together.

As we drove back to New York City, I was beaming. I had not only come out of that prison alive and unviolated but had actually managed to put on a show that everyone in attendance (other than Laura) seemed to really enjoy. But what was even more striking to me were the aftereffects of my visit to Sing Sing in the weeks that followed. My day-to-day anxiety seemed to be cut in half and I felt almost calm in situations that might have otherwise sent me into a panic. I didn't suddenly fancy myself some sort of tough guy or doer of good deeds or anything like that. It was more like the anticipation of performing in front of a few hundred violent felons had built up so much pressure inside me that I busted some sort of emotional gasket by actually going through with it. And with that pressure gone, I could suddenly breathe easy, walk with a more confident stride, and not freak out about everyday life so much. All of a sudden someone's overly loud headphones on the subway weren't quite so grating and those televisions some asshole chose to install in the back of every New York City cab weren't as annoying. I even found I could accept McDonald's completely unpredictable and seemingly arbitrary removal of the McRib from their menu as just a part of life.

I was almost embarrassed to bring up this newfound state of well-being to my therapist when I saw him the week after the show.

"They say prison changes you, but could four or five hours behind bars really count?" I wondered.

"You took a trip to the underworld," he said after squinting at me for a couple of minutes. "And it sounds like you had a really nice time."

It seemed so simple, but I had to agree with the guy. I *did* have a really nice time. And if I can have a really nice time in a room full of murderers, rapists, and other negative types, well, I reasoned, I can probably have a really nice time just about anywhere. In fact, part of me keeps wondering if spending even more time in prison, like maybe a few weeks or months, might have an even more positive effect on me.

Here's to never, ever finding out for sure.

• • • • • • • • •

Bunny[1]

I always thought I had a fairly reasonable understanding and acceptance of death. A person gets old and sick, hit by a bus, or accidentally
tossed over the side of a boat while tied up inside of a large burlap sack
late, late at night and next thing everyone knows he's dead. Even as a
little kid, I somehow got that dying was just another part of life, a sort
of victory lap at the end of a (hopefully) nice long stretch of time on
earth. When a relative would die, I'd have to put on my little navy
blazer and clip-on tie, my family and I would swing by the wake, hit
the funeral, and then afterward I'd get to hang out with all my rela-
tives and eat fancy little sandwiches, cakes, and other good stuff my
parents didn't normally keep around the house.

"Your great-grandmother died," my dad would tell me.

"Oh, cool, a party!" I'd reply. Come to think of it, I might have
been a little too accepting of death back then.

When my mother died last year, however, it was a whole other
thing. It was as if no one had ever died before in the history of time
and the very concept of death had never even existed. Learning that
my mother had died sounded about as ridiculous to me as if someone said, "Hey, Dave, did you know your mom used to play for the
Knicks? It's true."

---

1 My mom's given name was Bernadette, which was eventually shortened to Bernie,
which in turn somehow morphed into Bunny, the name everyone knew her by.

*This is me and my mom. For some reason,
I can't remember where or when this
picture was taken, but as best I can tell,
we were having a really nice time.*

"Huh?" I'd respond.

The idea of my mother being dead just didn't make any sense to me even though I saw her a few times after she died and she was about as dead as they come. I touched her, I held her hand, I kissed her. No two ways about it—dead, dead, dead. Still, I just couldn't wrap my head around the idea, so I decided it was easier to just tell myself she had moved without telling anyone. My mom had lived her entire life in Cleveland, so it seemed well within her rights to just throw a dart at a map and make a new home for herself wherever it landed, be it Paris, Paramus, or wherever.

As crazy as it sounded, the idea of my mother having moved instead of being dead was much easier to swallow. Of course I knew it wasn't true, but in the deep, dark trenches of my mind, I'd sometimes catch myself wondering how I might steal a few days and track my mother down wherever she had run off to.

"Mom, I've been looking all over for you," I'd say once I found her. "Why Akron?"

The idea that my mom had simply relocated stuck with me for months. Then one day I confronted reality. My mother was a nice lady, in fact, a great lady. She wasn't the type of person who would just move without telling anyone, leaving all her stuff behind, sticking my dad with all the house chores and making it pretty much impossible for me to borrow money from her anymore. She would have at least left some cash behind for me. It just wasn't like her at all. So, after mulling it over awhile, I finally decided to give in to the popular opinion that my mother had actually gone ahead and died. The stark truth was something I still couldn't quite comprehend, but compared to the idea that she'd just skipped town, it required much less detective work on my part. Accepting her death also made my family more comfortable letting me borrow my dad's car, handle sharp objects, and bathe without supervision.

My mother was a very spiritual and religious person, about as Irish Catholic as they come. I know she believed in an afterlife and, in fact, was pretty much counting on it, not necessarily as some sort of great reward or anything, but so she could at least have somewhere to go after she got done with earth. So, despite the various opinions on the subject, I very much hoped that she was at least enjoying a nice afterlife somewhere out there.

Of course, once I let the concepts of death and the afterlife settle in a bit more, I jumped to the next logical conclusion—that my mother could see me at any given moment. And once I began operating under that notion, I started to realize how much completely disturbing and upsetting stuff I do almost every second of the day— unthinkable, unspeakable things, many of which I should have probably closed the blinds for. At that point I decided I had to lay down some ground rules with the lady.

"Rule number one, Mom," I sighed under my breath, "stay out of the bathroom, even when I'm not in it."

To be honest, even I would rather not be around for most of the stuff I get up to in my bathroom, but I've got no choice. I was mortified to think that my mother would have to witness any of it—everything from typical, disgusting guy behavior to the application of more skincare products than any straight man should even be allowed to keep in his home. When it gets right down to it, my bathroom is just a house of shame.

Making matters worse is the fact that I live in a studio apartment.[2] My bed takes up about half the place and naturally that had to be off-limits to my mother's beyond-the-grave eyes, too. I'm not suggesting that I am in a constant state of flagrante delicto or other things requiring me to take my pants off.[3] It's just that I—like a lot of people, I'm assuming—have this habit of pulling my boxers down to my ankles in my sleep and then just letting all my various parts, both private and otherwise, hang right out there for anyone in the afterlife to see. Call me a prude or overly protective if you want, but I just don't think my mother should have to look at that sort of thing.

The rest of my apartment is mostly taken up by my desk, which is where my computer sits. And my computer, of course, is what I use to access the Internet. So, needless to say, I had to tell my mother the desk was off limits, too. I just didn't think she would understand the kind of important research I sometimes have to do.[4]

"Mom, I'm taking an online anatomy course," I'd have to tell her. She was a smart lady—I just don't think she'd buy it.

With my bathroom, bed, and desk all off-limits, that leaves my mom with just the entryway and kitchen. And, sure, me sitting on the floor tying my shoes or standing at the stove making spaghetti are both really great in their own way, what with all the grunting sounds and the way I check to see if the spaghetti is ready by throwing an entire handful at the ceiling. But I tend to think my mother deserves better.

Aside from my concerns about what exactly my mother can or can't see from the hereafter, though, I would really just love to be together with her one last time. It's not like we'd even have to do anything particularly fun or interesting, either. We could just sit in the den together and watch TV. We wouldn't even have to watch my shows or agree on something we both might like. We could watch

---

2 I know what you're thinking: but Dave, that's impossible because you're a major, major celebrity and there's no way you live in anything less than a sprawling New York City apartment like the one from *Three Men and a Baby*, where you do indoor rock climbing, work on choreography, and even put on the occasional laser show. But it's true.
3 As you can probably imagine, though, I do all right for myself.
4 See *Tasteful Nudes*.

all of her programs, even the sucky ones. I'd even let her have the remote. Right now, sitting quietly in a room with my mother watching *Antiques Roadshow* or whatever else might be on PBS seems like just about the greatest thing that could ever happen. Or maybe we could watch *Goodfellas* again—a movie that becomes twice as entertaining when you watch it with my mother as she claims to be repulsed by it while secretly delighting in every bloody, profanity-laced scene.

"This is awful!" my mother grimaced as we watched it together one night years ago. "Their language is horrible and they all just seem like really negative, terrible people."

"I can turn it off if you want."

"No. I don't want you to have to get up."

While my mom might be gone, my dad is thankfully still around, so I find myself determined to make the most of our time together, which, statistically speaking, is probably not going to be all that much longer. Before too long, one of us is going to be dead and—between you and me—the smart money is on him. Lately, we've been spending most of our time together at the house, chatting and drinking coffee of various strengths. And when that gets old, we usually grab some food together. And if there's one nice byproduct of my mother dying, it's that the idea of cooking or—even worse—heating up some leftovers, is one I can easily defeat with the mere suggestion of pulling the car out of the garage and heading someplace for breakfast, lunch, dinner, or, on a good day, all three.

"What should we get for lunch?" I'll ask him. "Italian? Mexican? Indian?"

"Yes," he'll reply.

"Oh, Davey, that's extravagant," my mom would have said were she still here, stopping our plan in its tracks. "Why don't we just stay home and I'll boil something?"

On his own, though, my dad is a total pushover. Still, things just aren't the same. For my entire life, it was a given that when the check came it was definitely my dad's problem, not mine. But from the time my mother was diagnosed with cancer a couple of years ago, straight up to the day she died and, now, over a year later, when all evidence seems to support the death theory, things have somehow changed.

It all started one night when my dad and I went out to dinner. We had a nice meal, and, when the check came I did my patented reach-for-the-wallet-like-I-might-actually-chip-in (yeah, right!) routine, and for the first time ever my dad didn't stop me. In fact, I was not only able to remove my wallet from my pocket, but I was able to set it down on the table, and—after a prolonged staring contest—I was actually able to use the money in it to pay for dinner. I figured it was just a fluke. But as we went out for meal after meal after meal, each time the check came my dad would just sit there like some kind of crazy person whose pockets weren't lined with cash.

"What the hell have you done with my father, mister?" I wanted to yell at him one night. But you just can't go doing that at P.F. Chang's. People get freaked out and the next thing you know they won't even let you pose for a photo with the big cement horses out front.

Naturally, this new pattern with me and my father had me worried. Not only had my father just lost his wife, but now it seemed like he didn't even have enough money to pay for Chinese food. I called up my brother Bob in a panic.

"Is Dad okay?" I asked him. "Is he having money problems?"

"No way," Bob said. "He's set for life. The guy could probably live another fifty years and still not run out of money."

I was relieved to hear this, but I also wondered what the hell was up. And it eventually occurred to me that the only possible reason my dad might have for letting me pick up the check if he wasn't broke was to show me respect, to let me know that he knew I was a financially secure and responsible adult who could take himself and his father out to a half-decent restaurant. That's nice and all, but I just wanted to tell my dad that I really don't need that kind of respect. I always thought we had a nice thing going with our old arrangement.

"I told you to just cook something at home," I could hear my mother say as I pondered my rapidly thinning wallet.

With my mother dead and gone and my dad slowly bleeding me dry, it's hardly a surprise that I became depressed. And to deal with it, I tried every possible method of dragging myself up from the depths—psychotherapy, acupuncture, homeopathy, holistic medicine, alcoholism, jai alai, prescription drugs, and just about everything else they sell at CVS, including that soap with the so-called "moisturizing beads." Nothing worked. Until I discovered running, that is, an activity I'd been vehemently opposed to my whole life. Even when chased by animals with an overabundance of strength, claws, sharp teeth, and almost no patience to speak of, I don't recommend it. Despite my disdain for it, though, running is the one thing that's gotten me to stop pondering the abyss and instead just go out for a sandwich or something.

Shortly after my mom died, I went running back home in Cleveland on an especially frigid day when it occurred to me that I might very well be freezing my dick off. I don't mean that in the figurative, colloquial sense, either. I was genuinely concerned that my member and I were about to part company for good. After patting my crotch in a panic, I determined that my penis, having shrunken down to little more than a cashewlike nub, was thankfully still where it had always been but was now seemingly fighting for its life, clinging to my barely warm body with all its might. It was like a scene from *Titanic,* all playing out within the confines of my trousers. And I decided the only way my penis—if you could even call it that by then—was going to survive was if I just sort of fluffed myself periodically in hopes that some blood might make its way to my downtown real estate. It occurred to me, however, that I was in public and people could totally see me. So, in order to avoid making the papers, I hastily devised a mathematical equation that told me if I only massaged my privates every hundred yards or so, it would look like I was just adjusting my pants and not actually fondling my goods in public. But, of course, then I remembered there was one person whose gaze never left me—my mother. Embarrassed, I tried to explain to her that desperate times call for desperate measures. Between already losing her and my dad making me pay for dinner all the time, freezing my John Thomas off was an indignity I just didn't think I could handle.

"Listen, Mom, you need to make a choice right here and now," I told her. "Would you rather have me run down the street massaging my genitals or lose the ability to ever use the group showers at the gym again with confidence?"

I chose to believe she preferred the former, so I continued down the street, huffing and puffing and vigorously rubbing my crotch area like it would be weird not to. Crisis averted.

Even greater than the fear that my mom's watching me doing something we both would rather not have her see, I struggled with not having her around. Aside from simply wanting to spend time with my mom, I wanted her to know everything was going to be all right with me, even though there are still moments when I'm not entirely sure of it myself. Despite occasional breakthroughs, I spent most of my life wishing I could know that my mother was proud of me, that she understood me, and that she wasn't worried that I was going to end up a criminal, a showgirl, or both.

Given my life pursuits—going into comedy, playing in rock bands, writing sometimes long and rambling essays, and other things that don't guarantee financial or emotional stability—my mother never seemed too crazy about my game plan for survival. Even when successes came, they seemed to confuse her more than anything else. In the last year or two of her life, my mom called to tell me a friend of hers had seen me on HBO.

"She was just clicking through the channels and there you were on HBO," my mom said, trying to sound impressed. "That's pretty good, right?"

"I think so," I answered. "Thanks."

"Cool, she's finally getting me and what I do," I thought. Then she dropped all pretense and asked, "What's HBO?"

My parents didn't have cable, so what I should have done to impress them was make the local news on one of my trips back home. To my mom, those people standing and waving behind the local newscaster reporting live from a Christmas tree lighting downtown were the ones with something to brag about. As long as she and her friends could tune in and watch it at six and eleven, it was the real deal. But some cable channel that you had to pay extra for? Not so much.

As hard as I tried to make her understand that I was one in an elite group of only several thousand people in America experiencing minor successes in the field of entertainment, she seemed prouder of my ability to do things like operate the microwave without supervision.

"Where did you learn to cook so well?" my mom would ask as I mixed some impossibly orange powdered cheese into a bowl of macaroni. "You should open your own restaurant! Bob, come here quick—our son's a gourmet chef!"

Once during my high school years, I decided to try my hand at baking cookies from scratch after everyone else in the family had gone to bed (a necessary prerequisite as my sisters would have attacked the dough like vultures before I would ever have had the chance to get it into the oven. It would have been like trying to grow a crop of marijuana in Snoop Dogg's backyard). As I sat in the kitchen salivating over two platefuls of slowly cooling chocolate chip cookies, my mom appeared in the doorway. She wasn't mad that I was messing up her kitchen, she was just looking to get in on the action. In an act of desperation, I offered her as many cookies as she wanted in exchange for not letting anyone else in the house know of their existence. There we sat at the kitchen table, knocking back cookie after cookie as if our lives depended on it while discussing their endless merits—how good they were just out of the oven, how good they were a few hours after they'd been out of the oven, how good they were when they were just barely cooked, and how good they were when they were cooked just a little too much.

"What makes them really good is if you throw in a little extra butter," my mother said, barely able to get the sentence out between bites. "Now promise me you'll only let me have a couple more before you get them out of my sight."

"I could just put them away now," I told her, crumbs spilling from my mouth.

"You do that and I'll stab you, David." She smiled before scooping up another handful, like one of those claw games at the amusement park.

And as we sat there chatting and laughing, a truly disturbing realization dawned on me: the woman sitting across from me was not just my mother, but also my friend. Of course, being a teenager, I couldn't bring myself to tell her that right there and then. Still, deep down inside I knew things would never be the same—we were, and always had been, friends for life. (I know, gross, right?)

In the last few months of my mother's life, once cancer and the several strokes that followed rendered her unable to stay at the house anymore, I began bringing bags of chocolate chip cookies to her in the hospital and we'd sit there eating them together one after another. The doctors told me not to feed her more than one or two a day, not because they might kill her—the cancer already had that covered—but because apparently even when you're dying, eating too many cookies is still a bad idea for some reason (science—will we ever really understand it?). Despite the urging of the medical community, though, I still gave my mother as many cookies as she wanted because I knew that—even by the time my mother was so sick she could barely speak—if she could eat cookies she was still my mother, my friend, that lady who was into *Goodfellas* way more than she'd ever admit.

On what turned out to be one of our last nights together, I stayed behind at the hospital after the rest of my family had gone home, and helped my mother eat her dinner. Like most people presented with a tray of steamed garbage, she wasn't too interested in any of it. Still, the doctors said it would be good if she could get it down, so I stood over her and made her eat every last bite, bribing her with the cookies the whole way. She kept her eye on the prize and eventually cleared her plate, so I broke out the cookies. There we sat together, mostly in silence, going cookie for cookie with each other. My mom was able to put away four cookies that night, which—given the size of the cookies and her current state—was pretty impressive. Even at my best, I'm good for only a couple before I get a stomachache.

As I set the cookies back on the counter in my mom's hospital room, I saw that she was about ready to conk out for the night. It was in that moment that I realized that none of that stuff I worried about—doing something to make my mom proud of me or have her understand me or know that I wasn't going to end up New York City's favorite deep-voiced call girl—really mattered at all.

"Are you sick of me?" I asked, pulling my coat on.

"Yes, I'm sick of you," she drawled. Then she stared at me for a few seconds and, with perfect comedic timing, said, "I love you."

I didn't plan either of these things, but those cookies were the last thing she ever ate and those words were the last she ever said to me. Sometimes even in darkness, a bright light will just come along and blind you.

Needless to say, I miss my mom terribly and even find myself sometimes forgetting she's gone as I absentmindedly reach for my phone to give her a ring until I think, "Oh . . . yeah." My only consolation is that if she were still alive, there's enough profanity and other bad stuff in this book that I'd be grounded for life.

"It's just not decent to talk like that, David," she'd say as she flipped through this book's pages. "And the title! What were you thinking?"

"I'm sorry, Mom," I'd say. "Do you want me to put the book away?"

"No. I don't want you to have to get up."

Epilogue

When my publisher told me I was contractually obligated to hand in between sixty thousand and eighty thousand words for this book, I told them to go fuck themselves. Again. I'm sorry, but it just seemed like a lot—like a word a day for the next two hundred years or something, which is insane given all the other stuff I've got going on. Even so, we did it. We really, really did it—we finished the book (I am referring to you and me now). It was a pretty wild ride, wasn't it? I mean, sure, I did the hard part, what with all the typing and everything, but you're the one who had to read it[1], which I realize is no easy feat considering the fact that I used a handful of big words that even I had to look up, and I threw in so much profanity that you would have thought I was rehearsing for a community theater production of *Scarface* (I bet that controlling bastard St. Martin is rolling over in his grave by now). Please know that I only added both of those things so my book would seem more sophisticated, which in turn makes for a richer literary experience for you, the reader. However, if you, like me, object to words like "honorificabilitudinitatibus"[2]

---

1 If you just skipped everything else before this part, that's not only cheating, it's just plain weird. Stop it or your funeral will almost definitely be poorly attended and those that do show up will only be there for the donuts and the dunking machine anyway. Don't say I didn't warn you.

2 I realize I didn't actually use the word honorificabilitudinitatibus anywhere in my book until now. But since it apparently means—according to its Latin origins anyway—something along the lines of "the state of being able to achieve honors,"

or any of the other sailor talk that wound up in here, I imagine you had to hold on extra tight just to make it here to the end. And for that I commend you. You are a champion and don't think I'm the only one who's noticed.

In addition to all the fancy language and swearing I've included in this collection, though, I feel like I covered a fair amount of ground while I was at it. In fact, I'd argue that I've told you what I would describe as "a lot of what there is to know about me, Dave Hill, a major, major celebrity, thinking man, and person of both great and wide-ranging influence." I realize this book wasn't exactly a "tell-all" or anything, but it was definitely a "tell-some." I would have written a tell-all, but then I would have been pretty much screwed when it came time to write the much-anticipated follow-up to this, my debut collection of important essays that I typed all by myself, as I wouldn't have had anything left to write about. Also, let's face it—they just didn't pay me enough money to go ahead and tell you my whole life story all in one neat little volume. (Sorry, Mr. Publisher, you're going to have to add another zero or two if you want me to write about all the stuff that happened while I wasn't wearing pants and may or may not have been wearing a mask.) I think I included most of the good stuff, though, and that's what really matters. Sure, I could have thrown in a few shower scenes or perhaps the graphic details of my many and frequent doctor appointments here and there to spice things up, especially for late-night reading, but I imagine I could do that for the European version. If the magazine store by my house has taught me anything, the people of Europe are a lot more accepting of nudity anyway, which—come to think of

---

I thought I'd throw it in now since I plan on achieving all sorts of honors and prizes and stuff for writing this book, some of which may come from Oprah or those Pulitzer bastards, some may not. Whatever. I've got plenty of space on the mantel and I'm not picky, so as long as the plaque or trophy goes with all the other stuff in my apartment, I'll probably hang onto it, at least until all that stuff I ordered from the Franklin Mint shows up. Also, as long as I'm on the topic, honorificabilitudinitatibus is the longest word in the English language featuring alternating consonants and vowels, which is not only something I just read on Wikipedia but also a really fun thing to bring up at parties, the free clinic, or wherever. Try it.

it—will be especially great when it comes time to do my book tour over there. But I digress.

All of the above aside, however, the greater question here is "What did we learn from my book?" I mean, sure, there are all those stories to cherish, ponder, and then twist and turn over in your head again and again like a maze you will never, ever solve no matter how hard you try. So there's that. But even besides the stories themselves, what did we learn from my incredible book in the larger sense, the sense that's bigger than the both of us or the both of us and also another person who happens to be standing nearby? Or—what the heck?—maybe even all of us put together (me, you, that other person I just mentioned, and also everyone else in the whole world, too, which ends up being literally thousands of people).

Unfortunately, I can't answer that question for you. I'm an artist, not a mind reader. It's something you need to decide for yourself and then talk about with other people as you repeatedly encourage them to buy my book even though you are finished with your copy and could easily loan it to them. (Seriously, don't do it. You're a human being, not a goddamn library.) And whatever you do decide, may I suggest to you that, as the words in this book grow in importance and resonance for you over time, perhaps you gently move it from wherever you tend to file contemporary nonfiction written by guys who smell really nice and possess what some people might call "offbeat good looks" over to the space on your bookshelf where you keep all the dusty old classics—stuff like *The Great Gatsby,* the works of Plato, the Bible (the real one, not the one with all the made up stuff in it), *How to Win Friends & Influence People,* or maybe even something by Hemingway or the Rock. Just don't put it up too high though. Next thing you know you're dragging over a stool so you can more easily reach it, you fall off, twist your ankle, hit your head, and wind up lying there in a pool of blood (yours) that's almost guaranteed to ruin a perfectly good rug. Keep my book on a lower shelf and we'll both sleep a little easier at night. Or you could maybe place it on an old wooden book stand with it opened up to one of your favorite passages. Next to it you can put an old magnifying glass, one of those pens made out of a feather that you have to dip into an inkwell, and maybe a big, melty candle, just to class things up a bit. It would be cool if somewhere around there you could have a human skull and a taxidermied bird of prey with its wings spread wide open, too, but ultimately I leave that up to you. Think about it, though, because it will look awesome. Ask anyone.

Getting back to the whole learning thing, though, I suppose I should just go ahead and tell you what I, Dave Hill, learned from this book. The simple answer is this—plenty. More specifically, however, I learned that sometimes you have to write your own story to really understand your own story. I also learned that sometimes the truth is far scarier than the most outlandish fiction you could ever imagine, even while hopped up on all the prescription cold medicine money can buy. Perhaps most of all, however, I learned that just because you type in a pair of skimpy briefs and one of those giant foam cowboy hats while you're at home, doesn't mean that sort of thing is gonna fly at your neighborhood coffeehouse or the public library, even if you are sitting in the New Age section and "everyone else is doing it." And, just to complete my thoughts on the topic, I should probably also point out that trying to write with one of those little white-headed capuchin monkeys sitting on your shoulder the whole time might seem great in theory, perhaps even necessary, but in practice it's next to impossible if you ever expect to get any real work done. Not only are all of his adorable little antics competely distracting, but—in the case of the monkey I rented anyway—all that pipe smoke makes it almost impossible to breathe. And all these months later, I still can't even hazard a guess at what I might have been doing that that damn monkey could have possibly interpreted as an invitation to sex.

Before I go and we both get back to doing whatever it was we did before agreeing to spend this time together, I would like to take a moment to address the elephant in the room, the one that exists in the form of you sitting there right now thinking, "Hey, Dave, how can I arrange to have you come speak at my institution of higher learning, church, and/or place of business as an elaborate means to try and have intercourse with you?" Well, first of all, thanks for asking. You are just the right combination of formal and naughty, and I love it. That said, however, I am not the kind of person who is likely to accept an offer of somewhere in the neighborhood of fifty dollars to roll into your town on anything less than a Greyhound bus, show up at your institution of higher learning, church, and/or place of business, speak for up to but no longer than three hours straight (including Q and A. No exceptions!), allow you to ply me with alcohol, shrimp cocktail, and Robitussin immediately following the lecture, and then stumble back to your house for what I can guarantee you will be the best nine or ten minutes of lovemaking you and your roommates will ever, ever experience.[3] But rather than just tell you no myself, I recommend you contact my public appearance agent instead so that he can field your potentially insulting offer and tell you in no uncertain terms that the odds of me agreeing to any or all of that as long as you pay in cash simply aren't very good at all even if you agree to pick me up at the bus station and allow me to take any leftover shrimp cocktail home with me the next day. Sorry, I have no doubt that that sort of thing might fly with Stephen Hawking, Salman Rushdie, and just about any current or former NBA player you can think of, but I am quite simply better than that.

> Stick around for the meet and greet,
> Dave Hill

---

3 It occurs to me that this book will also be read by dudes, something I am not only totally cool with but also encourage as they will no doubt find it instructive. However, I should probably tell you now that if you are a dude, the odds of me coming back to your apartment aren't very good, even if you live with "two totally hot twins who should be home from the Sunglass Hut any minute." But if you want to go for a quick drive around town in your car after the reading while taking turns giving the finger to other dudes we run into at stoplights and stuff, I'd be into it as long as I get to work the radio.

ACKNOWLEDGMENTS

Most people think writing a book simply entails one person with a lot of time on his or her hands sitting down at a desk and typing for three or four days straight, sometimes even longer, until the whole thing is done. And while that's pretty much the deal in a lot of ways, the greater reality is that it takes a bunch of other people to see to it that that dog-eared stack of ink- coffee- and sometimes even urine-stained paper sitting at the bottom of some desk drawer, perhaps otherwise never to be seen again, is somehow transformed into an attractive volume people are actually willing to pay as much as $24.99 (USD) for. In my case, there were many and I would like to take this opportunity to thank them now. Before I do, however, it should be noted that I'm not even including this section of the book as part of my contractually obligated word count, so please know this comes from the heart. Plus, while I realize I will probably one day be nominated for an Oscar, the Nobel Peace Prize, or some other cool award at some point in my life, there's no guaranteeing I will win, so I figure this is my chance to really swing for the fences in the thank you department.

Now let's get started.

The first person I would like to thank, of course, is you, the reader (especially if you actually paid for this book). But let's face it—that could potentially upset all the people who actually did something to help make this incredible book a reality, so if it's cool with you, please mentally and arbitrarily slip your name somewhere in the middle of this section (unless, of course, you didn't actually pay for this book, in which case I kindly request that you mentally put your name a little closer to the end where it belongs. Sorry, but I need you to be cool with that).

Okay, now that I've placated the reader, let's get down to brass tacks.[1] I would like to start by thanking my lovely and talented editor, Kathy Huck, who jumped into the breach when I found myself wandering the halls, stairwells, and basement of the Flatiron Building editorless and agreed to bring this ship into the shore as long as I wouldn't make her wear the lab coat and goggles I found on eBay. I thought they looked pretty cool, but whatever—you proved on a daily basis that you didn't need either of those things to do a super job and tear the world of publishing a new one in the process. The same goes for all the classy people you work with at St. Martin's Press who helped turn this book into an actual physical object that really hurts when it falls from a high shelf and hits someone on the head.

Next I would like to thank the lovely and talented Alison Strobel, my first editor on this tome, who plucked me from literary obscurity and set me on the path to becoming one of America's most cherished authors even though I was wasted and talking gibberish when we first met and for the majority of our meetings after that. And even though you decided to leave publishing altogether shortly after we began working together, I refuse to read into things. That said, if you didn't want me calling at three a.m., why did you always pick up the phone? It's a mixed message if you ask me.

I am also forever indebted to my lovely and talented manager, Kara Welker, who somehow managed to see what so many others failed to when I was doing summer stock in Reno all those years ago. Not only are you the world's best manager, but you are also the world's best-dressed manager, which is what really keeps me going on those days when show business seems cruelest. Sorry I blew that *Two and a*

---

1 What does this even mean? I looked it up on the Internet and all of the explanations sounded totally made up. I've had it!

Half Men audition, but, like you and that nutjob Redstone always say, I probably shouldn't have snuck onto the lot in the first place. We'll get 'em next time.

I'd probably be dead by now were it not for my lovely and talented lawyer, Amy Nickin, perhaps the only person I know willing to not only spring me from jail in the middle of the night, but also bring me an outfit that will allow me to leave that jail with dignity every time. As Abraham Lincoln once said, I have always found that mercy bears richer fruits than strict justice. I have no idea what that means, but I thought it would be pretty cool to say that here.

I am also totally indebted to my lovely and talented secretary, Shaina Feinberg, who heads up the Brooklyn office of Dave Hill International. Thank you for your unflagging dedication to helping me make this book even betterer. You are the greatest. Please help yourself to any leftover bagels in the pantry whenever you want. You've earned it. Also, we are out of toner.

And, of course, I cannot forget to thank my agent, Kirby Kim. Sorry to not mention you sooner in this section, but I know that you—like me—are a true gentleman and recognize that I'm running a ladies-first operation here despite my gruff, "bros before hos" exterior. Anyway, thank you for all your hard work and also for getting everyone else at William Morris Endeavor to wear suits to the office on days you knew I'd be stopping by. It really meant a lot. Ditto on the deli tray. Also, I have no idea what you said to St. Martin's Press to get them to cough up so much cash but I'm glad you did. Hardly a day goes by when someone doesn't compliment me on one of the many track suits I bought with the advance.

Lest anyone think it's all business all the time with me, I would also like thank the many friends, family members, and other assorted loved ones who offered their endless (within reason) love, support, and—in some cases—even their bodies throughout the writing of this very important work of literature. Some read early drafts and told me to finish the book anyway, some actually appear in these chapters by name (or by a name I made up so they don't sue me or get sued by somebody else or anything), and some just put up with me whenever

I'd announce really loudly how I was writing a book in the middle of a crowded restaurant, bus station restroom, or anywhere else I like a little extra attention. They include (in intentionally random order so as not to cause infighting) my siblings Miriam Hill (without you, I probably would never have written this book; take the credit or the blame; your choice), Libby Manthei, Bob Hill, Katy Wallace, Kathy Kato (thank you for not only picking up the phone but for staying on the phone through all the mumbling and the tears), Ira Glass and the staff of the popular public radio program *This American Life* (thank you for being the only radio show without the word "zoo" in its name to have me on with any regularity), Janyce Murphy (I consider you to be just like a real sister only less annoying), Fred Wistow (what started as fear has grown to include both love and admiration for you, but still mostly fear), Anaheed Alani and all my fellow teenage girls at Rookie (you "get me" and I appreciate that), my brothers-in-law Nick Simon, Jeff Manthei, and Rob Wallace (never anger a man who's got nothing to lose; if any of you ever do anything to hurt any of my sisters I will kill you all without even thinking about it), David Rakoff (compared to you, English will always be my second language), Will Tanous (you believed in me when I was just a guy from Cleveland with a bus pass and a dream; here's to none of that ever changing), Deirdre Dolan (sorry, not everyone gets a special parenthetical; starting with you, I'm just going to list names for the most part—deal with it), Carl Arnheiter, Stephen Sherrill, Tim Parnin, John Hodgman, Tony Kellers, Malcolm Gladwell, Nancy Southwell, Anne Fenton, Dale May, Mike Albo, the Laurent-Marke family, Todd Barry, Dick Cavett, Meredith Scardino, Kieran Blake, Dan Dratch, Beowulf Sheehan, Giancarlo DiTrapano, Chris March, Janeane Garofalo, Meredith Blake, Britt Bolnick, Paisley Gregg, Bridey Elliott, Stephanie Scott, Phil Costello, John Kimbrough, Doug Gillard, Pat Casa, Lucy Wainwright Roche, John Borland, Matt Stein, Gary Nadeau, Bob Bartos (I am working on getting a version of this book with your name mentioned first so calm down. I will be intimidated by you no longer), Walter Schreifels, Storme DeLarverie, Fran Illgen, Katherine Dore, Scott Guber, Leanne Shapton, John Herguth, Mel Robbins, the rest of my rock brothers (Rob Pfeiffer, Eddie Eyeball, Arthur Smilios, Moby, Tomato, Nash Kato, and even Drew Cardilicchio), Maura Maloney, Hal Sparks, Alex Gregor, the fine folks at Generate, Kyle Mizono, Patrick Ryan, Jody Jones, Miles Kahn, Leigh Arthur, Tig Notaro, Ryohei at Rimeout, Fuji at ThisTime, Koyo Fukamizu, Tim Fornara, Lisa Thomas Management, Thao Nguyen, Laura Krafft, Clark Caldwell, Lou Hagood, UCB Theatre, Jeff Sheehan (you facilitated my drinking throughout the writing of this book, which made me feel more like a real writer; thanks), Jeff Tomsic, Mike Gregg, Pete Walker, Mark Hall, Megan Madigan Roche, and, last but not least, Joe Randazzo, a sweet dude.

I realize I probably forgot some people, either intentionally (e.g. Harry Deansway) or in the way that sometimes happens when you have a gas leak in your apartment like I do. Don't worry, I'll get it right when the paperback comes out.

Before I go, I wanted to thank my nieces and nephews Anna, Eamon, Blake, William, Luke, and Lilah even though—let's face it—none of you did a single thing to help me write this book. In fact, half of you can't even read yet and the ones that can shouldn't be reading this book in the first place because it will haunt your dreams. But someday I may need you to testify on my behalf in court or—at the very least—see to it that my body is disposed of properly, so I just wanted to get it in writing now that I love you all very much.[2]

Finally, I would like to thank my parents, Bob and Bunny Hill. Dad, I realize you might have thrown this book in the trash several chapters ago, but if you made it this far please know that I love you and was just trying to do my best. Mom, nothing scares me more than the thought of you reading this book. Even so, I'd like to think you would have secretly enjoyed it despite the fact that you never would have let me borrow the car again. I love you and miss you every day.

Love,
Dave

---

2 Even those of you who appear to be going through some sort of awkward phase right now.